Freedom of Expression and the Law in Russia

This book discusses how Russia's legal system restricts freedom of expression.

As the author analyses legal amendments restricting the free flow of information since 2012, she draws upon Akerlof's framework of "Asymmetrical information" and Luhmann's "System Theory" to show how these amendments have deprived citizens of the opportunity to voice criticisms, influence public affairs, or take collective action against decision-makers. Among the innovations are the establishment of a "President Emeritus" institution and the introduction of laws through legislative processes already on hold – something we call "legislation through winter preservatives." The author provides a nuanced understanding of these and other processes that limit the free flow of information while simultaneously exploring the reasons why Russia's regime still endures.

The volume will be of interest to scholars and students of law, political science, international law, area studies, development studies, peace research, comparative politics/comparative area studies, citizenship studies, communication studies, social movements, and international organisations. Experts working with Russia in international organisations and the media will also find this systematic analysis of the transformation of Russian legislation and its consequences invaluable.

Mariya Riekkinen is Senior Researcher in Law at the Faculty of Social Sciences, Business and Economics, and Law, Åbo Akademi University, Finland.

Studies in Contemporary Russia

Series Editor: Markku Kivinen

Studies in Contemporary Russia is a series of cutting-edge, contemporary studies. These monographs, joint publications, and edited volumes branch out into various disciplines, innovatively combining research methods and theories to approach the core questions of Russian modernisation: how do the dynamics of resources and rules affect the Russian economy, and what are the prospects and needs of diversification? What is the impact of the changing state-society relationship? How does the emerging welfare regime work? What is the role of Russia in contemporary international relations? How should we understand the present Russian political system? What is the philosophical background of modernisation as a whole and its Russian version in particular?

The variety of opinions on these issues is vast. Some see increasingly fewer differences between contemporary Russia and the Soviet Union, while, at the other extreme, prominent experts regard Russia as a 'more or less' normal European state. At the same time, new variants of modernisation are espoused as a result of Russia's membership in the global BRIC powers. Combining aspects of Western and Soviet modernisation with some anti-modern or traditional tendencies, the Russian case is ideal for probing deeper into the evolving nature of modernisation. Which of the available courses Russia will follow remains an open question, but these trajectories provide the alternatives available for discussion in this ground-breaking and authoritative series.

The editor and the editorial board of the series represent the Finnish Centre of Excellence in Russian Studies: Choices of Russian Modernisation.

The Politics of the Pandemic in Eastern Europe and Eurasia
Blame Game and Governance
Edited by Margarita Zavadskaya

Freedom of Expression and the Law in Russia
Asymmetrical Information
Mariya Riekkinen

For more information about this series, please visit: www.routledge.com/series/ASHSER-1421

Freedom of Expression and the Law in Russia

Asymmetrical Information

Mariya Riekkinen

Routledge
Taylor & Francis Group
LONDON AND NEW YORK

First published 2025
by Routledge
4 Park Square, Milton Park, Abingdon, Oxon OX14 4RN

and by Routledge
605 Third Avenue, New York, NY 10158

Routledge is an imprint of the Taylor & Francis Group, an informa business

British Library Cataloguing in Publication Data
A catalogue record for this book is available from the British Library

Library of Congress Cataloging in Publication Data
Names: Riekkinen, Mariya, 1982– author.
Title: Freedom of expression and the law in Russia : asymmetrical information / Mariya Riekkinen.
Description: Abingdon, Oxon [UK] ; New York , NY : Routledge, 2024. | Series: Studies in contemporary Russia | Includes bibliographical references and index.
Identifiers: LCCN 2024027136 (print) | LCCN 2024027137 (ebook) | ISBN 9781032613369 (hardback) | ISBN 9781032613406 (paperback) | ISBN 9781032613383 (ebook)
Subjects: LCSH: Freedom of expression—Russia (Federation) | Freedom of information—Russia (Federation) | Assembly, Right of—Russia (Federation)
Classification: LCC KLB2470 .R54 2024 (print) | LCC KLB2470 (ebook) | DDC 342.4708/53—dc23/eng/20240729
LC record available at https://lccn.loc.gov/2024027136
LC ebook record available at https://lccn.loc.gov/2024027137

ISBN: 978-1-032-61336-9 (hbk)
ISBN: 978-1-032-61340-6 (pbk)
ISBN: 978-1-032-61338-3 (ebk)

DOI: 10.4324/9781032613383

Typeset in Times New Roman
by Apex CoVantage, LLC

Contents

Illustrations

Figures

Tables

Acknowledgements

To begin with, I wish this book were never topical due to the ongoing war in Ukraine, the continuing restrictions on free expression in Russia, and all the suffering they cause. However, for now, things are as they are, and my prayers are with the people.

My sincere thanks go to all those who have helped me along the way. Input from anonymous reviewers greatly improved the book, and I am grateful for their insights. The research was partially funded by a grant from the Modeen Foundation to the Law School of Åbo Akademi University. A generous Open Access grant from Åbo Akademi University has made this book accessible to all. Special thanks to an anonymous language and style editor – sorry you had to deal with Russian words and sources along the way, but you did a great job. Additionally, I would like to thank the Routledge team for their support and encouragement – I wouldn't be so confident about finishing the book without their friendly and warm communications.

Ultimately, it is my family's support that has made this book possible. I thank my children, spouse, and my mother. No words can adequately express how grateful I am for them.

In late April 2024, I wrote this all in Turku/Åbo, my second home, where there is snow now and nothing like summer to come in a month.

Acknowledgements

1 Introduction

1.1 Nuanced Socio-Legal Approach Towards Censoring Information

Partly because the topos of crisis now permeate our media and social lives, it is easy to forget that a crisis is not a discrete event or circumstance but rather a phenomenon that disrupts, inverts, or even undermines the logic deployed to understand and respond to life. In other words, a crisis questions our decision-making and evaluation systems. This is no more apparent than in the case of Russia's invasion of Ukraine, which undeniably challenges the conventional wisdom of global audiences and the perceptions of Russian citizens. On 24 February 2022, Russian troops invaded Ukraine, claiming to be engaging in a "special military operation," which escalated to be an unprecedented human rights and security crisis. In peacetime, decreasing military expenses and maintaining neutrality have been treated as a sign of democratisation (Clardie, 2011). However, even stable democracies like Sweden and Finland were inclined to increase military expenditures with accession to NATO membership.

Likewise, Russian citizenry has witnessed a radical change, with its government waging a de facto war against its neighbouring country, resulting in international sanctions. To make matters more unintelligible, international organisations previously supported by the government were immediately declared to be unfriendly. Access to international media has been banned, and any form of dissent is branded as foreign influence. Counteracting foreign influence goes along with fractious disputes over authentic Russianness (Alapuro et al., 2012; Laruelle, 2019), which reframe general legal principles, such as the rule of law, free expression, the legitimacy of parliamentary representation, and the impartiality of courts. All of these reforms have vast implications for the implementation of human rights.

True, there is a crisis when these developments occur. However, crises usually pass, and Russia remains after assimilating these changes. A more nuanced approach is required to understand how the authorities in Russia legitimise restricting the free flow of information. Selecting a relevant theoretical framework for researching these issues by examining prominent theories helps explain how authorities use censorship. The legislation tightening freedom of expression is examined in this book, starting from 2012. This examination is done through the

DOI: 10.4324/9781032613383-1

theoretical lens of asymmetrical information, as introduced by George Akerlof (1970), and within the methodological framework of the legitimation code theory (LCT) by Maton (2014; Maton et al., 2015). The year 2012 is linked to the pre-Crimea annexation, Putin's re-election, and the period of harshening freedom of speech, termed "new authoritarianism" (Lewis, 2020; van der Vet, 2018; von Gall, 2024). Such an approach allows for a holistic application of general theories of freedom of expression, access to information, and governance, detailed by several niche framework theories (e.g. dual state and legal dualism, communicative power, and agenda-setting) for data analysis and interpretation. Our framework of asymmetrical information is thus rooted in a substantive research theory based on supportive theories of free expression and access to information and elucidated by relevant specialised theories.

According to Akerlof (1970), asymmetrical information emerges when the providers of services have more information about the actual content and quality of these services than the consumers. A market system based on asymmetrical information risks becoming unsustainable. In market transactions, if one side has valuable information and the other does not, it can lead to an "adverse selection" problem. For instance, high-risk individuals predominantly take out insurance policies (p. 493). Importantly, Akerlof (1970, 1976, 1997) explores informational asymmetries in a context radically different from Russia's legal system. For our discussion, however, his insights mean a lot, pointing out that a good administration should be responsive to the needs of the people (e.g. security and economic stability). If the government exploits these needs as a pretext to gain and consolidate power, it delivers services of substandard quality, thereby generating informational asymmetry.

Akerlof further asserts that a market system based on information asymmetry would collapse. Consumers would only pay high prices for known quality goods, making it difficult for honest sellers, while dishonest sellers would look for another market to maximise profits. Even if honest providers are capable of offering services of actual quality, the general costs associated with asymmetrical information would result in both honest and dishonest providers being expelled from the system. Akerlof refers to this as "a loss of a legitimate market" (1970, p. 495).

Applying this to Russia, we might hypothesise that, first and foremost, when the government presents corrupt information to the citizens and silences the dissent, it is surrounded by a populace that is neither capable nor willing to counterbalance its actions and decisions. Such a government is more likely to take high-risk actions and policies that are contrary to the citizens' needs and interests, such as security, public order, and open public discussions. Under a façade, or lemon, using Akerlof's (1970) terminology, authorities make decisions to accumulate power, eliminating all possible decisions sponsoring human rights. Moreover, the leadership, bereft of public criticism and accountability, believes its actions are justified and supported by the populace, thus disconnecting itself from global norms of respecting human rights law and its principles.

The only way to sustain the system or compensate for the "cost of dishonesty" (1970, p. 495) is by symmetrising information, enabling free information flow. Even so, the current regime in Russia is barely capable of doing this, since asymmetries are what it is all about. This contradicts Black's (1961) median voter theorem, where he contends that the median voter ultimately decides the winner. Asymmetrical information-based systems can declare themselves winners by moulding the image of "median voter preferences" to assert that they are the popular choice in the absence of conditions for genuine elections.

Considering that Russia continues to operate without symmetrical information flow yet also without a major collapse, it is significant to examine whether Akerlof's ideas are relevant to Russia's context. If they are, what are the key features of the asymmetrical information technique in Russia that prevent the entire system from collapsing? The framework of asymmetrical information can provide new insights as, amidst constrained information flows, the citizenry is forced to either consume existing information or seek alternative means of finding information. As a result, it is probably reflected in citizens' actions and inactions concerning the Russian regime.

However, estimating the proportion of people supporting and opposing the regime is complex. Those who genuinely share the official narrative do not want to see alternatives, while those who see alternatives either speak up, constituting the vocal minority (Kohut & Bowman, 2017), or are silenced or choose not to speak out, instead finding new ways to practise silent resilience. While the official propaganda machine invents new ways to legitimise its actions by limiting freedom of expression, part of the citizenry also devises ways to resist, if not through protests, then by laying flowers to the dead oppositionist's Aleksei Navalny's grave (RFE/RL, 2004).

Although asymmetrical information in this context can refer to restrictions on free speech, propaganda, or censorship, it also provides a more detailed understanding of the processes governing these restrictions. Additionally, it may help explain why the autocratic regime remains viable. With that said, we analyse legislative changes aimed at restricting open society and the free flow of information since 2012 and help to explain the lack of active opposition to the regime.

1.2 Asymmetrical Information: A Working Concept, an Analytical Framework, and Our Goals Regarding Its Exploration

1.2.1 Our Goals

As mentioned, our ultimate theoretical dilemma is whether Akerlof's claims regarding asymmetrical information can stand within Russia's legal system. We use Niklas Luhmann's "systems theory" as an analytical tool. Involving Luhmann's insights is inevitable as we test Akerloff's market system ideas against Russia's legal system. For an in-depth understanding of Russia's legal system, an external observer can use asymmetrical information as a framework, which is nuanced and complex, involving a variety of other approaches related to communications and information. We return to these in Section 1.5. Therefore, we have the following key research questions:

- In the Russian legal system, what are the critical characteristics of asymmetrical information?

- What role do these techniques play in the system's survival?
- Are there specific asymetrising information techniques that this legal system went through?

In other words, we are not proposing or defending adjustments but analysing the legal system based on asymmetrical information. We are not trying to establish whether or when the system can collapse. We also approach the asymmetrical information-based legal system in Russia analytically because, in the end, no information can be completely neutral or complete. Our key intention is to see how the asymmetrising of information is performed with the help of law.

The question may, however, arise: What are the signs of asymmetrical information in its normal state, as it evolved post-2012 legal amendments, in limiting freedom of expression and entering a pathological condition? Peripherally, we will try to establish criteria for distinguishing the pathological condition. We can employ Luhmann's arguments, contending that a pathological sense arises only when "certain tolerance thresholds are exceeded" (Luhmann, 1992, p. 258). Using a methodological trick, we will also determine when the system might have been in a pathological state. This will be accomplished by analysing legal amendments using legitimation code theory (see Section 1.6). At this point, if the explanations for enacting new laws are nothing more than statements of fact, we could conclude that the system was busy with something other than inventing explanations.

1.2.2 The Working Concept of Asymmetrical Information

Taking Akerlof's ideas into account, we assume that information becomes asymmetrical due to the efforts of its transmitter, or the creator, in the case of a legal system, who is more aware of its asymmetrical nature than its receivers. Asymmetrical information in this book refers to information or data (e.g. amendments to laws that limit free speech, preparation materials, and court cases that enforce them). Secondly, asymmetrical information is more than merely a narrative; it is a way of narrating. In contrast to facilitating free information flow, asymmetrising information involves a set of actions that results in data lacking impartiality, objectivity, or completeness. Thirdly, these are data manipulated and transmitted (or communicated) asymmetrically within a legal system that includes laws and agencies responsible for creating, interpreting, amending, revoking, and enforcing them. When disseminating asymmetrical information, data in focus are communicated selectively, while other information is withheld or distorted to gain a strategic advantage. By considering Luhmann's "information-utterance-understanding" communication triad,[1] the utterance of asymmetrical information aims to manipulate information and individual perception of specific facts and events.

We demonstrate in this book that it is done by using specific language either too vague or, on the contrary, too bold in arguing for something as well as the amount of time and effort involved in "appearing" and "explaining oneself" behind legal amendments for making the essence of the narrative clear (Luhmann, 1992, p. 253). With all these extra marketing campaigns, asymmetrical communication of doctored data interferes with understanding events and forces those who disagree to express their perceptions only within the system's parameters. Regardless of what participants may understand in their self-referentially closed consciousnesses, the communication system works out its understanding or misunderstanding (1992).

As such, in this book, we treat asymmetrical information as a research phenomenon, or something normal, which concurs with Luhmann's functionalist approach and to some extent also with Akerlof's narrative, which claims that "in the real world . . . information is neither complete nor costless" (Akerlof, 1976, p. 599). As far as communication is concerned, he continues, "It is without goal or end, without immanent entelechy . . . . It occurs, or it does not-that is all that can be said about it" (Luhmann, 1992, p. 254).

1.3 Asymmetrical Information: From Market to the Legal System

Asymmetrising information in this book is studied as occurring within a legal system (a social system insofar as Luhmann's (1995) systems theory is applied). It thus depends on specific relationships between the system that is always autopoietic (i.e. capable of self-reproducing, operatively closed, and self-referential) and its environment (i.e. a product of the internal operations that are observed) (1995). This relationship that revolves around freedom of thought and expression creates and maintains the asymmetry. This is where Luhmann's and Akerlof's insights on asymmetrical information and adverse selection intersect, as legal and economic systems are social systems.

Luhmann argued that similar features apply to any social system, including law and economics (Luhmann, 1995). The proof for the feasibility of extending Akerlof's concepts to law undeniably goes beyond Luhmann's claim that all social systems follow his logic. Thus, references to other studies extend the application of Akerlof's ideas beyond second-hand car markets, which in one way or another highlight the problem of adverse selection that results from inaccurate information. For example, when institutions provide corrupt information about the premises to be insured from fire, this leads to incorrect risk assessment (Bartley & Schneiberg, 2002). Also, with health insurance relationships, when patients conceal information about the state of their health, which, when practised en masse, can impair the entire health insurance system (Horne, 2017). This idea applies Akerlof's ideas in studies dealing with the rationality of decision-making in the context of democracy studies (Pennington, 2010).

Akerlof saw a difference between social and economic systems when asserting that social decisions have social consequences, whereas economic decisions do not (Akerlof, 1997, p. 1006). However, Akerlof (1970) brought examples of adverse selection based on reluctance to hire minorities. He later expanded social science perspectives in his economic writings aimed at understanding how markets and employment work. In particular, he raised the issue of including knowledge about social systems, such as the role of stories, a battle between "us" and "them," and the search for self-respect, in the discourse on the economics of minority poverty (Akerlof & Shiller, 2010, p. 163).

The social sciences dimension of Akerlof's ideas rests on discourses that seem to have a standard line that certain countries from which migrants come are poorer because of a lack of skills, financial assets, and discrimination, ignoring the "thought patterns that animate people's ideas and feelings," or "animal spirits," as he called them (Akerlof & Shiller, 2010, p. 1). Akerlof approaches asymmetries via a concept of social distance. According to Akerlof, social decisions are influenced by people's dependency on the actions of others (Akerlof, 1997, p. 1005). In extreme cases, these interactions may create long-term traps, deviating from socially optimal outcomes. He further asserts that it is possible to make interventions in closed systems to achieve social transformation and provides several successful examples (p. 1021).

The asymmetrical information-based system in Russia illustrates this as accurate but in an adverse way. As a result of official narratives that call for social unity in Russia against Western values, such solidarity increases the distance between those who agree with the government's cause and those who believe in individual human rights. This imposed solidarity also counteracts dissent by making people agree with the prevailing viewpoint. These insights are similar to the effects of the spiral silence theory, where voices of dissent are silenced by fear of not being accepted (Noelle-Neumann, 1993). Moreover, they emphasise Luhmann's binary division between us and them to guarantee autopoiesis for the system.

According to Luhmann, asymmetry within a system is caused by distorted notions of equality. In highly differentiated societies (e.g. Russia), equality is not about recognising phenomena based on similarity and difference but about making the system constantly evaluate whether two similar cases are equal or not (Luhmann, 1993, p. 133). In an asymmetrical information-based system, unequal treatment thus requires justification, and such justification transforms into asymmetry through the constant "rule and exception" operations (pp. 132–134). This book does not lack examples of these operations when the laws and their application justify unequal treatment. For example, when the Constitutional Court agreed that banning criticism was illegal, it also claimed banning criticism of public officials was acceptable because of the public official's unique role (see Chapter 7 of this book on prohibitions of discrediting the military and the authorities). When equal treatment is not the rule but a reason to justify exceptions, there comes the demand for criteria of what is equal in this situation (p. 134), creating asymmetry. The foundations of asymmetrical information, as approached by Akerlof and Luhmann, are sketched in the Figure 1.1.

1.4 The Choice of Data for Analysis and Limitations

The choice of data for analysis (legal amendments introduced after 2012) is based on principles derived from several theories of freedom of expression and participatory governance. These theories foreground the interrelation between the right to freedom of expression, access to information, and participatory governance. Our attention is focused on legal amendments that limit citizens' avenues for free expression, specifically, public expression addressed to an unidentified circle of recipients, in line with Luhmann's distinction between the system and the

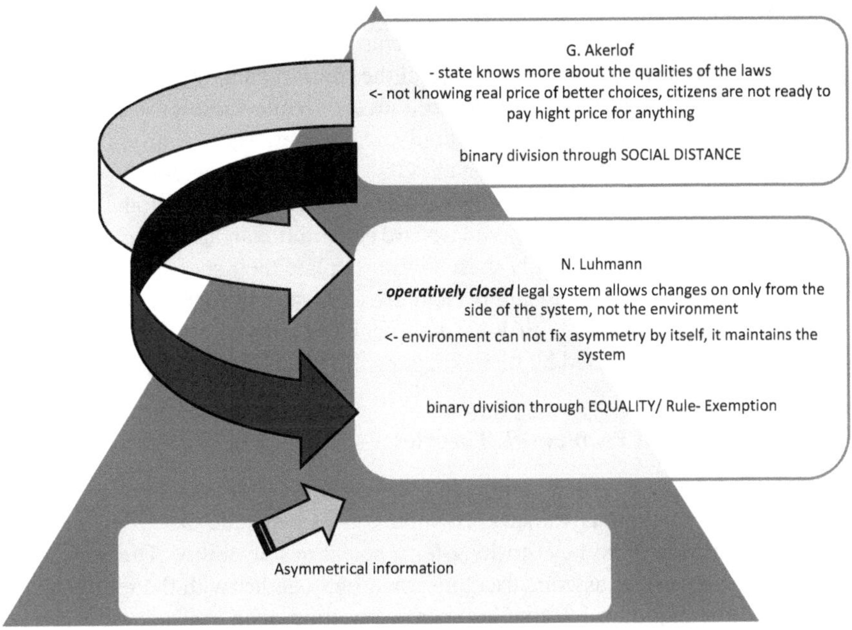

Figure 1.1 Foundations of Asymmetrical Information

environment. This attention implies that our discussions do not cover legal limitations on political party activities orchestrated by the authorities that are part of the system, nor how citizens can exercise their freedom of expression within their social circles, although both topics are undeniably important.

Thus, the choice of legal amendments for review is derived from, among other things, recent research on restricting the open society and freedom of expression by a diverse range of means, including creating a disreputable image of civil society actors receiving foreign funding. Matejova et al. (2018) studied governmental control over the activities of NGOs through legislation by grouping the means of the control into five categories: (a) administration, by introducing stringent requirements for registering NGOs; (b) finance, through controlling the economic foundation of NGOs; (c) communication, in limiting freedom of expression; (d) movement and activity, by restricting freedom of cooperating with other entities and NGOs; and (e) harassment, in introducing strict requirements for the staff, restricting personal freedoms. Moreover, Toepler and Fröhlich (2020) approached the issue of controlling civil society from the perspective of regulating the advocacy activities, which they divided into political, policy, and program advocacy, as well as case and public or community advocacy via the freedom of expression.

Of the multitude of legal amendments issued since 2012 that relate to freedom of expression and access to information, we chose the following: (a) regulating the so-called enlightenment activities, which involve information-sharing, often on political issues, and are pursued outside formal educational curricula through open lectures, discussions, and talks; (b) issuing a public register of traditional ethical and moral values; (c) tightening requirements for conducting public protests; (d) prohibiting criticism of the authorities and the military; and (e) extending foreign agent legislation concerning private individuals. While these laws have existed for some time, their use to suppress civil society grew significantly after Putin's election to a third term (McCarthy et al., 2023, p. 129). Our approach discusses in a nuanced manner how the authorities issuing laws, the Constitutional Court that is supposed to decide whether these laws are constitutional, and the administrative authorities and courts that apply these laws articulate their specific vision of why these laws are needed amidst the present crisis. Lastly, we parallel these amendments and interpretations with how the vocal minority of citizens try to argue against limitations imposed by them in courts of law and on the streets of Russia.

1.5 The Choice of Framework Theories

A broader range of socio-economic and sustainability studies examines different aspects of information asymmetry. However, most conclude that free expression and cooperation are the keys to long-term social sustainability. The substantive research framework of asymmetrical information, together with the following relevant theories inquiring into the issues of restricting open society and censoring public information, helps us understand how and with which narratives and triggers certain legal amendments can deprive citizens of the opportunity and willingness to criticise the government.

The prisoners' dilemma was formulated from the 1952 Flood and Dresher experiment (Flood, 1958), which suggested that two alleged perpetrators who cannot be proven guilty must choose between cooperating for mutual benefit or betraying each other for personal gain. If neither testifies against the other, they will each receive the mildest punishment (two years in prison). If one confesses to the principal charge and betrays the other, they will be pardoned, while the other must serve the full term (ten years in prison). The concept of adverse selection is employed by Akerlof (1970) to explain such stifling of mutually advantageous transactions. As a result of this dilemma, we see the benefits of symmetrical cooperation.

In this book, good faith cooperation means playing the game fairly and allowing the free flow of information. The prisoners' dilemma can also be interpreted by considering the value of punishing wrongdoings. If a government chooses only loyal supporters by corrupting information, it betrays the ideal of free information. Personal benefits from such cooperation will mean nobody will be held accountable for breaching the universal or social good, as embodied in international human rights norms. Open and fair cooperation is the premise of international economic organisations, like the WTO, which Russia still features. Sustainable resource consumption can only be achieved through cooperation and fair play. Defeating another party by consuming a shared resource will likely benefit one party. However, other parties can also deceive even more effectively and benefit more from consuming the same resource. In the end, the resource is consumed quickly without considering sustainability. This means that manipulating information could adversely affect regime supporters in the Russian context. Authoritarian leadership is even more susceptible to risky actions without checks and balances. Such a situation is dangerous for a nation with the largest nuclear arsenal in the world.

The theory of the dual state (Sakwa, 2010, 2011, 2021) and associated theories, for example, the informal network approach (Ledeneva, 2011), telephone justice (Ledeneva, 2013), the duality of control (Daucé, 2015; Salamon et al., 2015), and legal dualism (Hendley, 2017, 2022; McCarthy et al., 2023) contextualise more general theories of participation and access to information by underscoring the duality of Russia's administrative apparatus. These theories imply that governance in Russia relies on a mixture of formal institutions, primarily for routine cases, and informal administrative practices for serious political encounters (Sakwa, 2010, 2011).

An administrative regime tends to assume "extra-constitutional leadership in a divided society" (Sakwa, 2010, p. 191). The asymmetry of information resulting from a lack of legal certainty is enhanced by lacking remedies to protect human rights. The deeper the crisis, the greater Russia's emphasis on non-formal tools of governance (Sakwa, 2011). In a dual state, consolidation of the administrative authority is inevitable since other collective players (e.g. the wealthy Russians having extricated themselves from state control) are swept away (Tilly, 2007; Volkov, 2002). Where the channels of information, bereft of opposition, would have otherwise been taken by citizens, the dual state imposes its agents (Sakwa, 2010, p. 193), who can even profess to defend the constitutional democratic state.[2]

The appearance of individuals being essential for the state is reinforced by direct addresses to the citizens (Ibid.), underpinning the position of the administration, as illustrated by Putin's 2023 Address to the Federal Assembly, claiming that no ordinary citizen will sympathise with wealthy people whose wealth is currently held by Western states because of the sanctions against Russia. The dichotomy (or taxonomy as proposed by the Legitimation Code Theory (Maton et al, 2015)) between Russian and Western values, as exemplified by Russians who stayed in the homeland and Russians who chose to leave the country, allegedly lured by the material benefits of the West, is clearly illustrated in this statement. Explaining how the Russian government rationalises their regime's defence in the citizens' eyes, Sakwa proposes a concept of stabilocracy (*stabilokratiya*). This system is designed to maintain stability by manual or mechanical means (Sakwa, 2021), which implies the exploitation of Putin's government as an instance that created a stable economy with comfortable cities. This perspective also means one must not support the West to protect stability.

Although the idea of duality between the rule of law and orders by the administration has been invoked by several renowned scholars in various modifications to explain why Russia's regime remains viable, Sakwa's approach is more germane because he employs the concept of para-constitutional institutions and practices (Sakwa, 2011)[3] which are not prescribed by the Constitution but carry out significant tasks of strengthening the regime. Para-constitutionalism is essential for our analysis because the current regime in Russia seeks to "influence outcomes through a closed and shadow political system" (p. 3). The regime can achieve the desired effect in a dual state by circumventing popular choice. However, the 2020

Constitutional Amendments were a massive change. Earlier administrative methods relied on circumscribing the Constitution rather than changing it. After the 2020 Constitutional Amendments, it became clear that the administrative element began to take precedence over other measures. The revised constitution expanded the idea of Russia as being a "continuator" (*pravoprodolzhatel'*) of the Soviet Union and carrying out the task of protecting "historical truth" (Mälksoo, 2021, p. 83).

We explain how legislation legitimises the government's course by analysing the legal amendments controlling information flow. The concept of a para-constitutional institution – an arena for "intra-élite intrigues" (Sakwa, 2011, p. 50) – helps to account for how the regime can legitimise its actions by acquiring an institutional component. As a result, para-constitutional practices grant legitimacy to the system's preferences, instead of popular choice, using the veneer of public participation to control public affairs. This dynamic is similar to Black's (1961) median voter's theorem but in reverse.

Theories on access to information and influence through public discourse (i.e. citizen participation) also frame the process of understanding the broader societal implications of censoring information. The rights-based approach to free expression highlights the interrelations between freedom of expression and participation in public affairs (Matthies & Uggerhøj, 2014; Waldron, 1998, 1999), as guaranteed by Article 25 of the ICCPR, to which Russia is still a state party. The asymmetrical information-based system aims to preserve its existence by keeping its operations closed from the influence of actors other than those belonging to the system. Thus, limiting individual opportunities to exert influence on public decision-making is essential, and it is done through limiting freedom of expression since participatory rights are realised through adjacent freedoms (UHRC, 2006, par. 8). These theories help understand the interconnection between asymmetrical information and good and authoritarian governance. Without the opportunity for free expression of views that differ from those of the authorities, citizens are less likely to organise themselves to collectively and efficiently quash the official narrative. The current regime, hence, controls public engagement in politics by eliciting and containing citizen participation (Richter, 2009, p. 41), resulting in a controlled or managed society (Ledeneva, 2013; Petrov et al., 2010; Richter, 2009). Therefore, to have a managed democracy, Russia's regime controls participation by facilitating various institutionalised hubs (e.g. within the public chamber). In these hubs, however, citizens are not supposed to engage with the state but to act within the institutionalised ramifications under strict management (Richter, 2009, p. 60).

The idea of a controlled society intertwines with the theory of collective action (Coleman, 1966; Olson, 1965; Smelser, 1962). Most recently, Ekaterina Shulman (2022) invoked this theory to analyse citizens' reactions to the special military operation. Schulman, who specialises in decision-making mechanisms in autocratic regimes, is a scholar who is now in exile because of the uncertain position she and other scholars critical of the regime found themselves in foreign agents. In her recent interview, she invoked this theory to explain why Russian citizens have few chances to influence the current political situation. Participation should be on a mass scale to exert influence because individual action can lead only to persecution and oppression (Zhelnov, 2022). As an illustration, she revealed an open letter that the rectors of almost 600 Russian universities signed in Spring 2022 to support the special military operation in Ukraine (2022). If some of these rectors had not signed this letter, asserts Schulman, there is a strong possibility that these persons would suffer consequences and would have their positions in the university filled by someone else who is kindly disposed to the system and inclined to implement the official ideology (2022). However, Schulman concludes that the letter would not have been released if the majority had disagreed.

A lack of collective action also reflects the idea of a passive adaptation, "when actors take for granted, without questioning or apparent reflection on their presence or involvement" in political processes (Siisiäinen, 2014, p. 29; Volkov & Kolesnikov, 2023). A lack of collective action is thus something that maintains the asymmetrical information-based system's autopoiesis by holding an information monopoly (Shulman, 2022). Opposition figures like Aleksei Navalny or Vladimir Kara-Murza and many others who refused to adapt and have been arrested, yet still could exert an influence from prison. Their influence, counterbalanced by the official propaganda reinforcing the inviolability and righteousness of the regime, results in people who could otherwise be against the government refraining from expressing their opinions.

Citizens can choose not to oppose the regime for various reasons, which we, unfortunately, cannot systematically address in this book. However, one of the goals of asymmetrical information is to manage uncertainty by creating a quasi-statistical perception of opinions. When restrictions on the free flow of information create the official picture of what is right and what is not while assessed on the go by the courts in the absence of clear legislative provisions, any opinion at odds with the official line, thus, becomes unpopular. According to the spiral of silence theory, people tend to conceal their opinions if they appear unpopular. A silent opposition is thus a threat to the system, as it creates a vacuum that would prevent most citizens from openly and publicly reflecting on and redefining their actual position. Although there are individuals whose opinions remain unaffected by propaganda, such people are probably not in the majority position (McDonald et al., 2001). Thus, the system proceeds with increasingly broader restrictions, even starting to believe that they enjoy popular support. Nevertheless, the risk is that without adversarial groups, the government will be inclined to pursue even more dangerous policies with unpredictable consequences.

We assume that there are other states with policies that tend to restrict the open society and where widespread protests do bring certain results, for example, Iranian popular protest movements led the moral police to halt enforcing the compulsory hijab for women. This book attempts to explain how, through specific techniques of asymmetrising information, the current regime in Russia attempts to preserve itself. With his asymmetrical information theory, Akerlof explains that a vicious circle occurs when the government bans free media and punishes those who chat on social media or express themselves during protests or at various associations. At the same time, an alternative version of reality is represented via government-controlled media channels. Hence, Akerlof's ideas can also be viewed in light of communication theories and agenda-setting theories, explaining how targeted campaigns affect individual perspectives. In particular, Banas and Miller's (2013) inoculation theory explains how and when one can be inoculated against propaganda.

Finally, we put Russia's asymmetrical information practices in a broader context of repression as a coordinated communication power exerted via targeted media and military policies. This strategy continues to efficiently self-correct, learn from mistakes and failures as they go along, and get better each time (Rodgers & Lanoszka, 2023). While focusing on national law, this book also fills in the gaps left by ignoring Russia's power dimension during its international performance, during which it tries to consolidate support and exert influence. Various information manipulations in Europe have exposed Russia's involvement in influencing Western politics (Karlsen, 2019, p. 2). The recent crisis between Russia and Ukraine has reignited propaganda, which is not surprising in the middle of a war since propaganda research shows that signalling potential military deployments increases fight success (Slantchev, 2005).

To gain an edge in Ukraine, Russia seeks to project strength. Earlier, it was believed that signaling military might by autocratic states was often a bluff, as these states have low internal audience costs and are less concerned about losing credibility among oppressed citizens (Fearon, 1994). Recent research on propaganda as a strategic communication tool suggests that non-democracies can incur high "audience cost" even while tolerating street protests (Weeks, 2008; Weiss, 2013). Given Russia's history of ignoring opposition, international audiences have greater reasons to scrutinize its communication strategies – an opportunity explored in this book. Thus, asymmetrical information can be seen as a method by which Russia influences both internal and external policies through targeted communication (see our concept of asymmetrical information, which rests on three pillars: information, its asymmetrisation, and its communicating, in Section 1.2.2 "The Working Concept of Asymmetrical Information").

We return to Niklas Luhmann's idea that the law maintains the system's autopoiesis and operative closure by linking earlier and later decisions (Luhmann, 1993). Adjusting the narrative to align with environmental changes serves the system's essential needs. Our attempts to prove the validity of the asymmetrical information framework in the context of Russia's legal system rest on the premise that it serves to hibernate the opposition and manage the uncertainties which free information flow could bring in (Luhmann, 1992, p. 255). It is possible to stir strife deliberately and ridicule dissent through asymmetric information, like in Russia with its legislative amendments post-2012 limiting freedom of expression. This is how the system is both created and maintained.

1.6 Explaining the Data Analysis With the Help of the LCT Framework

This monograph's methodological framework draws on Karl Maton's work, particularly his LCT, which provides an interdisciplinary framework for analysing information about theories, laws, and practices. This is done by examining data (texts of legal amendments with preparatory materials, their interpretation by the Constitutional Court, and their application by courts of law) and structuring their contents into leading themes or legitimation codes that extend said principles across academic, practical, and national frontiers towards new forms of knowledge-building (Maton et al., 2015).

In our analysis, we use LCT to avoid arbitrariness, and our central justification for preferring this method is that it is topic-related. Asymmetrical information is understood in this book as data that have been modified (asymmetrised) and communicated so that one aspect of a topic is highlighted without mentioning the rest. Such asymmetries in modelling and communicating data can be tracked by LCT. As LCT maintains, the actor who issues a statement controls the process by establishing "specific legitimation codes as dominant and so defines what is legitimate, shaping the social field of practice as a dynamic field of possibilities" (Maton, 2014, p. 18). Each code has several dimensions, but the specialisation codes are especially relevant for our research since they allow the organising principles of practices to be conceptualised (p. 3). These codes position discourses in the structures of knowledge and knowers and establish independent relations to these two structures (2014). LCT recommends distinguishing between epistemic relations to knowledge structures (ER) and social relations to knower structures (SR). These relations can exhibit relatively stronger (+) or weaker (−) classification and framing. In other words, code dimensions in laws, interpretations, and the application of law may emphasise the knowledge structure, the social relations to knower structure, or neither. Depending on these modalities, we can assess our key findings and triggers to justify legal amendments. This assessment can be done by categorising the results:

1. using knowledge codes (ER+, SR−), in which specialised knowledge concerning concrete facts and events is underscored, and the attributes of actors are downplayed. Therefore, the more valorised shared knowledge is, like Western values emphasising pleasure or the West intimidating Russia, the more likely it is to have a significant impact, provided dissent is silenced.
2. relying on knower codes (ER−, SR+), in which specialised knowledge is downplayed but the attributes of actors are emphasised as measures of achievement. This would entail a classic example of bragging by emphasising the country's greatness while not mentioning the diversity of opinions or the value of individual rights.
3. employing élite codes (ER+, SR+), in which legitimacy is established based on both possessing specialised knowledge and being the right kind of knower (the term élite here refers not to social exclusivity but rather to possessing both legitimate knowledge and legitimate dispositions). Facts and claims are released that call for behaviour to support or stop certain actors (e.g. citizens protesting), but they are provocateurs and must be stopped.
4. acting through relativist codes (ER−, SR−), in which "legitimacy is determined by neither specialist knowledge nor knower attributes" (Maton et al., 2015,

p. 13). The latter codes are just data communicators announcing that the rules of behaviour are changing without any further explanation.

This book will provide numerous examples of how preparation materials for legal amendments or court interpretations allow such claims. However, if we identify examples from the previous three groups of techniques, we might discern that the system is in a creative phase, preparing to fine-tune the narrative. If we find a fourth example, it would mean that the system is too busy to invent creative ways to self-correct or that it is satisfied with its performance. Because of difficulties communicating, there is no way to further inquire and clarify in routine communication without causing emotional strain, which indicates an abnormal condition of the system. Methodologically, we perform LCT-grounded document analysis and organise data into topics of importance (or codes), with each topic further analysed according to four principal specialisation codes: ER+, ER−, SR+, and SR−.

While asymmetry of information by justifying the isolation of everything foreign is often at the forefront of contemporary discussions, using LCT will help us see this as only one of many elements in a matrix of stakeholders and considerations connected to how and why such a system could be created and survive. Such an approach can sustain a nuanced account of how disparate stakeholders articulate their needs and concerns in the face of any specific need or crisis and deliver research results with textual analysis of data that properly acknowledges the socio-political context. The LCT framework is beneficial for legal studies investigating limitations of free speech and access to information since it allows laws and regulations to be examined as an amalgam of connections between various research theories. LCT typically moves from social ontologies, such as theories of social systems and access to information, to explanatory frameworks, theories of the dual state and legal dualism, and theories of collective action and agenda-setting, to elaborating a substantive research area of asymmetrical information (Maton, 2014).

This process is not static or unidirectional: while social ontologies provide meta-theoretical implications for explanatory frameworks, the latter informs social ontologies by mediating their access to the social world. It is understanding how restricting the free flow of information is developed and not met with an adequate response by any independent entities where LCT can be fruitful, even essential, since the framework theories explain how the administration could control organised interest groups and replace them with its agents. Because the present status quo was established due to a lack of opportunities for determined opposition, any accurate analysis of this status quo will require an approach that can parse epistemic and social relations between different actors.

Perhaps most important is that although our research framework guides this study, the study also speaks back to theory and helps evaluate the data it provides (Maton, 2014). This dynamism is partly why LCT, applied and adapted in various ways, has proven to be a successful approach to human rights and information inquiries. Harzing (2016), for instance, used and adapted the LCT method to study the publication of academic sources, which provides a verified methodological apparatus for analysing data, nuancing the nature of academic and legal discourse, and developing insights into how objective information is accessed, shaped, and changed (Martin et al., 2020). The benefit of the LCT framework is its capacity to effectively apply the framework theory of asymmetrical information to publicly available data, revealing subtle assumptions, connections, and, ultimately, meanings.[4] See "Appendix" at pp. 148–149.

LCT-grounded examination of publicly available data (e.g. *travaux preparatoir*, subsequent amendments to other laws triggered by the law in question, public speeches of officials, interpretations of Richter (2009), Constitutional Court, and application of the law by the courts and administrative organs) allows further contextualising the meaning of the legal provision introduced in phase 1 and filtering out common topics with the CCA method as most speakers emphasised national security interests when justifying legal amendments related to foreign agent restrictions. Analysing each topic against four principal specialisation codes, ER+/– and SR+/–, can explore how the information security-based argument justifies why some persons should be labelled foreign agents. In statements made by A, B, and D, we could see either ER+/– meaning relatively strong or weak framing of the epistemic relationship. For example, quoting authoritative names indicates ruling out any possible foreign influence and either SR+/– meaning relatively strong or weak framing of social relationships by not mentioning any protest movement or NGO activity related to protecting freedom of speech.

Reading the findings in the context of the theories of access to information and the theories of the dual state, classified as knowledge-knower-élite-relativist codes, would lead to the formulation of new substantive research findings, demonstrating how exactly and with which triggers and techniques information released to the public is asymmetrised or moulded to persuade citizens to accept it uncritically.

Notes

1 As Luhmann wrote in his essay *What is communication?* (1993) and developed in further works, including *Law as a social system* (Luhmann, 1993), the three factors of communication are information, its utterance, and understanding. As he pointed out, this distinction is not new in linguistic communication; it was developed from works by Biihler, Austin, Searle, and Habermas, with Habermas adding a typology of implicit validity claims to his theory (Luhmann, 1992, pp. 252–254).
2 As one could witness in Russia when, for example, the trusted national political parties were strengthened while regional political agglomerations had to undergo severe restrictions.
3 The establishment of federal districts to control regional authorities' activities gradually elevated the Security Council's status, which ultimately sanctified the invasion of Ukraine.
4 See Wilmot (2020, p. 21), who demonstrates how to use LCT in moving from simple sentences ("I enjoyed the Tuesday reading group where I was able to learn from more experienced peers") to complex ideas ("Communities of practice are valued by postgraduate students"), often achieved by employing multiple theories within one stance.

References

Akerlof, G. A. (1970). The market for "lemons": Quality uncertainty and the market mechanism. *The Quarterly Journal of Economics*, *84*(3), 488–500.

Akerlof, G. A. (1976). The economics of caste and of the rat race and other woeful tales. *The Quarterly Journal of Economics*, *90*(4), 599–617.
Akerlof, G. A. (1997). Social distance and social decisions. *Econometrica*, *65*(6), 1005–1027.
Akerlof, G. A., & Shiller, R. J. (2010). *Animal spirits, how human psychology drives the economy, and why it matters for global capitalism*. Princeton University Press.
Alapuro, R., Mustajoki, A., & Pesonen, P. (Eds.). (2012). *Understanding Russianness*. Routledge.
Banas, J. A., & Miller, G. (2013). Inducing resistance to conspiracy theory propaganda: Testing inoculation and metainoculation strategies. *Human Communication Research*, *39*(2), 184–207.
Bartley, T., & Schneiberg, M. (2002). Rationality and institutional contingency: The varying politics of economic regulation in the fire insurance industry. *Sociological Perspectives*, *45*(1), 47–79.
Bikoue, S. M., & Bayemi, O. (2020). Bribery game in government secondary schools in Cameroon: An empirical investigation of Banfield's model. *Journal of Economic and Social Thought*, *7*(3), 110–124.
Black, D. (1961). The theory of committees and elections. *Philosophy*, *36*(137), 248–249.
Citroni, G., Spigno, I., & Tanzarella, P. (Eds.). (2022). *The right to political participation. A study of the judgments of the European and Inter-American courts of human rights*. Routledge.
Clardie, J. (2011). The impact of military spending on the likelihood of democratic transition failure: Testing two competing theories. *Armed Forces & Society*, *37*(1), 163–179.
Coleman, J. S. (1966). Individual interests and collective action. *Public Choice*, *1*(1), 49–62.
Daucé, F. (2015). The duality of coercion in Russia: Cracking down on "foreign agents". *Demokratizatsiya: The Journal of Post-Soviet Democratization*, *23*(1), 57–75.
Fearon, J. (1994). Domestic political audiences and the escalation of international disputes. *American Political Science Review*, *88*(3), 577–592.
Flood, M. M. (1958). Some experimental games. *Management Science*, *5*(2), 5–26.
Glaser, B. G. (1965). The constant comparative method of qualitative analysis. *Social Problems*, *12*(4), 436–445.
Hendley, K. (2017). *Everyday law in Russia*. Cornell University Press.
Hendley, K. (2022). Legal dualism as a framework for analysing the role of law under authoritarianism. *Annual Review of Law and Social Science*, *18*(1), 211–226.
Horne, L. (2017). What makes health care special? An argument for health care insurance. *Kennedy Institute of Ethics Journal*, *27*(4), 561–587.
Karlsen, G. H. (2019). Divide and rule: Ten lessons about Russian political influence activities in Europe. *Palgrave Commun*, *5*(19), 1–14.
Kohut, A., & Bowman, C. (2017). The vocal minority in U.S. politics.In E. C. Pease & E. E. Dennis (Eds.), *Radio: The forgotten medium*. Routledge.
Laruelle, M. (2019). *Russian nationalism. Imaginaries, doctrines, and political battlefields*. Routledge.
Ledeneva, A. (2011). Can Medvedev change Sistema? Informal networks and public administration in Russia. In V. Kononenko & A. Moshes (Eds.), *Russia as a network state* (pp. 39–61). Springer.
Ledeneva, A. (2013). *Can Russia modernize? Sistema, power networks, and informal governance*. Cambridge University Press.
Lewis, D. G. (2020). *Russia's new authoritarianism. Putin and the politics of order*. Edinburgh University Press.
Luhmann, N. (1990). The future of democracy. *Thesis Eleven*, *26*(1), 46–53.
Luhmann, N. (1992). What is communication? *Communication Theory*, *2*(3), 251–259.
Luhmann, N. (1993). *Law as a social system*. Oxford University Press.
Luhmann, N. (1995). *Social systems* (J. Bednarz, Jr. & D. Baeker, Trans.). Stanford University Press. (Original work published 1985)

Mälksoo, L. (2021). International law and the 2020 amendments to the Russian constitution. *American Journal of International Law, 115*(1), 78–93.

Martin, J. R., Maton, K., & Doran, Y. J. (2020). *Accessing academic discourse: Systemic functional linguistics and legitimation code theory*. Routledge.

Matejova, M., Parker, S., & Dauvergne, P. (2018). The politics of repressing environmentalists as agents of foreign influence. *Australian Journal of International Affairs, 72*, 145–162.

Maton, K. (2014). *Knowledge and knowers: Towards a realist sociology of education*. Routledge.

Maton, K., Hood, S., & Shay, S. (2015). *Knowledge-building: Educational studies in legitimation code theory*. Routledge.

Matthies, A. L., & Uggerhøj, L. (2014). *Participation, marginalization and welfare services: Concepts, politics and practices across European countries*. Ashgate.

McCarthy, L. A., Rice, D., & Lokhmutov, A. (2023). Four months of "discrediting the military": Repressive law in wartime Russia. *Demokratizatsiya: The Journal of Post-Soviet Democratization, 31*(2), 125–160.

McDonald, D. G., Glynn, C. J., Kim, S. H., & Ostman, R. E. (2001). The spiral of silence in the 1948 presidential election. *Communication Research, 28*(2), 139–155.

Noelle-Neumann, E. (1993). *The spiral of silence: Public opinion – our social skin*. University of Chicago Press.

Olson, M. (1965). *The logic of collective action*. Harvard University Press.

Pennington, M. (2010). Democracy and the deliberative conceit. *Journal of Politics and Society, 22*, 159–184.

Petrov, N., Lipman, M., & Hale, H. E. (2010). *Overmanaged democracy in Russia: Governance implications of hybrid regimes*. Carnegie Endowment for International Peace. https://carnegieendowment.org/files/overmanaged_democracy_2.pdf

RFE/RL. (2024, February 18). *Defying authorities, Russians pay tribute to Navalny; Hundreds detained*. www.rferl.org/a/russia-navalny-mourning-arrests/32824593.html

Richter, J. (2009). Putin and the public chamber. *Post-Soviet Affairs, 25*(1), 39–65.

Rodgers, J., & Lanoszka, A. (2023). Russia's rising military and communication power: From Chechnya to Crimea. *Media, War & Conflict, 16*(2), 135–152.

Sakwa, R. (2010). The dual state in Russia. *Post-Soviet Affairs, 26*(3), 185–206.

Sakwa, R. (2011). *The crisis of Russian democracy: The dual state, factionalism, and the Medvedev succession*. Cambridge University Press.

Sakwa, R. (2021). Heterarchy: Russian politics between chaos and control. *Post-Soviet Affairs, 37*(3), 222–241.

Salamon, L. M., Benevolenski, V. B., & Jakobson, L. I. (2015). Penetrating the dual realities of government-nonprofit relations in Russia. *Voluntas, 26*, 2178–2214.

Shulman, E. (2022, June 16). *The mobilisation of the demobilised. Neither society nor the political system are ready for ideological indoctrination, ideologies*. RE: Russia. https://re-russia.net/en/expertise/022/

Siisiäinen, M. (2014). Four faces of participation. In A. L. Matthies & L. Uggerhøj (Eds.), *Participation, marginalisation and welfare services: Concepts, politics and practices across European countries* (pp. 29–45). Ashgate.

Slantchev, B. (2005). Military coercion in interstate crises. *American Political Science Review, 99*(4), 533–47.

Smelser, N. J. (1962). *Theory of collective behavior*. Routledge.

Tilly, C. (2007). *Democracy*. Cambridge University Press.

Toepler, S., & Fröhlich, C. (2020). Advocacy in authoritarian contexts: The case of disability NGOs in Russia. *International Journal of Sociology and Social Policy, 40*, 1473–1489.

UHRC. (2006, July 12). *CCPR general comment No. 25: Article 25. (Participation in public affairs and the right to vote): The right to participate in public affairs, voting rights and the right of equal access to public service*. UN Human Rights Committee. www.refworld.org/docid/453883fc22.html

Van der Vet, F. (2018). "When they come for you:" Legal mobilisation in new authoritarian Russia. *Law & Society Review*, *52*(2), 301–336.
Volkov, D., & Kolesnikov, A. (2023). *Alternate reality: How Russian society learned to stop worrying about the war*. Carnegie Endowment for International Peace.
Volkov, V. (2002). *Violent entrepreneurs: The use of force in the making of Russian capitalism*. Cornell University Press.
von Gall, C. (2024, February 8). *Regime adaptation within Russia's judicial elites*. Verfassungsblog. https://verfassungsblog.de/regime-adaptation-within-russias-judicial-elites/
Waldron, J. (1998). Participation: The right of rights. *Proceedings of the Aristotelian Society*, *98*(3), 307–337.
Waldron, J. (1999). *Law and disagreement*. Oxford University Press.
Weeks, J. (2008). Audience costs: Regime type and signaling resolve. *International Organization*, *62*(1), 35–64.
Weiss, J. C. (2013). Authoritarian signaling, mass audiences, and nationalist protest. *International Organization*, *67*(1), 1–35.
Wilmot, K. (2020). Building knowledge with theory: Unpacking complexity in doctoral writing. *Critical Studies in Teaching and Learning*, *8*(2), 18–38.
Zhelnov, A. (2022, December 3). "People interfere with authoritarianism": Interview with recognized foreign agent Ekaterina Shulman. *Forbes*. www.forbes.ru/rubriki-kanaly/video/482006-avtoritarizmu-ludi-mesaut-interv-u-priznannoj-inoagentom-ekateriny-sul-man?ysclid=lfgwxkxfmj902580319

2 Context

2.1 General Remarks

In this book, legal amendments are discussed that have tightened freedom of expression since 2012. This is a period that included the forthcoming annexation of Crimea and Putin's re-election. To analyse Russia's asymmetrical information-based legal system, we need to understand the context in which it operates. As discussed in the introduction, Akerlof's idea of asymmetrical information, which he developed through concepts of adverse selection (Akerlof, 1970) and social distance (Akerlof, 1997), serves as the theoretical lens for this analysis. In considering the legal system, we also apply Niklas Luhmann's systems theory, which describes asymmetries in distorted equality and maintaining operative closure.

To summarise what was said in the introduction, legal regulation is crucial to maintaining the legal system's closure or the impossibility of changing it from the outside. One thing about Russia is that it often relies on information asymmetry to justify enacting laws. Some facts are shared selectively, while others are suppressed and distorted. It deviates from equal treatment because this approach justifies unequal treatment between wanted and unwanted political actors (Luhmann, 1993). According to Luhmann (1993), asymmetries like that happen in highly stratified societies, where equality can be shaped differently, leading to unequal treatment. Along the way, the system creates criteria for what is equal and what is not without figuring out what exactly these criteria should be since creating the form of equality (i.e. something moulded out of equality by authorities) emphasises the system's existing dynamics.

Therefore, equality becomes non-normative in the Russian legal system, with interpretations of vague laws acting as ad hoc norms. Chapter 7 shows how the Constitutional Court prohibited criticism of armed forces, citing their vital role in national security: criticism of the military should be banned, unlike other forms of criticism. Such interpretations become possible when legal norms are drafted to justify inequality using asymmetrical information techniques. Also discussed in this book is the issue of citizens being excluded from opportunities to exert influence through public discourse due to a broad definition of foreign agents. Along with other asymmetrical information techniques discussed in this book, these examples contradict the constitutionally guaranteed right to free expression.

DOI: 10.4324/9781032613383-2

Under Article 29 of the Russian Constitution, freedom of expression is guaranteed to everyone (RF Constitution, Article 29). The first paragraph of this article states that everyone is entitled to freedom of expression and thought. The second paragraph prohibits propaganda and agitation that incites hatred and hostility based on social, racial, national, or religious grounds. Additionally, it prohibits promoting social, racial, national, religious, or linguistic superiority. In accordance with the third paragraph, opinions or beliefs cannot be imposed or forcibly renounced. According to the fourth paragraph, individuals can seek, receive, transmit, produce, and disseminate information as they see fit. Federal law determines what information constitutes a state secret. According to Article 29's fifth paragraph, media freedom is guaranteed, and censorship is prohibited. In the following sections, the reader will be able to understand better how the current legislation allows such manoeuvres.

2.2 The "Not Possible to Change" Constitution

2.2.1 Rules on Changing the Constitution

Why Article 29 still exists in its current form despite heavy constitutional revisions in 2020 is easy to explain. There is no way the Federal Assembly or the Russian Parliament can change Chapters 1, 2, and 9 of the Russian Constitution (RF Constitution, Article 135, par. 1). In other words, the chapters that set out the state's foundations, fundamental human rights, and amendments to the Constitution can only be changed by revising the whole document. In this case, revision means creating a new draft of the Constitution, negotiating it, and getting it approved in all of Russia's regions. Moreover, a special Constitutional Assembly must approve a new constitution draft under specific federal constitutional (or organic) law. The assembly can only be called if both chambers of parliament approve the proposal to revise the mentioned non-amendable chapters (RF Constitution, Article 135, par. 2).

Currently, no organic law regulates how the Constitutional Assembly gets gathered. Given the current Russian legal environment, organic law can still be passed at any time (Chapter 7 of this book explains how the authorities can adopt the necessary legislation quickly through the existing legislative processes, a process we refer to as "legislation through winter preservers."). Most likely, this was not the main reason the Russian Constitution was not updated. Yes, the hypothetical constitutional assembly could either draft a new Constitution or confirm the invariability of the current one. However, each decision must be approved by more than half of the electorate in a national referendum. Considering that various unforeseeable circumstances could undermine the desired outcome, the current leaders may think revising the Constitution is too risky (see our discussion in Section 2.6.3 about adverse selection). Because of this, the current text of the Constitution, adopted in December 1993 and heavily amended in 2020, is inherently contradictory. Looking at its foundations should give us a better understanding of how asymmetrical information is used in law.

2.2.2 *Place of International Law and Role of Constitutional Court*

While the authorities might wish otherwise, Article 15, paragraph 4 of the Constitution, which cannot be amended, asserts a long-standing monistic principle regarding international law in Russia by stating that international law and international treaties are integral parts of Russian law. Article 15 of the 1993 Constitution remains the supreme legal authority over laws enacted in Russia (including ratification laws).

Even though this hierarchy existed, some scholars argued that international human rights should precede ordinary law in Russia. Smith (2007) argued that since Article 55 indicates that enumerating constitutional rights and freedoms should not negate or diminish other widely recognised rights, these rights should serve as a guiding framework for political actors. Specifically, Article 55 prohibits any law that diminishes or abolishes the rights and freedoms (para. 2).

This principle of international law being a part of Russia's legal system was introduced in 1993 to challenge Soviet time dualism, which viewed international law as a parallel system. Only the 1993 Russian Constitution has an "integration clause" relating to international law (Kalinichenko, 1998). While the Soviet Union ratified significant UN human rights treaties, no change to the law was required (Bowring, 2018). To monitor the Soviet Union's treaty compliance, treaty bodies reviewed compliance and made mild political decisions in individual cases where national authorities accepted the possibility of submitting individual complaints. As a result of censorship and controls over the third sector, shadow reports by NGOs could not counterbalance official reports. To erode international law's importance, Russia amended its Constitution as far as possible in 2020 to revert things to factory settings. In his address to the Federal Assembly, before the amendment was finalised, Putin announced his intention to maintain the supremacy of the Constitution (RF President, 2020). In his speech, the president stated that Russia can only enforce international legislation, treaties, and decisions that do not contradict the Russian Constitution. There is a limit on applying international law in the (revised) Russian Constitution:

> *Only if it does not limit human rights or freedoms or contravene Russian constitution principles can the Russian Federation belong to interstate associations and transfer parts of its authority to them.*
>
> (Article 79)

A new amendment to Article 125 of the Constitution strengthens the RF Constitutional Court's power to legitimise non-enforcement of international treaties when they violate the Constitution. A new paragraph 6 in Article 125 states,

". . . non-conforming international treaties and agreements cannot be enforced or applied." After amending the Organic Law of the Constitution in 2015, the courts now have the power to make non-executive decisions for interstate bodies and foreign or international courts, imposing obligations on the Russian Federation if those decisions violate Russian law and order. With the 2020 Constitutional Amendments, this power gained constitutional status in Article 125, paragraph 5.1 b.

Article 125 indeed elevates the Constitutional Court's role as interpreter and defender of the Constitution, but this role has also eroded and become asymmetrical. It is ironic, too, that before the Constitutional Court, the Committee for Constitutional Supervision of the Soviet Union initiated joining the optional protocols to UN treaties, which made it possible for citizens to submit individual complaints about violations of UN treaties (Bowring, 2018). This committee was also the last Russia-driven constitutional body that strove to remain apolitical before it folded in 1991. In its statement regarding the establishment of the Commonwealth of Independent States, the committee claims that the statement in the Belovezhsk Agreement that "the USSR ceases to exist as a subject of international law and geopolitical reality" is just a "political assessment of the situation, which has no legal force" (USSR, 1991). For example, in 1992, the Constitutional Court ruled in a compromise decision that Yeltsin had rightfully dissolved the Communist Party. Still, the party could continue at the local level, even though the applicants in a new Russia probably thought they would get a definitive condemnation of the party (Bowring, 2024). Neither did the Court become more robust or more independent when it received powers over international decisions; instead, it moved from legitimising public decisions to interpreting legal gaps and ambiguities even when no decision had been publicly announced.

Whether it was amending the Constitution (RF Constitutional Court, 2020), justifying the joining of East Ukraine's territories to Russia (RF Constitutional Court, Postanovlenie No. 36-P, 2022; RF Constitutional Court, Postanovlenie No. 37-P, 2022; RF Constitutional Court, Postanovlenie No. 38-P, 2022; RF Constitutional Court, Postanovlenie No. 39-P, 2022), or explaining why it was acceptable to be sentenced criminally for no crime except a series of minor violations of protest legislation (RF Constitutional Court, 2017) (see Chapter 5), the Court supported all kinds of decisions. In the end, the role of the Court became even more notable when it had to proclaim things the authorities would not say aloud, such as explaining how citizens would support Russia's enemies by criticising its government and military (RF Constitutional Court, 2023). Olga Podoplelova calls it a constitutional paradox: the more fervently the Court legitimises unconstitutional laws, the more quickly it loses its political influence (Podoplelova, 2024). This book also asserts that these developments are one of the guarantees of asymmetrical information. Niklas Luhmann pointed out that not all authorities' motives can be turned into law. There will never be a statement in a judgment that a legislative act was due to a party's manoeuvring or that it was now politically correct to take a stance on the matter. There is only one issue: how to limit moral zealots' active interpretation (Luhmann, 1993, p. 115). The Constitutional Court seems to handle this well.

2.3 Law and Accountability

2.3.1 Legal Dualism and Ways Around the Law

The 1993 Russian Constitution states that law-making is vested in the Federal Assembly, the country's representative and legislative body (RF Constitution, Article 94). Legislation is drafted and debated in the Federal Assembly, and then the president approves it (RF Constitution, Articles 104, 105, and 107). When the Council of the Federation fails to enforce the law it passed, the State Duma, the lower house, has a veto right (RF Constitution, Article 94, par. 5). However, the parliament does not have an absolute veto over the president's approval of the law (RF Constitution, Article 107, par. 2). On the one hand, if the president vetoes a law passed by parliament, the veto can be overridden by both chambers with a qualified majority. On the other hand, in 2020, the procedures were changed so that the president could submit a law he is not happy with to the Constitutional Court for review. If the Constitutional Court rules the law unconstitutional, the president returns it to parliament without signing it, effectively ending the legislative process for that law. With the president nominating the Court's members, it is more likely that the Constitutional Court will concur with him. Since the Constitutional Court was created in its current form, it "didn't condemn a single law that undermined democracy or curtailed public participation in politics" (Podoplelova, 2024).

As we will witness in this book, Russian law limits freedom of expression, the press, assembly, and association, and it relies heavily on the courts to enforce these limitations (Pomeranz, 2021). There is also a shift from normativity and legal certainty in applying law. For instance, McCarthy et al. (2023) and Hendley (2022) discuss the emergence of a politicised version of the law and legal dualism that coexists with a legal system and serves citizens' needs in ordinary, non-political situations. McCarthy et al. (2023, p. 127), nevertheless, point out that while the state has more latitude since the war began with censorship of anti-war criticism, the law still plays an essential role in Putin's Russia, whether to provide internal legitimacy, punish dissents, or to teach others.

When justifying the introduction of cumulative criminal liability after a series of minor administrative omissions, the Russian Constitutional Court articulated its interpretation of legal dualism. As discussed in Chapter 5 of this book on limiting protest activities, the Constitutional Court concludes that administrative law and criminal law "share the same duties, guiding principles, and goal of defending human rights." According to the Court, using administrative law liability as a basis for criminal liability or applying a dualistic approach is one way to prosecute offences. The law is dualistic when you have a dual state, as Sakwa calls Russia (Sakwa, 2007). It is an asymmetry where the law loses its role in setting mandatory rules, but courts mainly handle its role in deciding what is legal. It encroaches on the law's normative closure, in which facts and cases are distinguished as equal or unequal (Luhmann, 1993, p. 23).

Since the law picks facts and uses distinctions differently than ethics or politics, the distinction between equal and unequal should have a different meaning within the law (Luhmann, 1993, p. 23). This distinction does not exist in modern Russia. In

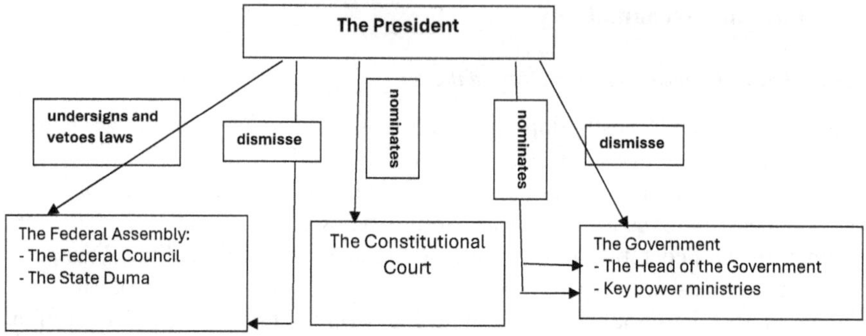

Figure 2.1 President's powers over all critical state organs

the event of a law that is inconvenient for calling legal what is illegal, asymmetrising information techniques help to justify and invent ways around it. Getting laws adopted quickly can be done interestingly if the circumstances are tight. On the one hand, the Constitution lays out a general framework for law-making, including a timeframe that cannot be rushed. These constitutional guidelines are detailed in legislation, including Parliamentary Rules of Procedure (RF State Duma, 1998). The State Duma registers draft laws submitted by authorised actors and refers them to the Duma profile committee for consideration. Once the committee reviews the draft, either amendments are made or it is added to the lower house schedule for the current or upcoming session (RF State Duma, 1998, chap. 12). Neither of these procedures requires a minimum timeframe, and a call for an extraordinary session of the lower house is permitted under Article 43 of the Rules of Parliament. Nevertheless, a minimum of 15 days is required to fix possible amendments after adopting the law in its first reading (RF State Duma, 1998, art. 119, para. 5).

Borzenko (2019) demonstrated in a study that, on average, a law takes 170 days to be adopted in Russia. On the other hand, authorities can circumvent legislative restrictions if there is an urgent need, like after the invasion of Ukraine, when military critics were silenced (see Chapter 7). There was a tactic used to speed up the legislative process. The authorities took materials associated with another draft law that was already pending. They incorporated them into the passage of the necessary statute after the blitzkrieg failed in Ukraine, intending to introduce legislation prohibiting defamation of military forces as soon as possible. Opening winter preserves is what we call this strategy, a phrase Petranovskaya used to describe similar legal manoeuvres. Therefore, the legislative processes are on hold to preserve supplies for the harsh winter. Figure 2.1 summarises the president's powers over all critical state organs.

2.3.2 Rule of Law

New legislation and legal institutions need new frameworks to tame old categories and justify them if they mean stepping away from the previous course.

Consider the following two quotes to understand how this works in Russia's asymmetrical information-based system.

> *Lawmakers must follow constitutional principles of equality, fairness, and proportionality when regulating public relations. Therefore, laws must be clear, adequate, reasonable, sufficient, proportionate, and legally certain, clear, and consistent across sectors.*
>
> (RF Constitutional Court, 2014)

We indeed quoted the 2014 Russian Constitutional Court ruling in these two sentences. It is only later that the Constitutional Court will refine and detail its understanding of the rule-of-law state, as we will see in Chapter 7 of this book on prohibitions of discrediting the military and the authorities. As the Court explained in 2023,

> *If citizens challenge public authority decisions, it means Russia isn't a rule-of-law state, the Constitution isn't supreme, and people don't obey it.*
>
> (RF Constitutional Court, 2023)

These two quotes perfectly illustrate Luhmann's idea of the system self-correcting to avoid collapse. Russia's constitutional architecture allows for this kind of self-correction since it has a weak system for holding executive bodies accountable despite the rule-of-law claim in Constitutional Article 1 (Sakwa, 2007, p. 7). By 2020, the Federal Assembly had the constitutional power to exercise parliamentary control and direct parliamentary inquiries to the government, local governments, and other authorities (RF Constitution, Article 103.1). All major branches of government, however, are controlled by the president. In his role, he is responsible for the general management of the government and makes resignation decisions (Article 83). The president holds the prime minister personally accountable (RF Constitution, Article 113). The president can issue mandatory edicts and decrees (RF Constitution, Article 90) and formulate international and domestic policies (RF Constitution, Article 80). The president can dissolve parliament's lower chamber.

Parliament became even weaker after the 2020 constitutional revisions because the president could now dismiss the lower house in three situations instead of two. It used to be that the lower house could be dismissed if the Duma rejected the candidate the president proposed as head of government (i.e. the Prime Minister) (RF Constitution, Article 111) or if parliamentarians voted with no confidence in the government (RF Constitution, Article 117). When the latter scenario happens, the president must choose between resigning and dismissing the legislature. With the 2020 amendments, the president can also dismiss the Duma if it rejects the candidacy three times of key deputy heads of the government and federal ministers in charge of defence, state security, internal affairs, justice, foreign affairs, disaster relief, and public safety (RF Constitution, Article 112). A change in the composition of parliament's upper house allowed the acting president to nominate up to seven senators for life (RF Constitution, Article 95).

The acting president nominates key officials: the head of government and deputies (whom he can dismiss), the president of the Constitutional Court, the Prosecutor General, and the chief leader of the armed forces (RF Constitution, Article 83). Besides running the State Council and Security Council, he upholds Russia's military doctrine. The impeachment process, or *otreshenie ot dolzhnosti*, involves high treason or another serious crime and must be approved by both chambers of parliament, with the Senate making the final decision (RF Constitution, Article 93). It is determined by the Supreme Court and the Constitutional Court (whose leaders are the president's picks) to regulate whether the process is legal.

2.3.3 The Novelty of the President Emeritus

A strong and largely irremovable president was to be the focus of stability in a 1993 Constitution adopted amid the chaos of the Soviet Union's collapse while the government had lost control of parliament (Sakwa, 2007, p. 7). In 1996, the 50% minimum threshold of electorate necessary for taking part in elections was abandoned, making it possible to decide election results based on any number of votes, thus preventing citizens from boycotting the elections. Taking proactive measures, the Constitution was amended to deal with the situation when Putin is no longer a president. In order to address this challenge, the President Emeritus institution will be constitutionally enshrined after the 2020 amendments. The revised Constitution does not mention President Emeritus as such. Still, several new provisions make it easier to get privileges, immunities, and guarantees for *"president Rossiiskoi Federatsii, prekrativshii ispolnenie svoikh polnomochii v sviazi s istecheniem sroka ego prebyvaniia v dolzhnosti ili dosrochno." In English,* "the Russian president whose powers have lapsed since the end of his term tenure or earlier."

As a result of renewed Constitutional Article 125, the Constitutional Court should assess the compliance with the Constitution of the process for bringing charges of treason or other serious crimes against the acting president and the president who ceased to exercise his powers. As part of the renewed Constitution, Article 92.1 gives the president immunity if he ceases to exercise power after his term ends or earlier if he resigns or becomes permanently disabled. Also, the President Emeritus received a lifetime seat in the upper house, the Council of the Federation. In theory, the immunity of the President Emeritus could be revoked. This can only be done through a complicated process outlined in Article 93 of the Constitution, in which the Constitutional Court plays a significant role. It is a further assurance for Putin since senators enjoy immunity, which means they cannot be detained, arrested, or searched, except for arrests at crime scenes and personal searches (RF Constitution, Article 98).

Other than the constitutional powers granted to the president, several different institutions and tools are in place, reviewed below, that were not, or are not, envisioned in the Constitution. With Luhmann's idea that systems are shaped by their environments, they help sustain the cycle of the story – the new legislative pressure – the new story to fix the old one that keeps the system going.

We do not argue that people are tangible assets for the system since they are labourers, taxpayers, and military forces. We claim that citizens and the system's environment, in Luhmann's words, also provide immaterial resourcefulness to keep it from collapsing, as Akrelof suggests an asymmetrical-based information system should. Our first step will summarise the ideology of the new authoritarian system to understand how it maintains its operational closure. By ideology, we mean a set of ideas that governs action or policy and beliefs that govern behaviour (Oxford English Dictionary, 2023).

2.4 Stratification Based on Traditional Values and Distancing From Foreign Affiliations and Values

A lack of equality and legal certainty keeps distance within society and between the system and its environment. As with any other system, asymmetrical information-based systems can only be changed from within or by the state, not the environment, thus widening this gap to give them more power. During his address to the Russian parliament on 21 February 2023, Putin condemned those Russians who shared Western liberal ideas as national traitors (Krupskiy, 2023, p. 55).

Russia's constitutional foundations are juxtaposed with the norms of international law and the decisions of international bodies, further exacerbated by the distinction between those who keep up with Russia's values and others. According to Luhman, strict adherence to traditional values is probably the strongest binary division or cause of enhancing social distance.

Several constitutional amendments refer to family values, high moral ideals, historical memory, and generational continuity, which the President identifies as traditional spiritual and ethical values (see Chapter 6 about codifying traditional values). Article 67.1 of the Constitution, which explains that Russia continues the Soviet Union, recognises that Russia has a thousand-year history, preserves the memory of ancestors who passed on their ideals and faith, and maintains continuity in development (RF Constitution, Article 67.1, par. 2). Respect for older people is interwoven with the obligation to look after the unmighty parents that the non-disabled children have (RF Constitution, Article 72, par. g. 1). In essence, it is a tautology of an obligation stated in Article 38 of the Constitution that cannot be changed. Moreover, Russia honours the memory of its defenders, guarantees the protection of historical truth, and does not tolerate any belittlement of the people's fight for their homeland (RF Constitution, Article 67.1).

The new rule of the Constitution also stipulates the power of the federal government to protect marriage as a union between a man and a woman, reinforcing the orthodox rejection of same-sex relationships (RF Constitution, Article 72, par. g. 1).

As a result of the 2020 changes, we can see what some researchers call the ethnic turn in the Constitution (Laine & Zamyatin, 2001), meaning the emphasis on Russian culture and language. According to the Constitution, Russian is the language of the state-forming people of the Russian Federation throughout its entire territory (RF Constitution, Article 68, par. 1). It is the state's responsibility to ensure and support Russian culture as unique heritage of its multi-ethnic citizens (RF Constitution, Article 68, par. 4). Furthermore, the Constitution reaffirms its commitment to support compatriots living abroad in implementing their rights, protecting their interests, and preserving their cultural identity (RF Constitution, Article 69, par. 3).

Several new amendments introduce restrictions regarding individuals holding citizenship in foreign countries. Several new amendments restrict high-ranking public servants from holding foreign citizenship, or opening foreign bank accounts. Only the candidate for an RF President position was given a preference not extended to other officials. Citizens of states that were either admitted or part of which were accepted to the Russian Federation are not subject to the requirement of lack of foreign citizenship (RF Constitution, Article 81, par. 2). The only way to understand this exemption is to wait and see who might be introduced as Putin's successor and whether their roots are from the territory annexed by Russia.

2.5 The "Balanced" Information Flow of the Soviet Era

The 2020 amendment to the Constitution added another novelty. Russia, based on the Constitution's new Article 67.1, paragraph 1, was now a continuator (*pravoprodolzhatel*) of the Soviet Union in terms of membership in international organisations and their organs, membership in international treaties, and when foreseen with international treaties concerning actions and obligations of the USSR beyond Russian border. As opposed to succession, with continuity, the previous subject continues to exist despite issues like revolution, temporary occupation, or territory loss (Mälksoo, 2021, p. 83). As demonstrated by the president's appeal to voters at a World War II memorial in Rzhev before the 2020 constitutional referendum, Russia's constitutional commitment to the Soviet legacy has become a cornerstone of state identity based on the Soviet victory in World War II (2021, p. 84).

Allusions to the Soviet Union in the amended RF Constitution recall when the Soviet leadership tried to prevent the principle of free flow of information from becoming part of the UN. The 1948 Geneva Conference on Freedom of Information attempted to propose a Special Convention on Freedom of Information, but disagreements arose due to Soviet lobbying, so it was not adopted (Riekkinen, 2017, p. 139). The Geneva Conference was triggered by the UN General Assembly recognising freedom of information as a fundamental human right in 1946 (UN General Assembly, 1946).

The conference proposed three conventions: the Gathering and International Transmission of News, the Draft Convention Concerning the Institution of an International Right to Correction, and our Draft Convention on Freedom of Information. The draft of the Freedom of Information Convention "hasn't even been finalised" (Eek, 1953, p. 11; Österdahl, 1992, pp. 28–29). Throughout the conference, democratic governments were "trying to develop freedom of information" (Kish, 1995, p. 41), and authoritarian states attempting to restrict it could not agree on what freedom of information meant. The first Draft Convention on Freedom of Information was approved 31 to 6 with two abstentions. It was the Soviet bloc that voted against the resolution with six votes (Eek, 1953, p. 19).

Amendments to the draft Convention were recommended by the General Assembly to be considered during its next session. In the meantime, the Soviet Union had established its official position on adoption, saying it was "for a convention on freedom of information to be drafted as soon as possible" (UN Secretary General, 1958). It did it for its own reasons. Freedom of information did not align with USSR politics, especially Article 2, which called for special legislation on freedom of expression. Among the special guarantees of Article 2 were prohibitions against censorship and government criticism, strengthening the link between freedom of expression and political participation, and keeping the links between free information, free speech, and political involvement strong by prohibiting censorship and criticising the government (UN General Assembly, 1960). In addition, the Draft Convention on Freedom of Information was based on the free flow of information. The Soviet Union, meanwhile, was pushing for a balanced flow (Kortteinen et al., 1992, p. 402) of information based on exchanges" between political actors. Adopting the Draft Convention stalled after 1971 (UN General Assembly, 1971).

The Soviet Union slowed down the process of universalising freedom of information once the International Bill of Human Rights was conceived and spread far beyond the 1948 Geneva Conference (Humphrey, 1979, p. 25). Despite being nominated by Chairman Roosevelt of the Human Rights Commission of ECOSOC as part of the drafting committee for the Universal Declaration of Human Rights, it refused to acknowledge the right to the free flow of information. In the alternative version of Article 19 of the Universal Declaration, the USSR promoted its favourite "balanced" flow of information. As a result of debates, the accepted draft was developed, but Soviet Ambassador Bogomolov objected saying, it was "full of solemn affirmations that lack sense" (Humphrey, 1979, p. 25).

Later, the Soviet Union supported the 1978 UNESCO Declaration on mass media and peace, human rights, and fighting racism, apartheid, and war. Although the Soviet Union was ready to adopt the declaration, they proposed changing the free flow of information to the exchange of information (Österdahl, 1992, p. 186). Even so, with the developments leading up to the collapse of the Soviet Union, by 1989, when the CSCE Information Forum was held in London, "it was evident that the Soviet position . . . had changed considerably in favour of information freedom" (1992, pp. 74–75). A well-known policy called *glasnost* had already been enacted by Gorbachev, which relaxed censorship in the media, introduced transparency in the government, and gave people the right to sue executive organs (McNair, 1991). Boris Yeltsin issued a decree on the right to information in December 1993, outlining a draft law that would not be adopted until 1995 (RF President, 1993). There would be a new federal law on information in 2006, where information is seen as an object of legal protection (RF Federal Law No. 149-FZ, 2006). According to Irina Maskaeva's analysis of this federal law in 2012, only its two articles, eight and nine, refer to 16 other laws, which were primarily federal ones (Maskaeva, 2012). As this book will show, the law relating to information has significantly been revised since the 2012 legal amendments tightened freedom of expression.

All the previous attempts to adopt international instruments regarding the freedom of information did not succeed because of a political conflict over press and information freedom, mostly because Communist ideology viewed the press and information as tools for ruling elites. At the same time, Western doctrine saw their freedom as tools for social progress and change, criticism, and dissent (Eek, 1953). Having the leadership of Russia more in tune with international human rights might have made it easier to accommodate free expression, free press, and freely flowing symmetrical information. After 2012, information again became a tool for the government, with laws restricting free expression. As evidenced by the Soviet time restrictions on free information flow, authoritarian regimes do, on the one hand, learn from each other (Hall, 2023, p. xiii). Still a technical detail about suppressing dissent by law: as opposed to the Soviet Union's almost exclusive (McCarthy et al., 2023, p. 129) reliance on criminal law, the current regime uses both criminal prosecutions and administrative liability, probably giving possible opponents a chance to back down after an administrative fine.

2.6 "Appearances" of Ideology

2.6.1 External Threat and Reliance on Power Ministries

In Russia, informal practices often overshadow formal ones, as Sakwa argues in his dual-state theory (Sakwa, 2011). There is a good chance these practices are motivated by a belief that Russia was weak under Yeltsin and is now strong under Putin (Taylor, 2011, p. 107), strengthening the power vertically (Fauconnier, 2020, p. 164). Since his first presidential term, Putin's main slogan marks a significant change from Yeltsin's era, when the government delegated coercive functions to regional governors rather than maintaining direct control over the power ministries (Partlett, 2021, p. 323; Taylor, 2011, p. 111). As the economy boomed following the fall of the Soviet Union and Russia was trading natural resources at high global energy prices, it may be argued that Putin's image gained momentum (Taylor, 2011, p. 108), a circumstance exploited to rationalise the regime of stabilocracy in the eyes of the citizens (Sakwa, 2021, pp. 222–241). This resource wealth also enabled the power ministries to spend more money, which some scholars have described as the resource curse (Treisman, 2010). From 2012 onward, regardless of terminology, the philosophy behind the official regime relying on the power ministries, albeit corrupted and divided among themselves, has been cultivating the belief that the state is under severe external threat (Treisman, 2010, pp. 107–108, 314).

Apart from being a formidable state, Russia is also promoting the idea of itself as a unique civilisation and a global multipolarity alternative (Kalinin, 2019, p. 461) with sovereign ideology as well as a sovereign internet (Allerson, 2022, p. 233) – all with a gradual erosion of the previously celebrated idea of sovereign democracy (Taylor, 2011, p. 109). Sovereign Internet Law is the informal name for the 2019 Federal Law's on Communications and Information legal amendments (RF, Federal Law No. 90-FZ, 2019). Under these amendments, Russia is building a national routing system for Internet traffic starting in 2023. The law protects the domestic portion of the Internet from outside threats. In the law, traffic routing rules are defined, compliance is controlled, and infrastructure is set up in case Russian telecoms cannot connect to foreign root servers. Under the law, Russian users' data can be transferred abroad as little as possible. Researchers call this approach state-sponsored civilisational nationalism (Linde, 2016, p. 606), which reached its political zenith in 2012 with Putin's presidential campaign articles. Russia's multi-ethnic civilisation and the role the Russian people played in uniting the country were emphasised in those articles. Eventually, the 2013 Foreign Policy Concept included the narrative of civilisational difference, highlighting the importance of global competition on a civilisational level, which implies a clash between various values and development models (RF, Concept of Foreign Policy of the Russian Federation, 2013). A year before invading Ukraine, Putin wrote a 2021 article titled "On the Historical Unity of Russians and Ukrainians," calling Ukraine's statehood artificial and a justification for the invasion (Putin, 2021).

With writing sources under heavy control and censorship and freedom of expression limited to the point where criticising the military or government is forbidden, disseminating such ideas through mass media is supposed to work as a catalyst of social memory, according to Luhmann (1993, p. 234), which swaps history. The state silencing possible opposition and selecting information with its own choice is also an example of asymmetrical information technique in Akerlof's sense. Akerlof says asymmetrical information happens when there is an imbalance in power and information between parties. As long as the state controls the dissemination of information and silences any potential opposition, individuals cannot make informed decisions, and the flow of information is skewed.

The selective information feed excludes other topics since "Russia is strong under Putin" makes a distinction between what is said and what is not. However, it could be more robust by avoiding war and keeping positive relationships with the rest of the world (Luhmann, 1992, p. 254). To achieve far-reaching goals, the authorities selectively share information, which allows them to minimise or ignore the difficulties that individuals are experiencing today. By omitting or distorting other information that would be useful for presenting an alternative viewpoint, this asymmetrising manipulation can heighten nationalistic feelings that could be used to silence dissent and minimise criticism. On the other hand, focusing on individual concerns would draw attention to individuals' immediate needs and experiences, potentially mobilising public opinion against governmental policies.

Every revised foreign policy concept has incorporated this approach, including the one from 2016 that is no longer valid (RF Concept of Foreign Policy of the Russian Federation, 2016) and the latest working concept from 2023 (RF Concept of Foreign Policy of the Russian Federation, 2023). According to the latest 2023 document, Russia is "a distinctive state-civilization, a vast Eurasian and Euro-Pacific power uniting the Russian people and other peoples that make up the Russian world's cultural and civilisational community" (RF Concept of Foreign Policy of the Russian Federation, 2023, par. 4). On the other hand, Europe is perceived as lacking sovereignty or somewhat unable to afford sovereignty because it depends on the United States (Lipman, 2016). Essentially, these approaches are only the appearances of ideologies or attempts to "transform own propaganda cliches into ideological platforms" (Shulman, 2022). Instead, the asymmetrical information (or propaganda) forms an ideological platform retroactively or attempts to do so.

2.6.2 Conceptual Framework(s): From Sovereign Democracy to New Eurasianism

No matter how resistant many citizens are to believing in new ideologies (2022), the balance between information flows and political expediency requires a conceptual framework for asymmetrical information to operate. Researchers have identified Vladislav Surkov and Alexander Dugin as the key designers of this framework.

It has been suggested that Vladislav Surkov, who went from being Putin's deputy chief of staff and deputy head of the government to becoming his advisor before he was arrested in 2022, was a critical proponent of an earlier version of the Kremlin's philosophy of sovereign democracy (Eltsov, 2019; Taylor, 2011, p. 109). Surkov's views on advocating Russian independence without external interference ranged from sovereign democracy to Putinism. His 2006 argument was that Russia's governance should be called a sovereign democracy so that Russia can be an open nation among other open nations, cooperating with them under fair rules and without being controlled from the outside (Surkov, 2006).

Already in 2019, in his article "The Long State of Putin," the meaning of sovereignty has been elevated to the concept of "Putinism." Surkov goes on to describe Russia's descending from the Soviet Union to its present state as a collapse (*obval*) that could still be halted by Russia's immodest role in world history (Surkov, 2019). He claims that by the mid-2000s, Russia had shaped into a state that did not exist. Surkov says Russians should stick to national interests, which have been proven by events like Brexit, not to be naïve in the face of globalisation. In addition, he argues that Russia's state is honest in justifying its coercive character because its most brutal power structures run directly down the facade without hiding:

> *[w]ith vast heterogeneous spaces and constant presence in the thick of the geopolitical struggle, the military-police functions of the state are essential and decisive.*
>
> (Surkov, 2019)

According to Surkov, there have been four main state models throughout Russian history: Ivan the Third, Peter the Great, Lenin, and Putin, all named after their long-willed creators. The Russian Federation will, therefore, remain Putin's Russia after many years, just like France, which still considers itself the Fifth Republic after de Gaulle. Consequently, Putin's rule embodies a complex ideology of the future and a system of dominion (*sistema vlastvovaniia*).

Even the least intuitive reader can see that dominion power has little to do with democracy, however sovereign both might be. To avoid raising eyebrows about where the sovereign democracy went, Surkov insists that Russians are not dependent on democratic institutions. In contrast to the West, where people trust institutions, Russians trust only the first person. In his words, Russians are "always canny (*sebe na ume*), untouched by social surveys, agitation, threats, or other forms of direct influence" (Surkov, 2019). People participate in party meetings, wars, elections, and economic experiments but live differently.

Surkov's mission was to "frame public thinking about contemporary domestic, regional and global political affairs through their representation of Russian state actions in light of Russian cultural traditions" (Silvius, 2017). He described it himself like this: "[p]eople need it. Most people need their heads to be filled with thoughts" (Foy, 2021). So, this mission fits the definition of propaganda. It has been found that relying on the leader's popularity is the best way to avoid overt repression (Frye, 2021). The idea of denying individual freedoms associated with democracy to concentrate on the collective values assured by Putin fits into the concept of diversion and mobilisation used as propaganda tools.

In the first case, attention is diverted from the current socio-economic problems within a country, while in the second, supporters are mobilised to overpower opposition (Hubb & Wang, 2023, p. 6). Public attention is likely to shift away from the grieving losses of family members on the battlefield, the high level of inflation, not to mention the possibility of removing the government of Ukraine (Kirby, 2023a) due to Putin's appeal to broader, far-flung goals of fighting nazism and liberating Eastern Ukraine territories (RF President, 2022). By focusing on Putinism, and later Neo-Eurasionism, as detailed below, instead of sovereign democracy, the communication of asymmetrised information aims to affect understanding of disturbing facts. This dynamic follows Luhmann's information-utterance-understanding that distracts the public from important issues and manipulates their perception of reality by manipulating their perceptions (Luhmann, 1992). It is possible to redirect attention away from pressing individual concerns by focusing on broader objectives and thus inflating the significance of the stated policy objectives.

In 2006, Surkov, the author of the sovereign democracy framework, claimed it was not different from European democracy (Surkov, 2006). He turned to conclude that democracy is not for Russians because it uses distrust to increase criticism and anxiety. Following this turning point, the invasion of Ukraine, expulsion from the Council of Europe, and constitutional changes that nullified Putin's two-term presidency seem to prove democratic peace theories, even though they are contested (Henderson, 2001).

Aleksander Dugin is the latest name associated with self-correcting the official ideological framework. The leading international media and research sources mention Alexander Dugin as Putin's current ideological architect (Auxier, 2023, Sands, 2022, Von Drehle, 2022). Dugin has called for invading Ukraine since 2012 to approximate a new system he designed (Camus et al., 2017, p. 227). In the wake of the (sham) referendums in Eastern Ukraine, Putin alluded to Dugin by saying the West fears Russia's philosophy and encroaches on philosophers (Beiner, 2023, p. 64). Darya Dugina, Aleksander's daughter, perished in a car bomb blast in August 2022, and it was speculated that her dad was the real target (Sands, 2022). On the other hand, research indicates Dugin was not close to Putin before the annexation of Crimea, and he is not in Putin's closest circles now (Camus et al., 2017, p. 230). Dugin rose to fame with the annexation of Crimea, his writings gained influence among Russia's ruling circles, and the heavily controlled state media treated him favourably, starting with Putin's return to power in 2012 (Kalinin, 2019).

A book published by Dugin in 1997 titled "Fundamentals of Geopolitics" argues that Russia should regain its dominance by seeking alliances and conquests against the rival North-Atlantic powers led by the United States (Dugin, 1997). In research, Dugin's ideology, which argues for building a different socio-political system model in Russia from liberal democracy (Mirtesen, 2022), is labelled neo-Eurasianism (Kalinin, 2019). This model encourages people to create a morally upright, spiritual, and just society by focusing on the future (Camus et al., 2017, p. 214). Dugin employs Russian Sovietism to argue for an anti-Western space that contrasts Eurasian and Anglo-Saxon power (2017, p. 214).

According to Dugin, the Orthodox Russia is a distinct civilisation competing for dominance among global powers. Dugin suggests a multipolar framework to promote communication between Russia and other civilisations (Donaldson et al., 2015). In his speeches, Putin often refers to a multipolar world, overtly disputing the dominance of the United States (Biscop et al., 2022; RG, 2023; TASS, 2022). The Gorbachev years, by the end of which the Constitutional Court applied international treaties directly, are seen as one of the most agonising geopolitical setbacks in the millennia-long history of Russia, East Asia, and the USSR (Dunlop, 2004) and a conscious transition from a bipolar to a unipolar world (Kalinin, 2019, p. 461). In one of his internet posts, Dugin praises Putin's commitment to enlisting traditional spiritual values, arguing that as liberalism focuses exclusively on individual morality, it resulted in an unprecedented decline in Russian moral values after the fall of the Soviet Union (Mirtesen, 2022).

2.6.3 Adverse Selection Effect: Widening Social Distance

It could be anything from a power play, or intra-elite intrigues (Sakwa, 2011) to an unlikely coincidence that Sovereign Democracy turned into Putinism and then new Eurasianism. In this book, we see these developments disseminate or "utter" in Luhmann's terms (Luhmann, 1992) asymmetrical information to ensure the system's viability through self-correction, which introduces the danger of adverse selection. According to Akerlof's adverse selection claim, if information is asymmetric between parties in a market, the party with better information will exploit the other party. At a minimum, when a state hires loyal advisors who follow the state's pattern of action, it will not get high-quality advice. Surkov himself was deposed and under investigation for embezzling funds intended for the Ukrainian region of Donbas (Stewart, 2022).

Potential rivals can be found within the system's structures during the adverse selection process. Adverse selection also affects the system's inner circle and can contribute to finding rivals within the system's structures. As laws are non-normative and vague and intended to impose fear and instil obedience, no one (e.g. the inner circle and the environment) has the ultimate threshold of what is permissible and what is not. Instead, everyone is left to determine the game's rules independently. Per the adverse selection idea, individuals driven solely by their interests rather than other motivations such as public duty, loyalty to superiors, or the greater good can be introduced into the system.

Morale can be eroded within the inner circle, resulting in decreased collaboration and increased instability. This prompts individuals to question their roles and responsibilities. In the absence of agreed-upon rules, exploitation and unfair practices can occur, further exacerbating inequalities and creating a hostile work environment. Power fluctuations may result in a new power struggle, threatening the system on its allies' side. A coup attempt has already been orchestrated by Putin's "chef," Mr. Prigozhin, who raged at Defence Minister Sergei Shoigu and Armed Forces Chief Valery Gerasimov for not supplying his mercenaries with sufficient equipment (Rosenberg, 2023a). Putin appeared confused, albeit for several hours, likely for the first time, as Wagner Group fighters crossed from occupied eastern Ukraine and passed by the observing Russian Army up the main motorway en route to Moscow in June 2023 (Kirby, 2023b). The Russian president accused Prigozhin of embarking on an armed rebellion and stabbing the back of the country. Despite Surkov's deposition not being made public, it is only possible to speculate about what occurred in the president's office. Other regime allies were also investigated for various crimes (Murray & Ford, 2023, Stewart, 2022).

Leonid Nikitinskiy, a Russian journalist and lawyer, disagrees that Putin created power verticals or police states since those would be strictly disciplined (Taylor, 2011, p. 313). Nikitinskiy asserts that the Russian system is more like feudalism, where officers might serve their bosses but not the whole administration. This system makes it possible to charge allies for things the state cannot do, which is perfect for asymmetrising information. Ekaterina Shulman also remarks that one of the features of the current Russia's system is turning propaganda cliches into ideologies (Shulman, 2022).

One can see better what we mean in the example below. The world media, for instance, reported that Russia's troll farm was involved in well-planned campaigns to influence the 2016 U.S. presidential elections (Lee, 2018). Over a dozen Russian nationals were charged with using stolen identities and social media strategies to influence American voters. It was alleged that the Russian Internet Research Agency (IRA) posed as U.S. volunteers, using shift work to divide and enrage people. Over 100 American real-life participants participated in the campaign, unaware they were playing pawns. Moscow denied interfering in the election. However, Yevgeny Prigozhin, nicknamed Putin's "chef," who headed the infamous Russian private military company Wagner, admitted to starting the IRA before his death (Krever & Chernova, 2023). In addition to tuning information flows internally, the system also pays attention to outside disinformation campaigns, and non-existent information freedom makes it possible.

Considering this in line with Akerlof's ideas of asymmetrical information, we can conclude that adverse selection among the system's supporters is also problematic, affecting citizens. If the same government is likely to continue to govern for another 12 years following the infamous nullification of Mr. Putin's presidency tenure, it becomes unnecessary to make further investments. Citizens who are apprehensive about something wrong around them do not seek to improve the system since they are unwilling to pay the price without guaranteeing a better lifestyle. Luhmann's understanding of asymmetry again helps us understand why such adverse selection occurs when information is asymmetrical (Luhmann, 1993, pp. 132–133, 136, 138).

Separating the system from its environment undermines equality: by sacrificing individual freedoms, obedience is guaranteed. Chapter 6 in this book details how the presidential decree enlisted traditional societal values. Moreover, throughout the present chapter, we can see how Russia's Strategy of National Security masterfully illustrates the dangers of Western ideas impinging upon moral principles and "emphasising pleasures" (RF President, 2021). Social distance, as asserted by Akerlof, will also increase whenever people are made to overlook their freedoms, advantages, or even pleasures, whether ideologically, economically, or through punishments or prosecutions. People with power, pleasure, and benefits are separated from those without; distance is also widening between those who are compelled to swallow their beliefs to appear obedient and those who are courageous enough to protest and fight for their liberties.

2.6.4 Autocorrecting the Story to Keep the System Going

There was a consistent focus on power verticals with "new authoritarianism" (van der Vet, 2018), a process (as illustrated in Chapter 6) where the values Putin took up during his 2012 re-election became part of the National Security Strategy and the Constitution, becoming a powerful ideological tool (Barry, 2012; RF President, 2021). Putin's image as a defender of traditional values and religion has also been exploited as a powerful ideological tool (Shuster, 2016). There were many issues with the official story, from minor technical errors to severe ideological gaps. The first example of Putin's reputation as a defender of traditional values does not require specific cases, just common sense. In the unlikely event that Russia allows free expression and democracy, it does not mean there will be more gays or fewer divorces. A democratic government means power is balanced and changed periodically without violence, but it does not mean that country A will become just like others.

The paradigm focuses on external threats and values. It does not leave room for questions like why values cannot be protected with rights and freedoms, not just alone, and why freedom of speech needs to be limited to protect Russia from external enemies with its impressive nuclear arsenal. Despite there being different ideological frameworks for explaining why, there is another case where the president divorced even though he promoted family values (Vasilyeva, 2013). There has been some skilful editing to accommodate these and other inconsistencies found along the way. As attributed to Soviet-era singer Iosif Kobzon, a Kremlin ally, the statement "Putin is married to Russia" (Milchanovska, 2015) intended to make Putin seem like one of us (Sharafutdinova, 2020). One appears to be concerned if the president is portrayed as a busy man promoting Russia's interests. Because of the system's inventiveness, the information has always been asymmetric to avoid causing problems.

Authorities also try to seem like they are listening, and plenty of examples exist. However, whether they target citizens or regional leaders supporting central power. Following the 2004 terrorist attack at the Beslan school, greater security-related authority for the power ministries was introduced (Gidadhubli, 2004, pp. 4705–4706), in addition to changing Chechnya's administration. To balance this, the president set up the Public Chamber, a consultative body composed of representatives from civil society and non-governmental organisations (Riekkinen, 2013, pp. 87–88). Russians make up almost a quarter of the members. The Public Chamber supports citizen initiatives and conducts zero hearings on draft legislation where civil society must provide input (RF Federal Law No. 32-FZ, 2005, arts. 2, 6). Almost a quarter of the Public Chamber are Putin's nominees (RF Federal Law No. 32-FZ, 2005, Article 7). Later in this book, we will see how the zero hearing regarding the introduction of exhausting legal regulation for the so-called enlightenment activities was an overwhelming justification for the amendment, with only a few courageous voices opposed (see Chapter 3).

Regarding more recent examples, although changing Chapters 3–8 of the Russian Constitution does not require a referendum, the 2020 amendments have nevertheless been put to a nationwide vote (Russell, 2020). It was beloved by people Valentina Tereshkova, the first woman to fly in space, who formally proposed the nullification amendment at the end of drafting the 2020 constitutional amendments (Mälksoo, 2021, p. 78). Under the 2020 constitutional amendments, the lower house gained the authority to recommend to the President candidates for deputy heads of government and federal ministers, which the latter is obligated to accept (RF Constitution, Article 112).

Nevertheless, Article 83 of the Constitution does not exempt the President from nominating exclusively the key deputies and ministers in charge of defence, state security, internal affairs, justice, foreign affairs, disaster relief, and public safety (RF Constitution, Article 83, par. d1). It is how this facade moves toward democratisation hiding its fundamental limitations. As soon as the current president announced his intentions to run for president in 2023, the idea of democratisation played out with the TV phone-in show. Many journalists, including a BBC Russia editor, were present in the studio where Putin acted as Russia's "Mr. Fix-it" (Rosenberg, 2023b). Text messages from citizens were displayed on the big screen, including ones criticising Putin's long-term rule. To temper this appearance of democracy, questions presented to the president were carefully selected, the BBC representative could not ask a question, and no one responded to critical comments projected on the screen (Rosenberg, 2023b).

Emphasising how the state looks out for its people makes the ideology's doctrinal vision more coherent. Some academics have viewed Russia's 1993 Constitution and admission to the Council of Europe as a sign of the country's transition to democracy from a Soviet system (Roter, 2017). The transition to democracy does not necessarily imply its attainment. Accordingly, others contend that Russia has never truly achieved democratic rule (Snegovaya, 2023) and state that Putin's rule past

2012 has amounted to a new authoritarianism (Lewis, 2020). Historically, there may have been a reason for this asymmetry: Democracy would have benefited the 1993 new Russian leadership as it sought support from and membership in the Council of Europe (Busygina & Kahn, 2020, p. 65; Taylor, 2011, p. 107). Yeltsin supported Gorbachev's idea of a Greater Europe with Russia as a party, whose purpose was to end European security cooperation with the United States (Menkiszak, 2013, pp. 9–10). Public officials initially hailed Russia's accession to the Council of Europe (Bowring, 2018). Even the early Putin expressed positive sentiments about Europe despite excluding liberal and democratic rhetoric and focusing on national interests (Menkiszak, 2013). When Putin became president, he explicitly spoke about ratifying the European Convention on Human Rights and Fundamental Freedoms (Bowring, 2018). However, later, Putin rarely mentions the Council of Europe except as an irritant. Those ideas implied Russia's dominance in Europe by differentiating between the Western and Eastern European pillars, thus undermining the U.S.'s importance (Bowring, 2018, pp. 5–6; Busygina & Kahn, 2020, p. 65; Taylor, 2011, p. 71).

Thus, despite the potential benefits of managing its domestic audience, Moscow remained hesitant to initiate a genuine political conflict with the West during the 2000s (Busygina & Kahn, 2020, p. 65; Taylor, 2011, p. 72). This can be attributed to the fact that the first European Court of Human Rights cases against Russia, those of Burdov and Kalashnikov, were not delivered until 2002 (Busygina & Kahn, 2020, p. 65). To authorities who believed Soviet-era international law was something of a fancy outfit one could put on occasion (e.g. operationalising foreign trade) and not requiring changes in legislation, becoming a pioneer of all cases tried by the international courts must have been something of a bad surprise.

As Moscow expanded in the 16th century, it was part of European politics and law, influencing and being influenced by everything, while now Russia sees itself as essentially Eurasian (Bowring, 2018). As Russia tunes its identity, there are more discrepancies between formal calls for more democracy and grassroots autocratic practices. These discrepancies may pose challenges to the stability of the system. A regime without a strong ideological commitment among its officials may not be able to provide a high standard of state quality. In the context of Russia, these drawbacks cannot be compelling enough. There are many ways in which a lack of commitment can manifest itself (Hollyer & Wantchekon, 2015), including promoting institutions that allow subordinates to coordinate the ouster of an autocrat if the leader promises to reward them (Myerson, 2008). Failures are easier to conceal if free expression is limited, and tuning is easier on the fly. It might seem counterintuitive, but despite its changing identity, Russia's sustainability can be explained by effective self-correction amidst non-existent criticism. Therefore, freedom of expression is the guarantee, or basis, of symmetrical information; only when it is limited will other tricks, techniques, and strategies of self-correction work.

2.6.5 "Creating an Audience": A Focus on Children

When it comes to the system's environment or the citizens, we cannot help but wonder why so many Russians disobeyed orders to observe self-isolation during the COVID-19 spread (Riekkinen, 2021), but fewer protested against the war. Certainly, there has been significant opposition, with 21,000 arrests and 370 prosecutions for anti-war statements in 2022, but you do not see huge crowds daily on the streets of Moscow or St. Petersburg (Kuleshova, 2023). In addition, it is interesting to note that most powerful opposition figures are over 45, as was Aleksei Navalny before his death. Answering these questions will reveal another feature of Russia's asymmetrical information system. There has been a significant investment in military-patriotic work with children since the late 1990s, when a federal law requiring such work was introduced. "Military-patriotic" work with children is required by the 1998 Federal law "On Military Duty and Military Service" (RF Federal Law No. 53-FZ, 1998, art. 14). In subsequent years, federal and regional programme documents emphasised the importance of explaining the foundations of patriotism and military service to children. Nationalistic rhetoric and patriotic education have increased since Putin was re-elected in 2012. As he put it in his 2012 address, the nation's consolidating base was national identity and patriotism (RF President, 2012).

There have been four successive 5-year federal patriotic education programs since 2001 in Russia. Government bodies and organisations are supposed to promote this kind of education to make people patriotic, loyal to their Fatherland, and ready to do their civic duties and constitutional obligations to protect the Motherland. The scope and focus of these five-year programs have evolved, addressing different aspects of Russian society, including children, youth, continuity with the Soviet experience, and upgrading teacher and professor training (Kviatkovskii, 2001; RF Government, 2005, 2010, 2015; RF Ministry of Enlightenment, 2020). Russia's national pride, patriotism, and support for strong leaders are still strong global forces, with many unaware of their names' actions and judging by state TV (Kizlova & Norris, 2022). When it tried to make Russians self-isolate amidst the COVID-19 outbreak, the Russian government did not have decades of propaganda behind it. People who are now in their 30s majored in the 80s or early 90s when the country was too busy with other political and economic issues to focus on gaining control of schoolchildren's minds.

Both examples show that critical thinking and dissent are possible when the system does not mould the environment. It is like McGuire's inoculation theory that insists, in a nutshell, that pre-emptive messages can protect attitudes from counter-attitudes (Papageorgis & McGuire, 1961). With McGuire's explanation and Akerlof's approach, we can see why working with consumers is a strategy for asymmetrical information holders to take advantage of consumers by changing the market. People are suddenly becoming aware that information asymmetry is not the market the system needs. Therefore, the system must keep its market from awakening. Investing heavily in patriotic education makes the soil absorb all the other possibilities in the official narrative by constantly interrupting the social memory chain sequence. In short, we used to be affiliated with the Council of Europe, but now we are not sad about breaking ties; we must protect our country. When patriotism is at the centre of attention, it is easier to explain sudden changes in political direction in a way that does not raise further questions. Ultimately, many will tell the same story, which coincides with official narratives. No one heals when they are exposed to constant and systematic propaganda. By restricting free speech, dissent is silenced so nobody can get vaccinated in the unlikely event the propaganda virus leaves the body.

An interesting study by Banas and Miller (2013) explains people's susceptibility to propaganda based on McGuire's inoculation theory. The University of Oklahoma's John Banas and Gregory Miller experimented to affect the perception of the 9/11 events through propaganda. A conspiracy story was invented and presented to two groups: familiars and newbies. The second group was more accessible for implanting a new narrative, while the first group was "vaccinated" with prior knowledge, so propaganda could not take hold. These findings give us an idea of why some people still support Putin: brought up in the spirit of military patriotism and listening to the same story daily; they become resistant to other views and explanations. Some even like the phrase special military operation because: "[w]e're liberating [Ukraine] from Nazis and fascists, not stealing anything" and "[t]hat's what Putin called it, so I trust him" (Volkov, & Kolesnikov, 2022, 2). Reports and narratives that are the bread and butter of Russian state media coverage of the war are not questioned by these people. Interventions reinforce their convictions instead of disenchanting them. This explains why many Russians living abroad (McCausland, 2022) or accessing freely available information oppose the leadership's current policies. Apathy is also a choice between the turbo-patriots and those who are openly against the current political course (Volkov & Kolesnikov, 2023, p. 1).

Being away from state TV and media, along with mastering access to technology, like VPN applications allowing international and social media following, is one of the reasons why young people risk slipping out of the Kremlin's hands (Milov & Khvostunova, 2019). This may explain why the 2020 constitutional amendments added Article 67.1 (par. 4), which states that children are the most crucial priority of Russian state policy, and adds that:

> *by instilling patriotism, citizenship, and respect for elders in children, the state creates conditions promoting holistic spiritual, moral, intellectual and physical development.*
>
> (RF Constitution, Article 67.1, par. 4)

Before these revisions, children were already seen as objects by Russia's law, which employed the term legitimate interests of the child instead of the internationally recognised "best interests of the child" (UN CRC Committee, 2014, par. 26 a). The 1998 federal law outlining guarantees of children's rights introduced this term. Interestingly, this federal law is titled not as concerning children's rights but as concerning basic guarantees of rights, focusing on regulating the process of implementing principal rights and legitimate interests, or the rights and duties of state organs in Russia, rather than those of children (RF Federal Law No. 124-FZ, 1998, art. 2). Would we consider the following to be a standard legal rule? The Child Ombudsman's activities also protect children's legitimate interests (RF Federal

Law No. 501-FZ, 2018, art. 2). These are the legitimate interests of the child, one of the child welfare agencies' top goals (RF Federal Law No. 48-FZ, 2008, art. 4, par. 2).

Both the 2015 Code of Administrative Procedure (RF Federal Law No. 21-FZ, 2015, art. 11, par. 10) and the 2013 Code of Civil Procedure (RF Federal Law No. 138-FZ, 2002; Kodeks administrativnogo sudoproizvodstva Rossiiskoi Federatsii No. 21-FZ, 2015) reference underage people's legal interests, exempting court decisions from public dissemination in cases involving their legitimate interests. Underage persons' legal interests are also referenced in the ode of Administrative Procedure, both providing an exemption from the principle of public promulgation of court decisions in cases involving the legitimate interests of underage persons. It may appear to be law at first glance. However, legitimate interests are defined in the law, while best interests are determined individually. In its 2014 report on Russia, the UN Committee on the Rights of the Child indicated that references to the legitimate interests of the child are not equivalent to the child's best interests (UN CRC Committee, 2014, par. 26 a). Hence, the child's interest is not considered a consequence of concrete circumstances and needs but a result of the architecture of concrete laws.

When it comes to Russian law, pursuing the legitimate interests of a child means interpreting it as restrictively as possible: the state makes sure that children only get everything the law specifies, including military-patriotic education. By regulating the type of information available to young people, the authorities can ensure they only access controlled information, thereby limiting their ability to receive diverse perspectives and critical thinking skills, and potentially restricting their exposure to dissenting voices or opposition movements. By manipulating the flow of symmetrised or free-flowing information, the government may have sought to control the younger generation and minimise their potential involvement in activities such as protests. As discussed in Chapter 5 of this book on limiting protest activities, this countered against Aleksei Navalny's attempt to address young people directly with his anti-corruption claims. The 2018 legislative amendments may have been introduced in response to those attempts to control the information flow to young people, limiting their access to certain information.

References

Akerlof, G. A. (1970). The market for "lemons": Quality uncertainty and the market mechanism. *The Quarterly Journal of Economics*, *84*(3), 488–500.

Akerlof, G. A. (1997). Social distance and social decisions. *Econometrica*, *65*(5), 1005–1027.

Allerson, E. (2022). Internet censorship in Russia: The sovereign internet laws and Russia's obligations under the European convention on human rights. *Minnesota Journal of International Law*, *31*(1), 233.

Auxier, R. E. (2023). The real fourth political theory. *Eidos*, *6*(4), 78–95.

Banas, J. A., & Miller, G. (2013). Inducing resistance to conspiracy theory propaganda: Testing inoculation and metainoculation strategies. *Human Communication Research*, *39*(2), 184–207.

Barry, E. (2012, December 12). Russia's history should guide its future, Putin says. *The New York Times*. www.nytimes.com/2012/12/13/world/europe/putin-tells-russia-to-seek-clues-from-its-past.html

Beiner, R. (2023). Fascist international: Why Steve Bannon's 2018 meeting with Aleksandr Dugin still matters. *Inroads, 52*.

Biscop, S., Dessein, B., & Roctus, J. (2022, March 7). *Putin is creating the multipolar world he (thought he) wanted*. Egmont Institute. www.egmontinstitute.be/putin-is-creating-the-multipolar-world-he-thought-he-wanted/

Borzenko, E. (2019, September 10). *At the speed of the president: The path of the bill in Russia*. Pravo. https://pravo.ru/story/212484/?ysclid=lpy2r3y5e910745935

Bowring, B. (2018). Russia and the council of Europe: An incompatible ideology, and a transplanted legal regime? In P. S. Morris (Ed.), *Russian discourses on international law: Sociological and philosophical phenomenon* (pp. 133–157). Routledge.

Bowring, B. (2024, February 11). What went wrong and what could be done? 30 years of the Russian constitution. *Verfassungsblog*. https://verfassungsblog.de/what-went-wrong-and-what-could-be-done/

Busygina, I., & Kahn, J. (2020). Russia, the council of Europe, and "Ruxit," or why non-democratic illiberal regimes join international organizations. *Problems of Post-Communism, 67*(1), 64–77.

Camus, J. Y., Lebourg, N., & Todd, J. M. (2017). *Far-right politics in Europe*. Harvard University Press.

Donaldson, R. H., Nadkarni, V., & Nogee, J. L. (2015). *The foreign policy of Russia: Changing systems, enduring interests* (5th ed.). Routledge.

Dugin, A. (1997). *Osnovy geopolitiki: Geopoliticheskoe budushchee Rossii* [Foundations of geopolitics: The geopolitical future of Russia]. Arktogeya.

Dunlop, J. B. (2004). *Aleksandr Dugin's foundations of geopolitics*. https://tec.fsi.stanford.edu/docs/aleksandr-dugins-foundations-geopolitics

Eek, H. (1953). *Freedom of information as a project of international legislation*. Acta Universitatis Upsaliensis.

Eltsov, P. (2019, August 3). The best way to deal with Russia: Wait for it to implode. *Politico*. www.politico.com/magazine/story/2019/08/03/russia-separatism-vladimir-putin-227498/

Fauconnier, C. (2020). The power vertical, strength and weakness of Putin's Russia. *Revue Internationale et Stratégique, 118*(2), 154–162.

Foy, H. (2021, June 18). Vladislav Surkov: "An overdose of freedom is lethal to a state". *Financial Times*. www.ft.com/content/1324acbb-f475-47ab-a914-4a96a9d14bac

Frye, T. (2021). *Weak strongman: The limits of power in Putin's Russia*. Princeton University Press.

Gidadhubli, R. G. (2004). Russia after Beslan. *Economic and Political Weekly, 43*(39), 4704–4706.

Hall, S. G. F. (2023). *The Authoritarian international. Tracing how authoritarian regimes learn in the post-Soviet space*. Cambridge University Press.

Henderson, E. A. (2001). *Democracy and war*. Lynne Rienner.

Hendley, K. (2022). Legal dualism as a framework for analyzing the role of law under authoritarianism. *Annual Review of Law and Social Science, 18*(1), 211–226.

Hollyer, J. R., & Wantchekon, L. (2015). Corruption and ideology in autocracies. *Journal of Law, Economics, and Organization, 31*(3), 499–533.

Hubb, A. C., & Wang, F. Y. (2023). Authoritarian propaganda campaigns on foreign affairs: Four birds, one stone, and the South China sea arbitration. *International Studies Quarterly, 67*(3), 1–15.

Humphrey, J. (1979). The universal declaration of human rights: Its history, impact, and judicial character. In B. G. Ramcharan (Ed.), *Human rights: Thirty years after the universal declaration* (pp. 21–39). Martinus Nijhoff Publishers.

Kalinichenko, P. (1998). The constitutional order of the Russian Federation and its adaptability to European and Eurasian integration project. In R. Petrov & P. Elsuwege (Eds.),

Post-Soviet constitutions and challenges of regional integration. Adapting to European and Eurasian integration projects (pp. 168–177) Routledge.
Kalinin, K. (2019). Neo-Eurasianism and the Russian elite: The irrelevance of Aleksandr Dugin's geopolitics. *Post-Soviet Affairs*, *35*(5–6), 461–470.
Kirby, P. (2023a, February 24). *Has Putin's war failed, and what does Russia want from Ukraine?* www.bbc.com/news/world-europe-56720589
Kirby, P. (2023b, June 24). Wagner chief's 24 hours of chaos in Russia. *BBC News*. www.bbc.com/news/world-europe-66006880
Kish, J. (1995). *International law and espionage*. Martinus Nijhoff Publishers.
Kizlova, K., & Norris, P. (2022). *What do ordinary Russians really think about the war in Ukraine?* London School of Economics. https://blogs.lse.ac.uk/europpblog/2022/03/17/what-do-ordinary-russians-really-think-about-the-war-in-ukraine/
Kodeks administrativnogo sudoproizvodstva Rossiiskoi Federatsii No. 21-FZ. (2015, March 8). Sobranie zakonodatel'stva Rossiiskoi Federatsii, 09.03.2015, No. 10 item 1391.
Kortteinen, J., Myntti, K., & Hannikainen, L. (1992). Article 19. In G. Alfredsson & A. Eide (Eds.), *The universal declaration of human rights. A common standard of achievement* (p. 402). Martinus Nijhoff Publishers.
Krever, M., & Chernova, A. (2023, February 14). Wagner chief admits to founding Russian troll farm sanctioned for meddling in US elections. *CNN*. https://edition.cnn.com/2023/02/14/europe/russia-yevgeny-prigozhin-internet-research-agency-intl/index.html
Krupskiy, M. (2023). The impact of Russia's "foreign agents". Legislation on civil society. *The Fletcher Forum of World Affairs*, *47*(2), 55–70.
Kuleshova, A. (2023, June 14). Why are Russians who oppose the war not taking to the streets? *Open Democracy*. www.opendemocracy.net/en/odr/ukraine-war-why-russians-are-not-protesting/
Kviatkovskii, I. K. (2001). *Patriotic education of citizens of the Russian Federation for 2001–2005*. Centre for Military Historical and Cultural Research under the Government of the Russian Federation. www.ainros.ru/ssylki/patr_vos.htm
Laine, V., & Zamyatin, K. (2001). *Russia's nationalities policy before and after the 2020 constitutional amendments. Is the "ethnic turn" continuing? 125 FIIA working papers* (pp. 1–14).
Lee, D. (2018, February 17). The tactics of a Russian troll farm. *BBC News*. www.bbc.com/news/technology-43093390
Lewis, D. G. (2020). *Russia's new authoritarianism. Putin and the politics of order*. Edinburgh University Press.
Linde, F. (2016). The civilizational turn in Russian political discourse: From Pan-Europeanism to civilizational distinctiveness. *The Russian Review*, *75*(4), 604–625.
Lipman, M. (2016). *What Russia thinks of Europe*. ECFR. https://ecfr.eu/article/commentary_what_russia_thinks_of_europe5084/
Luhmann, N. (1992). What is communication? *Communication Theory*, *2*(3), 251–259.
Luhmann, N. (1993). *Law as a social system*. Oxford University Press.
Mälksoo, L. (2021). International law and the 2020 amendments to the Russian constitution. *American Journal of International Law*, *115*(1), 78–93.
Maskaeva, I. I. (2012). Predely ogranicheniia prava na dostup k informatsii o deiatel'nosti organov gosudarstvennoi vlasti. In N. A. Sheveleva (Ed.), *Pravo na dostup k informatsii. Vozmozhnosti ogranicheniia v elektronnoi srede* (pp. 203–209). FGBU.
McCarthy, L. A., Rice, D., & Lokhmutov, A. (2023). Four months of "discrediting the military": Repressive law in wartime Russia. *Demokratizatsiya: The Journal of Post-Soviet Democratization*, *31*(2), 125–160.
McCausland, P. (2022, March 27). Russians who live abroad say Moscow is hardening the views of those back home. *NBC News*. www.nbcnews.com/news/world/russians-live-abroad-say-moscow-hardening-views-back-home-rcna20605

McNair, B. (1991). *Glasnost, Perestroika and the Soviet media*. Routledge.
Menkiszak, M. (2013). Greater Europe. Putin's vision of European (dis)integration. *OSW Studies, 46*. www.files.ethz.ch/isn/172280/No46-greater_europe_net.pdf
Milchanovska, E. (2015, January 7). *Joseph Kobzon: Putin has already married a second time*. Sobesednik. https://sobesednik.ru/obshchestvo/20150107-iosif-kobzon-putin-uzhe-zhenilsya-vtoroy-raz
Milov, V., & Khvostunova, O. (2019, June 17). Opinion: How Putin and the Kremlin lost Russian youths. *The Washington Post*. www.washingtonpost.com/opinions/2019/06/17/how-putin-kremlin-lost-russian-youths/
Mirtesen. (2022, November 23). UKAZ no. 809. Osnovanie suverennoi ideologii polozheno/Decree no. 809. The foundation of sovereign ideology has been laid. *Mirtesen*. https://vmestevselegche.mirtesen.ru/blog/43201812394/UKAZ-809-osnovanie-suverennoy-ideologii-polozheno?utm_referrer=mirtesen.ru
Murray, G., & Ford, G. (2023, April 14). Putin turning on inner circle as close ally who "made him president" arrested. *Hull Daily Mail*. www.hulldailymail.co.uk/news/uk-world-news/putin-turning-inner-circle-close-6955278
Myerson, R. B. (2008). The autocrat's credibility problem and foundations of the constitutional state. *The American Political Science Review, 102*(1), 125–139.
Österdahl, I. (1992). *Freedom of information in question. Freedom of information in international law and the calls for a new world information and communication order (NWICO)*. Iustus Förlag.
Oxford English dictionary (3rd ed.). (2023). Oxford University Press.
Papageorgis, D., & McGuire, W. J. (1961). The generality of immunity to persuasion produced by pre-exposure to weakened counterarguments. *Social Psychology, 62*(3), 475–481.
Partlett, W. (2021). Russia's 2020 constitutional amendments: A comparative analysis. *Cambridge Yearbook of European Legal Studies, 23*, 311–342.
Podoplelova, O. (2024, February 10). Legitimizing authoritarian transformation: Russia's constitutional court and the cost of compromise. *Verfassungsblog*. https://verfassungsblog.de/legitimizing-authoritarian-transformation/
Pomeranz, W. E. (2021). Putin's 2020 constitutional amendments: What changed? What remained the same? *Russian Politics, 6*(1), 6–26.
Putin, V. (2021). *On the historical unity of Russians and Ukrainians*. Presidential Library. www.prlib.ru/en/article-vladimir-putin-historical-unity-russians-and-ukrainians
RF Concept of Foreign Policy of the Russian Federation. (2013, February 12). *Kontseptsiia vneshnei politiki Rossiiskoi Federatsii*. Approved by the President of the Russian Federation. https://legalacts.ru/doc/kontseptsija-vneshnei-politiki-rossiiskoi-federatsii-utv-prezidentom/?ysclid=lrambtw91j258435702
RF Concept of Foreign Policy of the Russian Federation. (2016, November 30). *Konceptsiia vneshnei politiki Rossiiskoi Federatsii*. Approved by the decree of the president of the Russian Federation no. 640, Sobranie zakonodatelstva Rossiiskoi Federatsii, 2016, No. 49 item 6886.
RF Concept of Foreign Policy of the Russian Federation. (2023, March 31). *Koncept-siia vneshnei politiki Rossiiskoi Federatsii*. Approved by the decree of the president of the Russian Federation no. 229 of 31 March 2023. www.kremlin.ru/events/president/news/70811
RF Constitutional Court, Determination No. 14-P. (2014, May 13). *Po delu o proverke konstitutsionnosti chasti 1 stat'i 7 Federal'nogo zakona "O sobraniiakh, mitingakh, demonstratsiiakh, shestviiakh i piketirovaniiakh v sviazi s zhaloboi grazhdanina A.N. Iakimova* [On the constitutionality check of part 1 of article 7 of the federal law "on assemblies, rallies, demonstrations, processions and picketing" in response to a complaint from citizen A.N. Iakimov]. Rossiiskaia gazeta, 20.05.2014, No. 112 (6384).
RF Constitutional Court, Determination No. 1387-O. (2023, May 30). *Ob otkaze v priniatii k rassmotreniiu zhaloby grazhdanki Markus Kristiny na narushenie ee konstitutsionnykh prav chastiiu 1 statii 20.3.3 Kodeksa Rossiiskoi Federatsii of Administrativykh Pravonarusheniiakh*

[On inadmissibility of the complaint of citizen Markus Kristina concerning the violation of her constitutional rights by part 1 of article 20.3.3 of the Russian Federation's code on administrative offenses]. https://legalacts.ru/sud/opredelenie-konstitutsionnogo-suda-rf-ot-30052023-n-1387-o/?ysclid=lpsf30dclc88103881

RF Constitutional Court, Postanovlenie No. 2-P. (2017, February 10). *Po delu o proverke konstitutsionnosti polozhenii stat'i 212.1 Ugolovnogo kodeksa Rossiiskoi Federatsii v sviazi s zhaloboi grazhdanina I.I. Dadina* [Concerning the constitutionality of the provisions of article 212.1 of the criminal code of the Russian Federation in connection with the complaint filed by citizen I.I. Dadin]. Sobranie zakonodatel'stva Rossiiskoi Federatsii, 2017, No. 9 item 1422.

RF Constitutional Court, Postanovlenie No. 36-P. (2022, October 2). *Po delu o proverke konstitutsionnosti ne vstupivshego v silu mezhdunarodnogo Dogovora mezhdu Rossiiskoi Federatsiei i Donetskoi Narodnoi Respublikoi o priniatii v Rossiiskuiu Federatsiiu Donetskoi Narodnoi Respubliki i obrazovanii v sostave Rossiiskoi Federatsii novogo sub"ekta* [On verifying the constitutionality of the international treaty between the Russian Federation and the Kherson region, which has not entered into force, and on incorporating Donetsk people republic into the Russian Federation and establishing a new entity within the Russian Federation]. http://publication.pravo.gov.ru/Document/View/0001202210020002?ysclid=lt4jishlzd268998578

RF Constitutional Court, Postanovlenie No. 37-P. (2022, October 2). *Po delu o proverke konstitutsionnosti ne vstupivshego v silu mezhdunarodnogo Dogovora mezhdu Rossiiskoi Federatsiei i Luganskoi Narodnoi Respublikoi o priniatii v Rossiiskuiu Federatsiiu Luganskoi Narodnoi Respubliki i obrazovanii v sostave Rossiiskoi Federatsii novogo sub"ekta* [On verifying the constitutionality of the international treaty between the Russian Federation and the Kherson region, which has not entered into force, and on incorporating Luhansk people republic into the Russian Federation and establishing a new entity within the Russian Federation]. http://publication.pravo.gov.ru/Document/View/0001202210020003?ysclid=lt4ji6c13s129460455

RF Constitutional Court, Postanovlenie No. 38-P. (2022, October 2). *Po delu o proverke konstitutsionnosti ne vstupivshego v silu mezhdunarodnogo Dogovora mezhdu Rossiiskoi Federatsiei i Zaporozhskoi oblast'iu o priniatii v Rossiiskuiu Federatsiiu Zaporozhskoi oblasti i obrazovanii v sostave Rossiiskoi Federatsii novogo sub"ekta* [On verifying the constitutionality of the international treaty between the Russian Federation and the Kherson region, which has not entered into force, and on incorporating the Zaporozhskaia region into the Russian Federation and establishing a new entity within the Russian Federation]. http://publication.pravo.gov.ru/Document/View/0001202210020001?ysclid=lt4jjtlrs9725473289

RF Constitutional Court, Postanovlenie No. 39-P. (2022, October 2). *Po delu o proverke konstitutsionnosti ne vstupivshego v silu mezhdunarodnogo Dogovora mezhdu Rossiiskoi Federatsiei i Hersonskoi oblast'iu o priniatii v Rossiiskuiu Federatsiiu Hersonskoi oblasti i obrazovanii v sostave Rossiiskoi Federatsii novogo sub"ekta* [On verifying the constitutionality of the international treaty between the Russian Federation and the Kherson region, which has not entered into force, and on incorporating the Kherson region into the Russian Federation and establishing a new entity within the Russian Federation]. http://publication.pravo.gov.ru/Document/View/0001202210020001?ysclid=lt4jjtlrs9725473289

RF Constitutional Court, Zakliuchenie No. 1-Z. (2020, March 16). *O sootvetstvii polozheniiam glav 1, 2 i 9 Konstitutsii Rossiiskoi Federatsii ne vstupivshikh v silu polozhenii Zakona Rossiiskoi Federatsii o popravke k Konstitutsii Rossiiskoi Federatsii "O sovershenstvovanii regulirovaniia otdel'nykh voprosov organizatsii i funktsionirovaniia publichnoi vlasti", a takzhe o sootvetstvii Konstitutsii Rossiiskoi Federatsii poriadka vstupleniia v silu stat'i 1 dannogo Zakona v sviazi s zaprosom Prezidenta Rossiiskoi Federatsii* [On the compliance with chapters 1, 2 and 9 of the Russian constitution of the provisions on the law "on improving the regulation of certain issues of public power organization and functioning" that have not entered into force, and on the compliance with the constitution of the procedure for entering into force article 1 of this law, upon the Russian president's request]. http://publication.pravo.gov.ru/Document/View/0001202003160037?ysclid=lt4jc2wazx507880896

RF Federal Law No. 21-FZ. (2015, March 8). *Kodeks administrativnogo sudoproizvodstva Rossiiskoi Federatsii* [The code of administrative procedure of the Russian Federation]. Sobranie zakonodatel'stva Rossiiskoi Federatsii, 2015, No. 10 item 1391.

RF Federal Law No. 32-FZ. (2005, April 4). *Ob Obshchestvennoi palate Rossiiskoi Federatsii* [On the public chamber of the Russian Federation]. Sobranie zakonodatel'stva Rossiiskoi Federatsii, 2005, No. 15 item 1277.

RF Federal Law No. 48-FZ. (2008, April 208). *Ob opeke i popechitel'stve* [On custody]. Sobranie zakonodatel'stva Rossiiskoi Federatsii, 2008, No. 17 item 1755.

RF Federal Law No. 53-FZ. (1998, March 28). *O voinskoi obiazannosti i voennoi sluzhbe* [On military duty and military service]. Sobranie zakonodatel'stva Rossiiskoi Federatsii, 1998, No. 13 item 1475.

RF Federal Law No. 90-FZ. (2019, May 1). *O vnesenii izmenenii v Federal'nyi zakon "O sviazi" i Federal'nyi zakon "Ob informatsii, informatsionnykh tekhnologiiakh i o zashchite informatsii"* [On amending the federal law "on communications" and federal Law "on information, information technologies and information protection"]. http://publication.pravo.gov.ru/Document/View/0001201905010025?ysclid=lqgg7ye2rr307219917

RF Federal Law No. 124-FZ. (1998, July 24). *Ob osnovnykh garantiiakh prav rebenka v Rossiiskoi Federatsii* [On the main guarantees of the rights of the child in the Russian Federation]. Sobranie zakonodatel'stva Rossiiskoi Federatsii, 1998, No. 31 item 3802.

RF Federal Law No. 138-FZ. (2002, November 14). *Grazhdanskii protsessual'nyi kodeks Rossiiskoi Federatsii* [The code of civil procedure of the Russian Federation]. Sobranie zakonodatel'stva Rossiiskoi Federatsii, 2002, No. 46 item 4532.

RF Federal Law No. 149-FZ. (2006, July 27). *Ob informatsii, informatsionnykh tekhnologiakh i zashchite informatsii* [On information, information technologies and information protection]. Sobranie zakonodatel'stva Rossiiskoi Federatsii, 2006, No. 31 (part I) item 3448.

RF Federal Law No. 501-FZ. (2018, December 27). *Ob upolnomochennykh po pravam rebenka v Rossiiskoi Federatsii* [On child ombudsmen in the Russian Federation]. http://publication.pravo.gov.ru/Document/View/0001201812280003?index=3&rangeSize=1&ysclid=lt8lzuzflf450522940

RF Government, Decree No. 422. (2005, July 11). *On state program "Patriotic education of citizens of the Russian Federation for 2006–2010"*. http://docs.cntd.ru/document/901941206

RF Government, Decree No. 795. (2010, October 5). *On state program "patriotic education of citizens of the Russian Federation for 2011–2015"*. Sobranie zakonodatel'stva Rossiiskoi Federatsii, 1995, No. 41 (part II) item 5250.

RF Government, Decree No. 1493. (2015, December 30). *On state program "patriotic education of citizens of the Russian Federation for 2016–2020"*. Sobranie zakonodatel'stva Rossiiskoi Federatsii, 2016, No. 2 (part I) item 368. Not in force.

RF Ministry of Enlightenment. (2020). *Federal project "patriotic education of citizens of the Russian Federation.* https://edu.gov.ru/national-project/projects/patriot/

RF President. (2012, December 12). *Poslanie Prezidenta Federal'nomu Sobraniiu* [The address of the president to the federal assembly]. http://kremlin.ru/events/president/news/17118

RF President. (2020, January 15). *Poslanie Prezidenta Federal'nomu Sobraniiyu* [The address of the president to the federal assembly]. www.kremlin.ru/events/president/news/62582

RF President. (2022, February 2024). *Poslanie Prezidenta* [Address by the president of the Russian Federation]. http://en.kremlin.ru/events/president/news/67843

RF President, Decree No. 400. (2021, July 2). *O Strategii natsionalnoi bezopasnosti Rossiiskoi Federatsii* [On the strategy of national security of the Russian Federation]. www.kremlin.ru/acts/bank/47046

RF President, Decree No. 2334. (1993, December 31). *O dopolnitel'nykh garantiiakh prav grazhdan na informatsiiu* [On additional guarantees of citizens rights to information]. Sobranie aktov Prezidenta i Pravitel'stva RF, 1994, No. 2 item 74.

RF State Duma of the Federal Assembly. (1998). Postanovlenie of 22 January 1998 no. 2134-II GD. *O Reglamente Gosudarstvennoi Dumy Federal'nogo Sobraniia RF* [On the rules of procedure of the federal assembly of the Russian Federation]. Sobranie zakonodatel'stva RF, 16.02.1998, No. 7 item 801.

RG. (2023, October 16). *Vladimir Putin: Sozdanie mnogopoliarnogo mira neizbezhno* [Vladimir Putin: Creating a multipolar work is unavoidable]. https://rg.ru/2023/10/16/vladimir-putin-sozdanie-mnogopoliarnogo-mira-neizbezhno.html?ysclid=lr4ys9k2hi323672627

Riekkinen, M. (2013). Russian legal practices of citizens' involvement in political decision-making: Legal study of their genesis under the influence of international law. *The International Journal of Human Rights*, *17*(1), 79–112.

Riekkinen, M. (2017). Living off the Soviet legacy: Confidentiality-based approach towards access to information in Russia. In A. S. Lind, J. Reichel, & I. Österdahl (Eds.), *Transparency in the future – Swedish openness 250 years* (pp. 137–157). Ragulka.

Riekkinen, M. (2021). Attitudes of Russian speakers in Finland towards AntiCOVID-19 restriction measures in Spring 2020. *Russian Journal of Comparative Law*, *8*(1), 11–16.

Rosenberg, S. (2023a, June 24). Putin under pressure as ally Yevgeny Prigozhin turns rebel. *BBC News*. www.bbc.com/news/world-europe-66007017

Rosenberg, S. (2023b, December 14). Inside Putin's carefully choreographed annual news conference. *BBC News*. www.bbc.com/news/world-europe-67718655

Roter, P. (2017). Russia in the council of Europe: Participation à la carte. In L. Mälksoo & W. Benedek (Eds.), *Russia and the European court of human rights: The Strasbourg effect* (pp. 26–56). Cambridge University Press.

Russell, M. (2020, May). *Constitutional change in Russia. More Putin, or preparing for post-Putin?* European Parliament Briefing. www.europarl.europa.eu/RegData/etudes/BRIE/2020/651935/EPRS_BRI(2020)651935_EN.pdf

Sakwa, R. (2007). Constitutionalism and accountability in contemporary Russia: The problem of displaced sovereignty, In R. Sharlet & G. Smith (Eds.), *Russia and its constitution: Promise and political reality* (pp. 1–12). BRILL.

Sakwa, R. (2011). *The crisis of Russian democracy: The dual state, factionalism, and the Medvedev succession*. Cambridge University Press.

Sakwa, R. (2021). Heterarchy: Russian politics between chaos and control. *Post-Soviet Affairs*, *37*(3), 222–241.

Sands, L. (2022, August 21). Darya Dugina: Daughter of Putin ally killed in Moscow blast. *BBC News*. www.bbc.com/news/world-europe-62621509

Sharafutdinova, G. (2020). *The red mirror: Putin's leadership and Russia's insecure identity*. Oxford University Press.

Shulman, E. (2022, September 22). *The mobilisation of the demobilised. Neither society nor the political system are ready for ideological indoctrination*. RE: Russia. https://re-russia.net/en/expertise/022/

Shuster, S. (2016, September 12). Russia's President Putin casts himself as protector of the faith. *TIME*. https://time.com/4475613/putins-pilgrimage/

Silvius, R. (2017). *Culture, political economy and civilization in a multipolar world order: The case of Russia*. Routledge.

Smith, G. B. (2007). The promise of the Russian constitution. In R. Sharlet & G. Smith (Eds.), *Russia and its constitution: Promise and political reality* (pp. xxiii–xxvi). BRILL.

Snegovaya, M. (2023). Why Russia's democracy never began. *Journal of Democracy*, *34*(3), 105–118.

Stewart, W. (2022, April 13). Putin 'arrests the man who invented Putinism' in purge of 150 spy chiefs as he turns on his inner circle in hunt for scapegoat for disaster in Ukraine. *Daily Mail*.

www.dailymail.co.uk/news/article-10714319/Putin-arrests-man-invented-Putinism-purge-150-spy-chiefs-turns-inner-circle.html
Surkov, V. (2006, June 29). Vladislav Surkov ruined democracy. *Kommersant*. www.kommersant.ru/doc/686274?ysclid=lr7v7nsnh0802197789
Surkov, V. (2019, November 2). Dolgoe gosudarstvo Putina, Rossiiskaia gazeta. *Nezavisimaya Gazeta*. www.ng.ru/ideas/2019-02-11/5_7503_surkov.html
TASS. (2022, November 30). *Putin zaiavil o formirovanii mnogopoljarnoi sistemy mira* [Putin claimed about creating a multipolar world system]. https://tass.ru/politika/15082807?ysclid=lr4ynn0dt987594583
Taylor, B. D. (2011). *State building in Putin's Russia: Policing and coercion after communism*. Cambridge University Press.
Treisman, D. (2010). Is Russia cursed by oil? *Journal of International Affairs*, *63*(2), 85–102.
UN CRC Committee. (2014, February 25). *Concluding observations on Russia*. UN Doc. CRC/C/RUS/CO/4-5.
UN General Assembly. (1946, December 14). *Calling of an international conference on freedom of information*. Resolution A/RES/59(I).
UN General Assembly. (1960, December 9). *Draft convention on freedom of information*. Third Committee, Report A/4643.
UN General Assembly. (1971, December 18). *Freedom of information: Human rights and scientific and technological developments; elimination of all forms of religious intolerance*. Resolution A/RES/2844(XXVI).
UN Secretary General. (1958, August 8). *Views and suggestions of governments concerning the draft convention on freedom of information*. Report by the Secretary-General, UN Doc. A/3868, reproduced in the official UN Official Document System database. https://documents-dds-ny.un.org/doc/UNDOC/GEN/N58/188/73/pdf/N5818873.pdf?OpenElement
USSR. (1991, December 11). Statement by the Committee of Constitutional Supervision of the USSR, Russian Federation State Archives, Archival Fund R9654, Inventory number 6, case number 76, pp. 48–51; Archival Fund R9654, Inventory number, case number 749, pp. 134–135. The document was distributed to the deputies but not published in the central press. Reproduced. https://sssr.su/1991-12.pdf
van der Vet, F. (2018). "When they come for you": Legal mobilization in new authoritarian Russia. *Law & Society Review*, *52*(2), 301–336.
Vasilyeva, N. (2013, June 7). Putin's divorce breaks taboo in Russian politics. *San Diego Union Tribune*. www.sandiegouniontribune.com/sdut-putins-divorce-breaks-taboo-in-russian-politics-2013jun07-story.html
Volkov, D., & Kolesnikov, A. (2022). *My country, right or wrong: Russian public opinion on Ukraine* (pp. 2, 23). Carnegie Endowment for International Peace.
Volkov, D., & Kolesnikov, A. (2023). *Alternate reality: How Russian society learned to stop worrying about the war* (pp. 1, 21). Carnegie Endowment for International Peace.
Von Drehle, D. (2022, March 23). The man known as "Putin's brain" envisions the splitting of Europe – and the fall of China. *Washington Post*. https://link.gale.com/apps/doc/A697860738/AONE?u=aboacad&sid=bookmark-AONE&xid=a9a5cbe2

3 Analysing Legal Amendments Since 2012

Regulating Enlightenment Activities

3.1 Legislative Amendments

To control even those discussions outside the education curriculum, a new set of legislative amendments was introduced on 5 April 2021 (RF Federal Law No. 85-FZ, 2021). More particularly, the Federal Law "On Education in the Russian Federation" (hereinafter: The Federal Law on Education) was amended to regulate discussions targeting intellectual and moral development within an educational context, which became classified as enlightenment activities. These activities can take various forms, such as lectures, seminars, masterclasses, roundtables, or other formats. A comprehensive regulation was provided by adding Article 12.22 (i.e. general requirements for enlightenment activities) and amending Article 2 with paragraph 35 (i.e. basic concepts used in this Federal Law). In the following year, the government of Russia published a decree that formalised procedures for conducting the activities in question and ensured that these were performed under conditions stipulated by the government and monitored accordingly (RF Government, Decree No. 1195, 2022). This package of amendments was part of a broader set of legislation aimed at tightening regulations regarding non-governmental organisations, public meetings, media operations, and freedom of expression in general.

Justifying the rationale for amending the Federal Law on Education, its explanatory note stated that Russia's current laws lack "procedures for conducting enlightenment activities" and "requirements for their participants."[1] Russian citizens, especially pupils and students, should be kept away from anti-Russian propaganda in teaching materials with the new amendments, according to the note:

> *Since there is no appropriate legal regulation, anti-Russian forces can uncontrollably conduct propaganda activities at schools and among pupils under the guise of educational activities.*
>
> (Explanatory Note to the Draft Law No. 1057895-7)

Following the authors of this draft law, these forces can rely on propaganda sponsored by foreign states to discredit the Russian Constitution, distort history, and discredit official policies.

DOI: 10.4324/9781032613383-3

With the amendments of 5 April 2021, coming into legal force, enlightenment activities are currently legally defined by the Federal Law on Education as:

> *carried out outside the framework of educational programs activities that disseminate knowledge and experiences, develop skills, values, and competencies for intellectual, spiritual, moral, creative, physical, and (or) professional development, fulfil the educational needs and interests of the individual, and affect relations governed by this Federal Law and other regulatory legal acts of the Russian Federation.*
>
> (RF Federal Law No. 273-FZ, 2012)

Public authorities and authorised organisations should carry out these activities. (Federal Law No. 498-FZ, 2022). Conducting enlightenment activities by individuals is subject to several restrictions obligating natural persons to pursue these activities "subject to the requirements outlined in this Federal Law and other normative acts of the Russian Federation" (Federal Law No. 498-FZ, 2022, Article 12.2, par. 1). Candidates for the role of enlighteners must meet specific requirements before agreeing with an educational institution that outlines their role and responsibilities. They must have good legal standing and at least two years of experience in enlightenment activities, demonstrating involvement in socially significant initiatives. In addition, this person should be able to conduct teaching activities without legal restrictions. Article 331 of the Russian Federation's Labour Code lists these restrictions. The enlighteners are thus no longer just individual researchers and activists but are government-authorised agents of enlightenment and education.

In December 2022, an additional legal amendment was introduced, restricting the conduct of enlightenment activities by individuals identified as foreign agents who became prohibited from conducting enlightenment activities for minors (Federal Law No. 498-FZ, 2022). When enlightenment is in question for adults, foreign agents must declare their responsibility as foreign agents for preparing and delivering messages and materials during enlightenment activities. Enlightenment activities include lectures, presentations, seminars, masterclasses, round tables, and discussions through various methods, including the internet, and all statements made by foreign agents on the internet are considered enlightenment activities (RF Government, Decree No. 1195, 2022).

When legal persons wish to pursue enlightenment activities as organisations, they need to meet the following criteria: (a) not being enlisted on the Ministry of Justice's register of foreign agents; (b) not being in debt for taxes, fees, or other obligations that also extend to individual employees; (c) having employees meeting the requirement of Article 331 of the Labour Code regarding a lack of obstacles for teaching activities;[2] (d) having an updated website with the following information: the date of establishment of an organisation, information on its founders, its location, contact information, information about the employees who plan to conduct educational activities, their education, qualifications, experience, and information about contracts with educational personnel.

Since the amendments require that the government must issue special regulations for their implementation, the latter becomes a key player in operationalising enlightenment. Specifically, the federal executives are given the authority to coordinate the participation of educational institutions in international cooperation (RF Federal Law No. 273-FZ, 2012, Art. 13.2). Organisers of enlightenment activities involving budget funds must notify the Ministry of Enlightenment, along with a schedule of activities. The Ministry reviews these schedules to ensure compliance with Russia's legislation and strategic planning documents. Depending on the need, such an evaluation can involve other Ministry-authorised organisations. Since notification of the forthcoming enlightenment activities should be submitted no later than 30 working days before the expected start date and are to go through a review procedure, it virtually excludes the possibility of immediate discussion of any urgent matter of public significance.

Moreover, a concluding statement should be obtained from the Ministry of Enlightenment whenever an educational institution contracts with foreign persons (organisations or individuals) to conduct enlightenment activities on its behalf (RF Federal Law No. 273-FZ, 2012, Art. 105, par. 4). In the first year following the entry into the legal force of the amendments, all educational institutions were required to obtain such statements from the Ministry of Enlightenment.[3] When foreign persons perform enlightenment activities, this requirement applies in the following areas, outlined in Part 3 of Article 105 of the Federal Law on Education:

- collaboration with foreign or international organisations to develop educational and scientific initiatives;
- exchanges among students, faculty, and researchers, including those between foreign countries;
- collaborative scientific projects, fundamental and applied scientific research in the field of education;
- joint implementation of innovative activities;
- participation in network educational program implementation;
- participation in international educational, research, and scientific-technical projects in international congresses, symposiums, conferences, seminars, and independent organisation of these events, as well as the exchange of scientific and educational literature on a bilateral and multilateral basis.

Additionally, the amendments may have maximised efforts to ensure the purity of education discourses by considering the methodological support provided for formal education. Amendments required a distinct inventory of organisations supporting educational activities in public institutions with scientific and methodological expertise. In addition to approving the rules for selecting organisations for this inventory, the Russian Ministry of Enlightenment must also approve the inventory itself. The Ministry maintains this inventory and adopts regulations regarding the selection and inclusion of specific organisations, including the requirements for the reporting forms.

The amendments brought in a strict set of rules governing the content of the enlightenment activities. Such activities are forbidden from spreading false information about historical, national, religious, or cultural traditions of peoples, inciting racial, religious, or social hatred, or agitating against citizens based on their social, racial, national, religious, or linguistic affiliation, or their attitudes toward religion, as they promote exclusivity, superiority, or inferiority (RF Federal Law No. 273-FZ, 2012, art. 12.22, par. 2). There are no official guidelines for determining what information qualifies as false in disseminating historical information. Given the current practice of rewriting history books to justify the war against Ukraine, the question of which year or edition to use safely can be particularly confusing. Moreover, the rules for the implementation of enlightenment activities, introduced by the government, stipulate that those activities should be carried out following traditional Russian values, also outlined in the legislation of the Russian Federation. Rules for the implementation of enlightenment activities were upheld by the government (RF Government, Decree No. 1195).

The issue was important enough for the people to call a zero hearing of the draft law in question within the Public Chamber. The Public Chamber is one of the initiatives the authorities present to strengthen democratic institutions. It was founded in 2004 in the wake of the Beslan tragedy in which children and teachers were taken hostage by terrorist groups, causing significant casualties and calling for more transparency in decision-making. These hearings were a novelty within the Chamber's practices, introduced in 2014 as modified public expert examinations to assess acts and decisions made by authorities and verify compliance with legislation, human rights, and NGOs' interests. As a variant of public hearings, these hearings aim to facilitate civil society-authorities dialogue (RF Public Chamber, 2021).

The session called together representatives of the Ministry of Enlightenment, the Public Chamber, regional public chambers, and representatives of research institutions and civil society organisations. At the beginning of the session, Maxim Grigoryev, a director of the Moscow-based non-profit Foundation for Research on Democracy with a Ph.D. in political science, spoke strongly in support of the draft law (RF Public Chamber, 2021, 0:20:00 on recording). The participants generally supported the draft. However, Olga Orlova (Public Chamber in Kurgan Region of Russia) (RF Public Chamber, 2021, 01:03:38 on recording), Irina Bergovskaya (Public Chamber in Kaluga Region) (RF Public Chamber, 2021, 01:20:00 on recording), Sergey Popov (professor of the Russian Academy of Sciences, whose popular science releases are well-known in Russia) (RF Public Chamber, 2021, 39:06:00 on recording), along with Ilya Ferapontov, the only journalist on the meeting ("N+1" media outlet general editor) (RF Public Chamber, 2021, 01:45:00 on recording) remained critical of it. The majority of sceptics, however, appeared outside the session as YouTube commenters under footage of zero hearings, commenting on the draft law and the noncritical opinions from participants. Many critics have argued that excessive regulation of freedom of speech slows down education and development by introducing more bureaucracy.

In its conclusion on the already adopted legislative amendment related to the enlightenment activities, the Federation Council's Committee on Constitutional Legislation and State Building found no contradictions with the Constitution, federal constitutional laws, or federal laws (RF The Federal Assembly of the Russian Federation, 2021). In the final third reading, 308 members of parliament voted in favour, and 95 voted against it, including the draft law's authors Nikolai Ryzhak and Rizvan Kurbanov (who voted against their own bill). A single vote was abstained. The Communist Party and Liberal Democratic Party representatives expressed concerns about bureaucratisation, shrinking free discussion spaces, and stifling valuable programs (Smith & Mahlay, 2021).

3.2 Reactions from the NGOs and Individuals

Cases in which individuals defend their rights to engage in enlightenment activities or challenge sanctions imposed for violating enlightenment regulations are not yet included in publicly accessible legal databases. The Constitutional Court has not examined the constitutionality of these legal amendments. Nevertheless, it was possible to find information about the 15th December 2021, case from the Moscow City Court in which a citizen was penalised for violating protest regulations after participating in demonstrations against the adoption of amendments to the Federal Law on Education to formalise the conduct of enlightenment activities (Ovd.info, 2022).

Moscow City Court, on appeal, cancelled a fine imposed on an activist for protesting the new law on enlightenment activities (under Article 20.2, par. 5 of the RF Administrative Code). After the said protest held on 16 May 2021, near the Moscow State University Lomonosov Complex, at least 26 people were detained by police and fined (Ovd.info, 2021). The cancellation of the fine for the applicant in the case under consideration (₽ 20,000) was not substantiated by the unjust limitation of freedom of expression expressed in the protest demonstration but by violations of the fine-imposing procedure. Procedural omissions were made during the drafting of the protocol, which is necessary in administrative cases. Although the authorities redrafted the protocol after the Nikulinsky District Court ordered them to, they did not invite the person accused of a violation, which was another abuse of the procedural rules.

Aside from public protests, there were many social media discussions and petitions against the draft law (*Deklaratsiia uchenykh i populiarizatorov nauki*; *Otkrytoe pis'mo ob otklonenii zakonoproekta nomer 1057895*). For instance, on 5 January 2021, a public petition opposing this law-making initiative was launched on the portal Change.org. Authored by Sergey Popov, an astrophysicist and professor of the Russian Academy of Sciences, it received more than 247,632 signatures before being closed (petition against the amendments to the law regarding the enlightenment activities). The law was criticised for its isolationist nature, potential censorship increase, broad and vague scope, and unconstitutionality. As the multiple open letters noted, the law could rob Russian society of various academic resources (Smith & Mahlay, 2021).

3.3 Communicating Data Analysis Findings Back to the Theory

3.3.1 Separating the History of Enlightenment in Russia From Related Legal Amendments

The attempts to combat historical knowledge with the new legislative changes take on an intriguing new meaning when considering the historical origins of enlightenment in Russia. To demonstrate how far the system can go in re-narrating the past in order to self-correct, we need to look back in history up to the Imperial times. In contrast to current practices, the Russian Enlightenment may have triggered, rather than distorted, rule-of-law awareness before the Great Reforms in the middle of the 19th century. In those times, the enlightenment was confined to a small group of jurists, enlightened bureaucrats, reformist officials, professors, and others (Poole, 2021, p. 5). Although there were no social groups that could help balance power distribution, the Enlightenment was crucial as an intermediary between the people and the Absolute.

Orthodox Canon Law was not a significant source of this development, but it was an inspiration for Russian religious philosophy (initiated by Vladimir Solovyov in his 1880 "A Critique of Abstract Principles"). The concept of enlightenment was first encountered through Feofan Prokopovich (1681–1736), a theologian, a head of the Kyiv Theological Academy, and Peter the Great's friend and supporter. It provided the groundwork for practical enlightenment, which was the idea of applying knowledge and education in practice to achieve the goal of working for the welfare of the state under the direction of a Tsar who received European education (Dmitrieva, 2023, p. 162).

Approximately a thousand books were printed in Russian until 1700, but over 600 publications were published in the first 25 years of the 18th century (Danilevskiy, 1954, p. 27). The Enlightenment under Peter the Great increased the translations of secular literature: manuscript works were an exceptionally high proportion of political treatises translated during this period. During this period, the political lexicon evolved: by the 1760s, educated elites had embraced the new ideas borrowed during Peter's reign. The reigns of Elizabeth and Catherine deduced the new lexicon and made them widely available during these eras because of their definitions (Polskoy, 2020). As Peter the Great introduced modernisation to Russia, he embraced the tenet of rule of law rather than rule by law (Kahn, 2006). Respectively, the Enlightenment of those days encouraged the education of the clergy, albeit the Russian autocrats ran the risk of people discovering that the law served a higher purpose than the current needs of an absolute (Poole, 2021, p. 8).

3.3.2 Enlightenment, Civil Society, and Universal Education for All

Civil society may have been fostered by informal aristocratic learning societies that supported orphanages, schools, libraries, and museums. The 18th century saw these societies emerge as saloons or living rooms, producing a group of social critics who could shape Russian social philosophy in the future (Jones, 1998). During the second half of the 18th century and the early 19th century, the Russian concept of enlightenment was probably closest to its European counterpart, based on either the state of Russian society at the time or the ideal social structure that would characterise an enlightened society. In particular, Alexander Radishchev (1749–1802) and his famous 1790 novel *Journey from St. Petersburg to Moscow* exposed the misuse of authority by the government, the demagogic nature of Catherine II's enlightenment programs, and the gravity of the enslavement of peasants (Dmitrieva, 2023, p. 163).

A full-fledged Russian popular science magazine was first published in St. Petersburg: from 1755 to 1764, the Imperial Academy of Sciences published the journal *Monthly Essays for the Benefit of and Entertainment of Servants* (Vaganov, 2016, p. 69). In its first issue, published in January 1755, the magazine's motto was short and unambiguous: "For All." During Alexander I's liberal aspirations at the beginning of the 19th century, the system of enlightenment was reformed. A system of state secular schools was established through the 1803 Preliminary Rules of Public Enlightenment and the 1804 Charter of Educational Institutions (Kusber, 2021). The continuity of education connected parish schools, district schools, and gymnasiums for one, two, and four years, respectively (see Riekkinen & Riekkinen, 2022). The progress made during this period, however, did not endure. Even though by the early 20th century, the saloon informal learning societies had spread beyond living rooms despite repressive laws and government distrust (Lindenmeyr, 2012), late imperial Russia severely restricted workers' socialising chances.

3.3.3 Dissent Suppression: Old Decembrists Versus New Views

What connects the history of the Enlightenment to present-day practices is that social critique, which arose from Enlightenment concepts, has been later suppressed along with free speech. As a result of their failed 1825 uprising, the famous Decembrists, members of oppositional secret organisations founded between 1812 and 1825, were severely punished. As a movement composed primarily of young noblemen, the Decembrists were educated during the relatively liberal reign of Alexander I. Sharing the ideas emerging from the French Revolution promoted social critique as an enlightenment principle that would lead to social transformation (Lincoln, 1976). Plans and prospects for universal enlightenment occupied a special place in the Decembrist program documents.

After their revolt was suppressed in 1825, the Decembrists were banished to Siberia, where the living conditions were harsh. The Decembrists, originating from wealthy noble families, were likely among the most educated individuals of their time, contributing to the enlightenment of Siberia, which was then rural, cold, and mostly uneducated. Despite the regime's oppression in the cities, the exiles promoted enlightenment in remote Siberia, where literacy rates were only 1.5–2.0% at the dawn of the 19th century (Vasilieva, 2014, p. 32). However, the exiles were able to build schools, libraries, and cultural centres in Siberia and teach the locals basic literacy. They were the Decembrists who began introducing modern educational methods, including the system of public primary schools.[4] By providing access to books and resources, the Decembrists hoped to create a more informed and educated population of rural Siberia. Thus, the discussion of enlightenment initiatives and Russia's long history of penalising descendants are closely related. Asymmetrising information in the modern Russian Federation parallels these historical repercussions of dissent.

Since the 2020 constitutional amendments, new textbooks have been approved by the federal authorities, providing, among other things, new interpretations of the enlightenment activities in exile. For example, the 2023 textbook on the foundations of Russian statehood published by the Russian Academy of National Economy and Public Administration under the President of the Russian Federation asserts that "the rebels were deported to Siberia, where they built churches, opened schools, and served the Russian state" (Uvarov, 2023). Moreover, the popular science journal *Zagadki Istorii* (Mysteries of History) further aggravates the image of Decembrists by putting on the first-page material alleging that the West sponsored their uprising (Zagadki istorii, 2023). Sporadic comments on Russian policy back this notion via the internet. Nikolai Starikov, who has appeared on the Ukrainian and Aleksey Navalny Anticorruption Foundation's list of people who have called for war, raised this topic in 2010 in *the Komsomolskaya Pravda* periodical (Kaftan, 2010).

3.3.4 Enlightenment and the Soviet "Entertaining Science"

There is little mention of the term "enlightenment" in the Soviet period except when it is strongly associated with popularising science, with the new Marxist state focusing on technology and strengthening the Communist Party. Many saw the new Marxist state as a suitable ally in their efforts to educate an uneducated public after the 1917 Bolshevik Revolution. Soviet authorities believed scientific and technological progress could help strengthen the Communist Party's goals and revive the industrial sector (Andrews, 2013). During the early to mid-1920s, 60% of Soviet workers lacked access to books, with the remainder consumed mostly political literature. However, by 1922, popular science books had outperformed political literature by a noticeable margin. In 1926, the publisher Vremya began a series called *Entertaining Science*, which included *Entertaining Physiology*, *Entertaining Aviation*, *Entertaining Mineralogy*, and even *Entertaining Technology in the Past* (Andrews, 2013). The series aimed to provide scientific information in the most lively and understandable way possible, in such a way that reading the book would not be tedious work but a form of relaxation and entertainment even for readers most distant from science. Educators, enlighteners, and unprepared readers used these books (Block, 1929).

When it comes to popular science, its revival in the Soviet period corresponds to the emergence of new public science and technology policy in the aftermath of the world wars (Vaganov, 2016, p. 69). Consequently, Stalin launched a brand-new popularisation campaign focused on technology (Andrews, 2013). During the Khrushchev era, Soviet leaders realised that technology could be used for global competition, promoting extensive campaigns to publicise their achievements (2013). This was especially true about nuclear power and space programs.

Thus, during different historical junctures of the Soviet period, enlightenment aligned with the paradigmatic goals of mass education and propaganda. By the mid-1980s, popular science had become the dominant genre in the Soviet Union, with publisher Znanie producing half of its publications (Vaganov, 2016, p. 71). Communist Party congresses, plenums, and Central Committee meetings issued directives on propaganda and agitation activities across the country. In 1947, the All-Union Society "Znanie" (i.e. the All-Union Society for the Dissemination of Political and Scientific Knowledge) was established as an enlightenment organisation (Seleznev, 2018, p. 2). But at other times, it was contentious in promoting freedom of expression, conscience, and pluralism. Eventually, over 218 million copies of popular science literature were released on the eve of the collapse of the USSR in 1990 (2018, p. 2). After the collapse of the Soviet Union, even given the abandonment of the one-party system and overwhelming communist ideology, the term "enlightenment" was not featured in public discourses until the early 2000s and the popularisation of science. By 2015, Putin issued an edict revitalising the "Znanie" society (RF President, 2015), charging it with the tasks of: (a) popularising science in an educational context, introducing innovations, and informing citizens of scientific achievements; (b) facilitating the integration of older people with modern information technology; (c) supporting teachers and pupils; (d) funding promising educational projects; (e) promoting a healthy lifestyle among the younger generation; nurturing patriotism; (f) preserving natural and historical monuments; (g) fostering interethnic harmony; and (h) combating pseudoscience and falsifying history.

3.3.5 From Civil Liberties to Sovereignty Protection: The Enlightenment Aligns Formal Narrative

A key question remains: should legal enlightenment, as outlined in various federal laws, be considered equivalent to general enlightenment? According to Article 28, par. 2, legal clinics within higher education organisations and non-state centres of free legal assistance are entitled to provide law-related information and legal enlightenment (RF Federal Law No. 324-FZ, 2011). Many non-state organisations monitoring human rights have been declared non-grata as foreign agents, reducing some of the risks that legal enlightenment might pose to the official narrative. For law clinics within universities, it is unrealistic to expect them to seek licenses from the Ministry of Enlightenment to provide individual legal advice. Additionally, under the Federal Law on the Basics of Crime Prevention, both public authorities and persons involved in crime prevention, namely citizens, public associations, and other organizations, may pursue legal enlightenment to inform citizens and organizations about "protecting rights and freedoms, society, and the state from unlawful attacks" (RF Federal Law, 182-FZ, 2016, Art. 18). While such enlightenment may be communicated through various educational and informational measures, the law does not require special permission from the federal executive for these activities. The contradiction between Enlightenment activities and legal enlightenment appears to have been overlooked in the legal amendments.

Additionally, it is problematic that the new legal provision regulating Enlightenment activities has been added to Section 12 of the Federal Law on Education, which governs educational programs.[5] Section 12 regulates formal programs, while the enlightenment is expected to occur outside of formal education by its very new legal definition. Authorities seemingly see no contradictions and even take pride in not regulating enlightenment activities as they do formal education. For example, the Ministry of Enlightenment is in the process of developing a draft regulation to eliminate unnecessary regulation in the area of enlightenment activities (RF Ministry of Enlightenment, 2022). This draft aims to ensure the openness and transparency of the enlightenment activities.

Meanwhile, this draft is being worked on by the temporary commission of the Federation Council for the Protection of State Sovereignty headed by Andrey Klimov, who is one of the co-authors of the legal amendments to regulate these activities. Among the hurdles that lawmakers must overcome is eliminating unnecessary requirements for educational activities (Egorova, 2022). The people behind the proposed regulation are glad they decided against adding standards for enlightenment activities that would have resembled those for educational activities despite associating state sovereignty with restrictions on discourse about society and the state, even outside the classroom.

3.3.6 Counteracting Pseudoscience

According to the authors of the amendments in question, they are preventing violations of Russian law by countering the dissemination of various types of fakes and information meant to incite hatred, hostility, and the like. During the early 2000s, when enlightenment as a social endeavour became discussed publicly, it became synonymous with popular science, which also increased citizen science projects. It could have responded to the rapid decline of the prestige of science. Thus, in 2011, only 13% of Russians were interested in space exploration, down from nearly 100% 25 years earlier (Vaganov, 2016). In 2013, almost 80% of people interviewed by sociologists could not name even one domestic scientist (n=1,600 in 138 populated areas surveyed by the All-Russian Centre for the Study of Public Opinion) (2016). However, pseudoscience was widely disseminated during that period, which served as an efficient pretext for officials to pass these amendments.

Thus, in response to pseudoscience's spread, the Presidium of the Russian Academy of Sciences established a Commission on Combating Pseudoscience (KLNRAN, 2024). Founded in 1998 and reorganised in 2018, it identifies and counters pseudoscience and pseudoscientific publications through analytical, methodological, and expert work. In addition to speaking out against pseudoscientific beliefs, the commission condemns ufology, astrology, alternative medicine, and the use of religion in science and education. Its most recent Memorandum No. 3, published in 2023, exposes the pseudoscientific basis of astrology (KLNRAN, 2023).

The task of counteracting pseudoscience was reiterated during the discussion of formalising enlightenment activities. For instance, at the zero hearing as mentioned above held by the Public Chamber, Tatyana Chernigovskaya, a professor at Saint-Petersburg State University, and a television host for science-related programs (yet ambiguously perceived for her strong statements), defended the enlightenment amendments. When defending the amendments in question, she relied on the argument that pseudoscience was being combated (RF Public Chamber, 2021, 01:26:41 on recording). Similarly, Artyom Kiryanov, representing the Public Chamber, supported the amendments (Klyuchevskaya, 2021). As a result of these changes, Kiryanov believes the internet will be cleansed of phoney seminars, courses, and other events.[6]

3.3.7 The Dictatorship of Law Presumes All Enlighteners Guilty?

However, the idea that all enlightenment should be monitored for disseminating fake information implies that they are not acting in good faith. In this regard, we again see a sharp binary division between enlighteners deemed credible by the state and all the rest who are left outside of this realm. Thus, disapproved enlightener candidates only care about protecting their interests and not those of Russia and its citizens, who are believed to share these values. It is also implied that the authorities are concerned with protecting their visions and narratives through law. It satisfies Putin's view of the rule of law, which he refers to as a dictatorship of law aimed only at protecting law-abiding citizens after they have proved to be law-abiding (Kahn, 2006).

Even when international law was respected most during the early Yeltsin years, including due to the desire to join the Council of Europe, this stance still prevailed in independent Russia. It may have been Yeltsin's difficulty accepting limitations to his executive power that a rule-of-law state necessarily imposed upon him, or maybe it was a general difficulty balancing institutional realities with the ideal of the rule of law. However, his famous phrase, "the state should be bound by the law," still stands out as a replacement for what was intended by his legal advisors, who were bound by the rule of law (Kahn, 2006, p. 390).

The following is a real example of counteracting phoney events under Yeltsin's regime. Upon adopting the new Constitution in July 1993, the framework legislation on citizen health began to regulate the practice of traditional medicine, or healing *tselitel'stvo*, following the rise in mass healing sessions in the early 1990s (RF Fundamentals of Legislation of the Russian Federation, 1993). Anatoly Kashpirovsky was probably the most acclaimed healer who filled concert halls with people willing to be enlivened with his healing energy. Channel One invited Mr. Kashpirovsky to hold TV séances (Huxtable, 2017). In these sessions, for instance, the healer would look into TV viewers' eyes and send positive energy to them during moments of silence.[7] According to surveys, almost the whole country watched these programs, with over one-third stating they were beneficial (2017).

Having gained fame in 1988 by performing two operations without anaesthesia on the Soviet current affairs program Viewpoint/*Vzgliad* (2017), Kashpirovsky eventually became a parliamentarian and joined the state Duma's health committee. Healing has acquired an uncontrollable sense in the society of those days. Thus, to counteract harmful practices, it was legally defined as methods of healing, prevention, diagnosis, and treatment based upon the experiences of many generations of people, established in folk traditions and not registered according to law. All healers were obligated to obtain licenses based on statements from medical professional associations. Most importantly, mass healing sessions, including media, were explicitly prohibited by Article 57 of that framework legislation.

The aforementioned is thus a way to control a concrete social hazard. It is excessive to certify all educational discourses when combating false science or limiting foreign discourse influence on children. In an open legal system, one can prohibit harmful actions, such as mass healing sessions, while teaching children and students how to evaluate information critically and strengthening the ability to detect fraudulent information. There would, however, be a greater risk for the system in question since citizens may come across web resources containing analytics that the Ministry of Education does not approve.

3.3.8 Asymmetrical Information via Many-Sided Control

Although studying judicial techniques to analyse the legal logic of introducing the Enlightenment into the Federal Law on Education is worthwhile, we should also consider the broader picture of freedom of speech being curtailed. Shulman (2022) suggests that educational indoctrination is among the main tools used by the current regime to reshape its approach to education on the way from a semi-authoritarian into a totalitarian model. As a result of formalising any form of exposure learners may have to ideas outside those that fit official narratives, authorities may be able to systematically asymmetric information entirely under the guise of aligning formal and informal education to counteract lawbreaking and spread disinformation. Through the new amendments, the executive authority will not only be able to exert strict pre-emptive control over enlightenment activities by reviewing the preliminary programs for enlightenment, but it will also be able to conduct ex post facto reviews by looking at the reports on how those activities were implemented.

The amendments also encourage citizens to snitch on one another: the governmental rules for implementing enlightenment activities stipulate that public authorities and natural persons have the right to inform the Ministry of Enlightenment about any facts or allegations of enlightenment activities contrary to legislative regulations (RF Government, 2022, par. 9). The Federal Law on Education as amended, is broad in formulating what qualifies as violating the legislation on enlightenment activities (RF Federal Law No. 273-FZ, 2012, art. 12.2, par. 2). Incitement of hatred on social, racial, national, or religious grounds, promotion of exclusivity, superiority, or inferiority based on social, racial, national, religious, or linguistic affiliation, and religious views, including by spreading false information about historical, national, religious, and cultural traditions, as well as encouraging actions that violate the Constitution, are prohibited by this paragraph. When applied to, for example, the prohibition to incite actions contrary to the Constitution, these requirements ensure that no room is left for discussions of societal changes that would contradict the official position.

As an example, let us look at a hypothetical scenario. A 2020 constitutional amendment initiated by Putin before launching the aggressive campaign against Ukraine states that marriage is a union between a man and a woman. Should one conclude that Article 12.2 of the amended Federal Law on Education (RF Federal Law No. 273-FZ, 2012) means that citizens do not have the right to discuss issues such as legalising same-sex unions or homosexuality in general? Considering that enlightenment activities are precisely those that seek to promote social and political change, this may be consistent with the general policy of severely restricting freedom of expression adopted by the officials before the invasion of Ukraine.

Thus, with regulating the enlightenment activities, no threat can be ruled out as a potential danger to official discourse in today's social reality shaped by oppressive legislation and practices, on the one hand, and modified truths, which one hears every day, on the other. It is the responsibility of federal bodies to coordinate the speeches of enlighteners, as submitted by rectors, deans, and other administrators of educational institutions beforehand. Ultimately, only a proven orator who is government-friendly will be invited to speak to individuals. Still, while these changes can be viewed as ensuring that everyone receives pre-approved information, they seem excessive since most educational institutions[8] and religious organisations support the power (Smith & Mahlay, 2021).

Furthermore, the amendments under review are excessive, considering that Russia already has regulations governing how children should be raised. In 2015, shortly after Crimea's annexation, the Russian Federation adopted the Strategy for Establishing an Enlightened Russia by 2025 (RGRU, 2015). As outlined in this document, Russia's priority task in raising children is to develop highly moral individuals who share Russian traditional spiritual values, possess modern knowledge and skills, can realise their potential in contemporary society, and are prepared to create and defend the Motherland peacefully. As a strategic national priority, raising children requires consolidating efforts of civil society institutions and departments at the federal, regional, and municipal levels, according to the said document. Before the invasion of Ukraine, the goal of encoding traditional values in the minds of minors had been set.

According to Luhmann's view of communication, excessive legal control is one of the characteristics of autopoietic self-referential systems. Luhmann states that communication can heighten sensitivity rather than cause rejection in cultures where communication that can lead to rejection is avoided or wishes are met before expression occurs (Luhmann, 1992, p. 255). Therefore, if they believe that adding more laws will strengthen the official narrative even if they do not change overall circumstances, Russia's parliamentarians who are loyal to the leader will do so to comply with his wishes before those expressed.

3.3.9 Exempting Religious Organisations in a More Asymmetrical Manner

Further, asymmetry is created by the detail, which can go unnoticed at first glance. The rules on enlightenment activities do not apply to "relationships associated with enlightenment activity within the framework of culturally enlightened activities of

Table 3.1 A Summary of the Enlightenment-Related Legal Amendments

Amendment	*Contents of Enlightenment*
Enlightenment activities are carried out outside the framework of educational programs, activities that disseminate knowledge and experiences, develop skills, values, and competencies for intellectual, spiritual, moral, creative, physical, and (or) professional development, fulfil the educational needs and interests of the individual, and affect relations governed by this Federal Law and other regulatory legal acts of the Russian Federation	Definition
Forbidden from spreading false information about historical, national, religious, or cultural traditions of peoples, inciting racial, religious, or social hatred, or agitating against citizens based on their social, racial, national, religious, or linguistic affiliation, or their attitudes toward religion, as they promote exclusivity, superiority, or inferiority, should be implemented, taking into account traditional values	Special Prohibitions
Amendment	Affected Persons
Obtain approval from the Ministry of Enlightenment for enlightenment initiatives to be pursued with budget funds	Educational Institutions
Obtain the Ministry of Enlightenment's conclusion whenever foreigners attempt to promote enlightenment	
Make contracts on enlightenment activities	
Prohibited from enlightening minors	Persons Recognised as Foreign Agents
Obliged to declare responsibility as foreign agents for the preparation and delivery of messages and materials during enlightenment activities for adults	
Obligation contracts with educational institutions	Individual Educators
Special requirements: good legal standing; meeting the requirement of Article 331 of the Labour Code regarding a lack of obstacles for teaching activities; at least two years' experience in enlightenment activities; demonstrated involvement in socially significant initiatives	
Obligation to make a contract with the educational institution	Organisations
Special requirements: not being on the Ministry of Justice's register of foreign agents; not being in debt for taxes, fees, or other obligations; having employees meeting the requirement of Article 331 of the Labour Code regarding a lack of obstacles for teaching activities; having an updated website with the required information, including, among other things, about contracts with educational personnel	
Being enlisted in an inventory of organisations that support educational activities in public educational organisations with scientific and methodological expertise	Organisations Supporting Educational Activities with Scientific and Methodological Expertise
Amendment	Exempt Organisations
	Religious Organisations

religious organisations" (Smith & Mahlay, 2021). According to Smith and Mahlay (2021), the Orthodox Church appealed to authorities to exempt Sunday schools from upcoming legal changes. In this case, we can see that the exemption was much broader than just Sunday schools. Taking into account the authorities' ties with Orthodox Church leaders (Agadjanian, 2017), this exemption for religious organisations may suggest the intended elimination of all possible weak points to influence citizens outside of loyal educational institutions, which can disapprove of the official narrative. Continuous religious enlightenment can target even those who may not adhere to traditional morality but may still sympathise with the idea that this morality is a shield from the allegedly deteriorating Western values narrative.

Religious organisations are called to play an essential role in the state's policy to preserve and strengthen traditional values, which rest on the foundations of state policy according to Presidential Decree No. 809 (RF President, 2022). As stated in paragraph 26(e) of this decree, religious institutions and other institutions of civil society are required to participate in state policies that uphold and promote traditional values. This could give the authorities greater control over the narrative. As a reminder, religious organisations remain among the five institutions Russians trust the most. As a result of a recent sociological study conducted by the Levada Centre in Russia (September 2023), the following institutions are highly trusted: the president (76%), the army (72%), state security agencies (60%), government (56%), and religious organisations (55%) (Levada Centre, 2023)

Considering Russia's current censorship of freedom of expression, sociological surveys should be analysed carefully for bias: those who disagree with the government are unlikely to participate in surveys because they fear sanctions. However, in the absence of other verifiable data, Levada Centre's data, which has been acknowledged as a foreign agent, is considered the most credible by the European Parliament, which regularly monitors public opinion regarding Russia's war against Ukraine.

In conclusion, the legal amendments in question have now renamed the word enlightenment to *prosveshchenie*, which carries a positive connotation, implying the charitable and noble goal of spreading knowledge with features of caution, threat, control, and limitation. A summary of the enlightenment-related legal amendments can be found in Table 3.1 (Smith & Mahlay, 2021).

Notes

1 An initiative for this project was initiated by senators A. Klimov, E. Afanasyeva, A. Vainberg, L. Glebova, O. Melnichenko, along with members of the State Duma of the "United Russia" party: A. Iisaev, V. Piskarev, A. Alshevskikh, A. Shkhagoshev, and the "Just Russia" party; N. Ryzhak, A. Chepa, and R. Kurbanov of the Communist Party; and I. Belykh and D. Savelyevof the Liberal Democratic Party. Natallia Poklonskaya, member of parliament, withdrew her name from the list of authors on 24 November 2020.

2 Several factors make certain individuals ineligible to participate in teaching activities under this article. These include being denied the right to teach due to a court verdict in a criminal case, having a criminal record, being prosecuted for crimes against life, health, freedom, honour, dignity, sexual integrity, family members and minors, public health, morality, constitutional foundations, state security, peace and security for mankind, and

public safety. An individual with an unexpunged conviction or outstanding conviction for another intentional grave crime, a diagnosis of legal incompetency, or a condition approved by the federal executive body can also be admitted to teaching activities if the Commission on Minors and Their Rights makes a decision.

3 The obligation does not apply to agreements supplying educational services to foreign citizens or agreements that expire before September 1st, 2021.

4 Among other things, the Decembrists established the first public library in 1842 in the town of Tobolsk, Siberia, where locals could see and handle books. The wives of Decembrists often accompanied them into exile, and their children often grew up there. Women educated their children at home, where children of locals were also invited.

5 Similar to the solution aligning the enlightenment with formal education programmes in Section 12 of the Federal law on education, Chapter 7 of the Russian Constitution covers both the judiciary and the Prokuratura – two bodies that do not represent the same branch. The Constitution includes the Prokuratura in the judiciary chapter, even though it is not a judiciary. The Constitution only mentions the Prokuratura in one article, so no separate chapter was allocated to it.

6 Individuals have, for instance, paid for an internet course on tax avoidance strategies and then had issues with the tax authorities. Even though these courses harm the public interest in equitable taxation policies (just as self-medication courses can harm public health), heavy regulation of all extracurricular learning is excessive.

7 "Charged" photos of Mr. Kashpirovsky, sold in U.S. dollars, could also be purchased. The author remembers her grandmother putting a 3-liter glass of water in front of the TV during prime time. The entire family was supposed to drink the "charged" water in order to heal. The popular practice of drinking water blessed by the Orthodox church today can be explained by religious motives, but charging from a TV transmitting the image of an unlicensed healer has no rational explanation and can become a health and life hazard in cases where healing is preferred over doctor visits.

8 A few years ago, the rectors of Russian universities signed a letter supporting the invasion of Ukraine. Since then, no one from the educational establishment has openly criticised the government.

References

Agadjanian, A. (2017). Tradition, morality and community: Elaborating Orthodox identity in Putin's Russia. *Religion, State & Society*, *45*(1), 39–60.

Andrews, J. T. (2013). An evolving scientific public sphere: State science enlightenment, communicative discourse, and public culture from imperial Russia to Khrushchev's Soviet times. *Science in Context*, *26*(3), 509–526.

Block, G. P. (Ed.). (1929). *Science for entertainment. Catalogue of the book series*. Vremya Publishing.

Danilevskiy, V. V. (1954). *Russian technological literature in the first quarter of the 18th century*. Academy of Science of the U.S.S.R.

Deklaratsiia uchenykh i populiarizatorov nauki [Declaration of scientists and popular scientists]. https://trv-science.ru/2021/01/declaration/

Dmitrieva, N. A. (2023). The changing concept of enlightenment in Russia: An outline. *SHS Web of Conferences*, *161*, 1–11.

Egorova, V. (2022, March 29). *Among the hurdles lawmakers will overcome is derailing unnecessary requirements for educational activities*. RGRU. https://rg.ru/2022/03/29/zakonodateli-otkazhutsia-ot-izlishnih-trebovanij-k-prosvetitelskoj-deiatelnosti.html

Explanatory Note to the Draft Law No. 1057895-7. *On amendments to the federal law "on education in the Russian Federation" (on the introduction of enlightenment activities)*. https://sozd.duma.gov.ru/bill/1057895-7

Huxtable, S. (2017). Remembering a problematic past: TV mystics, perestroika and the 1990s in post-Soviet media and memory. *European Journal of Cultural Studies*, *20*(3), 307–323.

Jones, W. (1998). Enlightenment, Russian. In *The Routledge encyclopedia of philosophy*. Taylor and Francis. Retrieved October 9, 2023, from www.rep.routledge.com/articles/thematic/enlightenment-russian/v-1; https://doi.org/10.4324/9780415249126-E043-1

Kaftan, L. (2010). *Vosstaniem dekabristov rukovodila zagranica? Kak mogli oficery-patrioty svergat' carja i ubivat' pobedonosnuju russkuju armiju [obsuzhdenie]* [Is the uprisal of the Decembrists being handled by foreign states? In what way could the patriot officers kill the victorious Russian army and overthrow the Tsar? [discussion]]. www.kp.ru/daily/24609.3/778204/www.kp.ru/daily/24609.3/778204/?ysclid=lqasgpyr8q535942339

Kahn, J. (2006). The search for the rule of law in Russia. *Georgetown Journal of International Law*, *37*, 353–409.

KLNRAN. (2023, December 18). *Komissiia po bor'be s lzhenaukoi pri Prezidiume Rossijskoj akademii nauk* [Commission to combat pseudoscience at the presidium of the Russian academy of sciences]. Pseudoscience of Astrology Memorandum No. 3. Retrieved December 18, 2023, from http://klnran.ru/2023/12/memorandum-3-astrologija/

KLNRAN. (2024). *Commission to combat pseudoscience at the presidium of the Russian academy of sciences*. http://klnran.ru/category/commission/

Klyuchevskaya, N. (2021, April 16). *Amendments on educational activities: Expert disagreements and unresolved issues*. Garant. www.garant.ru/news/1457445/?ysclid=lp2o4roj1m39707003

Kusber, I. (2021). *Vospitanie elit i narodnoe obrazovanie v Rossiiskoi imperii XVIII – pervoi poloviny XIX veka*. LitRes.

Levada Centre, Institutional Trust. (2023, September). www.levada.ru/2023/10/12/institutsionalnoe-doverie-sentyabr-2023/

Lincoln, W. B. (1976). A Re-examination of some historical stereotypes: An analysis of the career patterns and backgrounds of the Decembrists. *JGO*, *24*(3), 357–368.

Lindenmeyr, A. (2012). Building civil society one brick at a time: People's houses and worker enlightenment in late imperial Russia. *The Journal of Modern History*, *84*(1), 1–39.

Luhmann, N. (1992). What is communication? *Communication Theory*, *2*(3), 251–259.

Otkrytoe pis'mo ob otklonenii zakonoproekta nomer 1057895 [An open letter on rejecting the draft law no. 1057895]. http://aroundart.org/2021/02/04/otkry-toe-pis-mosoobshhestva-s-trebovaniem-otklonit-zakonoproekt-1057895-7/

OVD.INFO. (2021, May 16). *In Moscow, protesters against the law on educational activities were detained near the Moscow State University building*. https://ovd.info/express-news/2021/05/16/v-moskve-u-zdaniya-mgu-zaderzhali-protestuyuschikh-protiv-zakona-o?_gl=1%2Akkld1o%2A_ga%2AMTMzNjYzNTY5NS4xNzAwNTc0OTU2%2A_ga_J7DH9NKJ0R% 2AMTcwMDU3NDk1Ni4xLjAuMTcwMDU3NDk2NS41MS4wLjA

OVD.INFO. (2022, January 17). *The Moscow city court canceled the fine for an activist who spoke out against the law on educational activities*. https://ovd.info/express-news/2022/01/17/mosgorsud-otmenil-shtraf-aktivistu-vystupivshemu-protiv-zakona-o?ysclid=lp8ef3j3xy87060812

Petition against the Amendments to the Law Regarding the Enlightenment Activities. www.change.org/p/%D0%B3%D0%BE%D1%81%D1%83%D0%B4%D0%B0%D1%80%D1%81%D1%82%D0%B2%D0%B5%D0%BD%D0%BD%D0%B0%D1%8F-%D0%B4%D1%83%D0%BC%D0%B0-%D1%80%D1%84-%D0%BF%D1%80%D0%BE%D1%82%D0%B8%D0%B2-%D0%BF%D0%BE%D0%BF%D1%80%D0%B0%D0%B2%D0%BE%D0%BA-%D0%BE-%D0%BF%D1%80%D0%BE%D1%81%D0%B2%D0%B5%D1%82%D0%B8%D1%82%D0%B5%D0%BB%D1%8C%D1%81%D0%BA%D0%BE%D0%B9-%D0%B4%D0%B5%D1%8F%D1%82%D0%B5%D0%BB%D1%8C%D0%BD%D0%BE%D1%81%D1%82%D0%B8-1e6d7a97-a61a-49b9-a7a7-80da49172ccf

Polskoy, S. (2020). Translation of political concepts in 18th Century Russia: Strategies and practices. *Kritika*, *21*(2), 235–265.

Poole, R. A. (2021). Introduction. A Russian conception of legal consciousness. In P. Valliere & R. Poole (Eds.), *Law and the Christian tradition in modern Russia*. Routledge.

RF. The Federal Assembly of the Russian Federation, the Committee of the Federation Council on Constitutional Legislation and State Building. (2021, March 30). Conclusion N. 3.1–06/1102 on the federal law "on amendments to the federal law "on education in the Russian Federation," adopted by the State Duma on 16 March 2021". https://sozd.duma.gov.ru/bill/1057895-7

RF Federal Law No. 85-FZ. (2021, April 5). *O vnesenii izmenenii v Federal'nyj zakon "Ob Obrazovanii v Rossiiskoi Federatsii*" [On amending the federal law on education in the Russian Federation]. Sobranie zakonodatel'stva Rossiiskoi Federatsii, 2021, No. 15 (part I) item 2452.

RF Federal Law No. 273-FZ. (2012, December 29). *On obrazovanii v Rossiiskoi Federatsii* [On education in the Russian Federation]. Sobranie zakonodatel'stva Rossiiskoi Federatsii, 2012, No. 53 (part I) item 7598.

RF Federal Law No. 324-FZ. (2011, November 21). *O besplatnoi iuridicheskoi pomoshchi v Rossiiskoi Federatsii* [On free legal Ais in the Russian Federation]. Sobranie zakonodatelstva Rossiiskoi Federatsii, 2011, No. 48 item 6725.

RF Federal Law No. 498-FZ. (2022, December 5). *O vnesenii izmenenii v otdel'nye zakonodatel'nye akty Rossiiskoi Federatsii* [On amendments to certain legislative acts of the Russian Federation]. http://publication.pravo.gov.ru/Document/View/0001202212050039?ysclid=lu9wf8sy5r497894126

RF Fundamentals of Legislation of the Russian Federation No. 5487. (1993, July 22). *Ob okhrane zdorov'iia grazhdan* [On protecting citizens' health]. www.kremlin.ru/acts/bank/3980. Not in force.

RF Government Decree No. 1195. (2022, July 1). *Ob utverzhdenii pravil osuchshestvleniia prosvetitel'stkoi deiiatel'nosti* [On upholding the rules of pursuing the enlightenment activities]. Sobranie zakonodatel'stva Rossiiskoi Federatsii, 2022, No. 28 item 5112.

RF Ministry of Enlightenment. (2022, March 23). *Opublikovan proekt pravil osuschestvleniia prosvetitelskoy deiatelnosti* [The draft rules of pursuing the enlightenment activities is published]. https://edu.gov.ru/press/4875/opublikovan-proekt-pravil-osuschestvleniya-prosvetitelskoy-deyatelnosti

RF President, Decree No. 617. (2015, December 11). *O sozdanii Obshcherossiiskoi obshchestvenno-gosudarstvennoi prosvetitelskoi organizatsii Rossiiskoe obschhestvo "Znanie"* [On establishing the All-Russia public enlightenment organization "Znanie"]. http://publication.pravo.gov.ru/Document/View/0001201512110006

RF President, Decree No. 809. (2022, November 9). *Ob utverzhdenii Osnov gosudarstvennoi politiki po sokhraneniiu i ukrepleniiu traditsionnykh rossiuskikh duhovno-nravstvennykh tsennostei* [On upholding the foundations of state policy on preserving and strengthening traditional Russian spiritual and moral values]. www.kremlin.ru/acts/bank/48502

RF Public Chamber. (2021). *Popravki v zakon o prosvetitel'skoi deiatel'nosti v Rossii* [Zero hearings of the draft legislaton on the enlightenment activities]. www.youtube.com/watch?v=f9QsC6n5EzE

RGRU. (2015, June 8). *Strategy for the development of education in the Russian Federation for the period until 2025. No. 996-r*. https://rg.ru/documents/2015/06/08/vospitanie-dok.html

Riekkinen, M., & Riekkinen, P. (2022). Basic education for all. Looking for shared elements of equality of opportunity in legislation of Finland and Russia. *European Journal of Comparative Law and Governance*, *9*(4), 409–445.

Seleznev, A. V. (2018). Periodizatsiia istorii Vsesoiuznogo obshchestva "Znanie" na osnove analiza ego tselei, organizatsionnykh osnov i sruktur [Periodization of the history of the all-union society "Znanie" based on an analysis of its goals, organizational foundations, and structures]. *Chelovek i kul'tura*, *1*, 1–17.

Shulman, E. (2022, September 28). *The Mobilisation of the demobilised. Neither society nor the political system are ready for ideological indoctrination, ideologies*. RE: Russia. https://re-russia.net/en/expertise/022/

Smith, K. E., & Mahlay, O. (2021, October). Shooting at sparrows with a cannon: Russia's counterproductive law on education. *Kennan Cable*, *72*, 1–11. www.wilsoncenter.org/sites/default/files/media/uploads/documents/KI_210927_Cable%2072_V1.pdf

Uvarov, P. U. (Ed.). (2023). *Osnovy rossiiskoi gosudarstvennosti. Uchebnoe posobie dlia studentov estestvenno-nauchnyh i inzhenerno-tehnicheskikh spetsial'nostei*. Delo and Ranhgnis.

Vaganov, A. G. (2016). Evopution of the modes of popularizing science in Russia: XVIII-XXI/Evoliutsiia form populiarizatsii nauki v Rossii: XVIII-XXI vv. *Almanakh "Nauka. Innovacii. Obrazovanie"*, *3*, 64–77.

Vasilieva, S. A. (2014). Prosvetitelskaia deiatelnost dekabristov v sibirskoi ssylke [The enlightenment activities of the Decembrists in Siberian exile]. *Vedomosti ugolovno-ispolnitelnoi sistemy*, *12*.

Zagadki istorii. (2023). *V novom nomere/Contents of the New Issue, 50 Zagadki istorii*. https://zagadki.media/?ysclid=lqas88s5s1922374628#new

4 Analysing Legal Amendments Since 2012

Extending Foreign Agent Legislation to Individuals

4.1 Background

Russia's foreign agent legislation covers NGOs, mass media, and, since 2022, individuals receiving foreign aid, being under foreign influence, and engaging in political activities, both broadly and vaguely defined as specified below. The foreign agent procedure is routinely invoked so that any NGO, mass media, or individual the authorities define as a foreign agent is included in a special registry maintained by the Ministry of Justice. It must comply with obligations (e.g. regular activity reports) and restrictions (e.g. using the foreign agent label when releasing information to the public). Failure to comply with the restrictions may entail the dissolution of a legal entity, high fines, or even imprisonment for individuals.

Foreign agent legislation initially consisted of provisions in several federal laws and regulations introducing significant restrictions on the said individuals and organisations. The development of this legislation dates back to a 2012 revision of the federal laws on non-commercial organisations and public associations. Each status, depending on whether its bearer is an NGO, a member of the media, or an individual, has specific features and a regulatory framework that includes legislative regulation and is subject to relevant acts of the Ministry of Justice.

Thus, until December 2022, the status of foreign agents was regulated by several federal statutes: Federal Law "On Non-Commercial Organizations" (RF Federal Law No. 7-FZ, 1996); Federal Law "On Public Associations" (RF Federal Law No. 82-FZ, 1995); Federal Law "On sanctions for persons involved in violations of fundamental human rights and freedoms, rights and freedoms of citizens of the Russian Federation" (RF Federal Law No. 272-FZ, 2012); Law of the Russian Federation "On the mass media" (RF Law of the Russian Federation No 2124-I, 1991). In 2022, the consolidated Federal Law "On the control of the activities of the persons influenced by foreign entities" was adopted (Federal Law of 14 July 2022 No. 255-FZ). Compared to the previous items of legislation that dealt with the status of foreign agents, this federal law, which entered into force on 1 December 2022, introduced one more qualifying feature

DOI: 10.4324/9781032613383-4

to define foreign agents – being under foreign influence. Article 1 defines a foreign agent as:

> *A person who receives support and is under foreign influence in other forms carries out political activities, collects targeted information on the military and military-technical activities of the Russian Federation, distributes messages and materials intended for a wide range of people, or (or) participates in making such messages and materials.*
>
> (RF Federal Law No. 255-FZ, 2022, Art. 1)

The concept of "support" comprises "funds and (or) other properties provided to a person by a foreign source, as well as organisational, methodological, scientific, and technical assistance provided by a foreign source" (RF Federal Law No. 255-FZ, 2022, Art. 2). Article 4 of this Federal law specifies that political activity entails activities "related to establishing a state, protecting the constitutional foundations, ensuring the sovereignty of the country, and protecting its territorial integrity." In addition, it "entails ensuring legality, law and order, public and state security, national defence, foreign policy, socio-economic and national development, as well as the political system of the country, as well as the activities of the public authorities, legislation regulating the rights and freedoms of citizens in order to influence public policy, the creation of public authorities, their actions and decisions" (RF Federal Law No. 255-FZ, 2022, Art. 4).

The 2022 consolidated federal law also introduced the requirement for a unified registry of all categories of persons addressed by the foreign agent legislation. Before, there were four registries for each category: registered non-commercial organisations, non-registered public associations, mass media, and natural persons. It also introduced one more criterion for recognising a person as a foreign agent, which was lacking until then. Namely, being under foreign influence is defined as an "act of supporting or influencing a person by a foreign source, including through coercion, persuasion or other means" (RF Federal Law No. 255-FZ, 2022, Art. 2).

Its Article 8 also introduced a set of six criteria upon which a person can be unlisted from the registry:

- termination of activity of a legal person after its dissolution;
- termination of activity of the unregistered public association and other entities;
- the death of a natural person;
- not receiving any foreign aid for one calendar year before the submission of an application for unenlisting, as confirmed with the results of a non-planned inspection by the authorised body;
- not receiving any foreign aid for three calendar years before the submission of an application for unenlisting by a person who had already been unlisted from the registry, as confirmed with the results of a non-planned inspection by the authorised body;
- the return of the foreign funds within three months of their receipt, provided that no other (technical, methodological, etc.) aid has been provided by the foreign

person or organisation, as confirmed by the results of an unplanned inspection by the authorised body (RF Federal Law No. 255-FZ, 2022, Art. 8).

In an explanatory note accompanying this federal law, it was noted that its adoption was necessary because current legislation contains "disparate provisions" that are enshrined in different federal laws and establish different approaches to essential elements, making a person a foreign agent (Explanatory Note to the Federal Law No. 255-FZ). The note focuses on its innovations and contents instead of explaining why this law was introduced. In the end, this law concludes that the measures proposed will protect and guarantee Russia's security, sovereignty, territorial integrity, and rights and freedoms, as well as ensure a prompt response to "internationally wrongful acts" by preventing foreign interference in Russian society and state affairs, and ensuring that citizens' rights and freedoms are implemented (Explanatory Note to the Federal Law No. 255-FZ).

As of 1 March 2024, 774 entries are listed in the registry of foreign agents maintained by the Ministry of Justice (in January 2023, there were 522 entries when the author of this book did her research), including entries on persons who had been unlisted (RF The Registry of Foreign Agents, 2023). The list has been growing unevenly. For example, in 2016, the number of *organisations* included in the registry almost tripled, amounting to 154 (Brikul'skii, 2022). In January 2023, there were 73 organisations in the registry with several members of the mass media, who were difficult to identify, being listed as foreign agents (because both legal entities and natural persons are enlisted in the same registry), which is probably due to the liquidation of foreign agent organisations, either voluntarily or based on a court decision for various violations of the foreign agent legislation (2022).

From the beginning, Russian authorities attempted to publicly legitimise the enactment of foreign agent legislation, providing explanations in response to the arbitrary actions of U.S. officials. At issue was registering Russian-sponsored news media outlets as foreign agents in the United States. Russia, thus, claimed its foreign agent restrictions "mirror those in other countries, mainly the US" (RFERL, 2017a). Under the 1938 Foreign Agents Registration Act (FARA), U.S. officials can require an entity to register under foreign agent requirements (Robinson, 2020). At least six foreign media outlets are known to be registered under FARA in 2017, including Canada's CBC, Japan's NHK, and the China Daily (RFERL, 2017b). However, unlike what is happening in Russia, where the enactment of foreign agent status is "simply triggered when an entity or an individual engages in political activity," the U.S. legislation, first, requires a proven connection with foreign governments, and second, registering under FARA legislation does not affect the ability to report news and information (RFERL, 2017b). However, these two distinctions do not prevent Russian officials from invoking "mirror" arguments. For instance, when the Russian state-funded "RT" television network was suggested to register under the U.S. FARA legislation for spreading misinformation, several senior Russian officials publicly announced future legislative amendments in response to the U.S. limitations on RT, enabling Russia to declare foreign media outlets as foreign agents (RFERL, 2017a).

The amendments extending the foreign agent legislation to individuals mean that organisations and physical persons who negatively comment on the Russian military or security services and their employees can be named foreign agents (Roth, 2023). Following the aggression against Ukraine, these amendments were adopted without offering significant public explanations. Considering the timing when these amendments were enacted and their targeting of critics of the state, these amendments were deemed to be repressive. Simple data analysis can show that the critical underpinnings of these legislative amendments went further to de-symmetrise information to strengthen the authorities' position vis-à-vis possible opposition.

4.2 Extending Foreign Agent Legislation to Individuals to De-Symmetrise Information

The foreign agent legislation, when read in conjunction with other laws subsequently amended, indicates a total prohibition for individuals listed in the foreign agent registry from pursuing any activities that allow free direct or indirect participation in the conduct of public affairs. It also precludes an opportunity for free public dissemination of political opinions.

Attempts to manipulate public opinion in Russia by dramatising the role of foreign agents lead to the propagation of such binary oppositions as Russia versus foreign states and law-abiding Russian citizens versus those who are under foreign influence. Labelling individuals as foreign agents, thus, excludes any possibility of expressing a dissenting opinion in public. With restrictions imposed on foreign agents, Russian authorities seek to undermine human rights, as well as diversity, which the authorities consider foreign values.

Not surprisingly, access to direct democracy is prohibited to those the state declares as foreign agents. The electoral laws related to electing the President and the members of the State Duma had been gradually amended with particular articles explicitly prohibiting foreign agents from direct participation in elections (RF Federal Law No. 19-FZ, 2003, Art. 11; RF Federal Law No. 20-FZ, 2014, Art. 11). Not only foreign agents themselves but also those individuals who, two years before the start of the electoral campaign, were founders of an organisation or members of the mass media recognised as foreign agents or individuals receiving funding from foreign agents are also among those who are prohibited from running for office. In this regard, a new category of persons before the law was introduced in 2021, persons "*affiliated with foreign agents*" (i.e. Article 2, para 35.1 of the Federal Law of 12 June 2002 No. 67-FZ. "On the basic guarantees of the electoral rights and the right to take part in the referendum of the citizens of the Russian Federation").

Restricting the possibility of exerting influence through public debate indirectly is enforced in several significant ways:

- The obligation to use the badge every time information is released to third parties via the media and when communicating in social networks is introduced, warning that "this information was conveyed by a person recognised as a foreign agent."

- Introducing a prohibition on disseminating information and educational activities for under-aged persons.
- Prohibition of carrying out pedagogical activities in state and municipal educational organisations.
- Introducing a ban on foreign agents operating significant objects of critical information infrastructure and carrying out activities to ensure the security of such objects.

Using a foreign agent label is also required from citizens should they wish to address public authorities. The foreign agent law obligates the citizens recognised as foreign agents to make notes of their special status in any communication with public authorities.

Furthermore, foreign agents are prevented from organising public gatherings.

Foreign agent restrictions prevent individuals from membership in various public organisations, consultative organs, and commissions whose principal aim is to defend human rights. These restrictions eliminated the ability of foreign agents to nominate candidates for public commissions under the aegis of public associations.

Foreign agents, meanwhile, seem to be considered outside the realm of personal data protection since the government adopted a regulation on publishing foreign agents' dates of birth, tax numbers, and pension certificates in December 2022, all of which allow these individuals to be personally identified (RF Government, 2022). This is even though the Russian Federation's Code of Administrative Offences punishes violations of personal data protection (RF Federal Law No. 195-FZ, 2001, Art. 13.11).

The Ministry of Justice had adopted a procedure for maintaining the foreign agent's register and posting the information on the official website (RF Ministry of Justice, Order No. 307.2022, November 29). In these regulations, among other things, the register is maintained on paper and electronic media. It has also been determined how an individual may be excluded from the register for the first time and how foreign agents may apply for exclusion from the register. This was done as part of implementing the Federal law "On the control of the activities of the persons influenced by foreign entities" (RF Federal Law No. 255-FZ, 2022).

4.3 Interpretations by the Constitutional Court

In 2014, the RF Constitutional Court delivered its judgment on a case initiated by the Ombudsman and the regional foundation "Kostroma Center for Support of Public Initiatives." The case concerned the constitutionality of the laws "On non-commercial organisations" and "On public associations" insofar as they relate to the status of foreign agents. In its Ruling No. 10-P, the Constitutional Court confirmed the constitutionality of the legislation on foreign agents (RF Constitutional Court, 2014a). The Court adjudged that the registration as a foreign agent, with all its associated responsibilities and restrictions, not to mention the sanctions for breaching these, conforms with the Constitution. Justifying this conclusion, it invoked the human right to association, as guaranteed by international law and protected by the ECtHR. As for the Court's principal stance on the purpose of foreign agent legislation, the Court ruled that the registration of an entity as a foreign agent does not imply any "negative assessment" of its activities, while the laws in question do not intend to form "a negative attitude" towards the political activity of such organisations (RF Constitutional Court, 2014a, par. 3.1). The Dissenting Opinion of Judge Yaroslavtsev, however, is significant not only for finding the "foreign agent" concept unconstitutional but also for the way this conclusion is grounded.

Yaroslavtsev maintains that the legal norms under consideration violate the constitutional right to association, which, in turn, is a motivation to participate in public and social life based on free formation and expression of opinion as guaranteed by international human rights law. Unlike the majority decision, which uses proclamations and statements of fact, this dissenting opinion relates the information mentioned above embedded in international law to the views of the knowledge-holders and, expressly, the ECtHR, stating that the said freedoms are at the core of a democratic society. Above all, he also appeals to the Russian classics in Ivan Turgenev's novel *Fathers and Sons*, which cites the moderate liberal Pavel Kirsanov. In particular, the quote states that "without dignity and respect for oneself . . . there is no solid foundation for the public good" (RF Constitutional Court, 2014a). This reference implies that by denying freedom of conscience and opinion, the state denies human dignity, without which there is no firm basis for the state. This dissenting opinion reveals another essential contradiction, pointing out that, based on the 2008 Governmental Decree No. 485, necessary universal and regional human rights and cooperation organisations, such as UNESCO, the European Commission, the Council of the Baltic States, the Nordic Council of Ministers, and other entities, constituted a list of organisations for cultural and scientific cooperation for which the government allocated special funding. Yaroslavtsev refers to the latter as follows:

> *Authoritative international organisations, which one would not believe, would negatively impact the fragile souls of Russians and even more so on representatives of the state power, who are confident in the "flawlessness" [nepogreshimost'] of their own decisions.*
>
> (RF Constitutional Court, 2014a)

The above statement implies that people who legitimately choose the government are expected to believe in its decisions, and no outsider, especially those who enjoy public trust, can undermine this belief. It also spotlights the policy reversal by stressing that those the government once regarded as trustworthy would later proclaim these entities as harmful. Finally, Yaroslavtsev further reveals this contradiction by observing that governmental decisions, flawless or weighed and justified, should not be influenced by external entities.

Likewise, in the 2019 Ruling No. 4-P regarding the application of foreign agent-related limitations to Radio "Chance" Ltd., the Constitutional Court asserted that legal provisions restricting the influence of foreign organisations and their agents on the "adoption of strategic decisions" in, *among other things*, shaping public discourse via mass media, especially those decisions concerning elections, aim at protecting the security of information of the Russian Federation (RF Constitutional Court, 2019). Such a conclusion is, however, questioned by Justice Aranovsky, who ultimately resigned from the Court in September 2022. He maintained that the 2016 Doctrine of Information Security cannot be used to justify the constitutionality of legal restrictions on foreign agents, as this doctrine was adopted two years after the foreign agent legislation had been introduced. Following Aranovsky, the necessity of such restrictions is unjustified because any threats to national security are merely risks, and their possible consequences need to be proven. The foreign origin of persons, funds, or ideas cannot per se prove a threat to the constitutional order. On the contrary, the dissenting opinion argued that isolation from the rest of the world deprives the constitution of meaning since it is addressed to the multinational peoples of Russia.

While the Constitutional Court, in the 2019 Ruling, limited itself to general proclamations, the 2014 Ruling mentioned above No. 10-P is an example of applying several new rules to foreign agent legislation (RF Constitutional Court, 2014a) that had not been prescribed by federal legislation.

First, the Court declared that no specific feature of foreign aid, be it duration and regularity, amount and volume, or the type of funding (donations, grants, bonuses, etc.), should be relevant for enacting foreign agent legislation which, as such, excludes the possibility of its arbitrary application. Second, foreign aid should be accepted by the entity, not merely transferred to its accounts, which implies that if a person returns foreign funds before starting a political activity, there are grounds for enacting foreign agent legislation. Third, the Court specified the features of activity that should be defined as political to enact foreign agent legislation. It started by reinstating that such activity relates to participation, including financing, in arranging political events to influence the adoption of decisions by public authorities and change their state policy, as well as shaping public opinion on the said matters. It further detailed that the forms of such participation can vary by extending the involvement in public events and can include (a) campaigning for elections or referendums, (b) publicly petitioning public authorities, (c) distributing their assessment of decisions, policies, and other actions by public authorities, which cannot be enlisted in a detailed manner.

Fourth, it established that when assessing the political nature of events in which non-commercial organisations participate, the focus of these actions should be decisive. Moreover, the focus should be on influencing directly or via the shaping of public opinion and the adoption of decisions by public authorities. Fifth, activities in the areas of science, culture, art, healthcare, welfare, motherhood, and childhood, as well as protection of persons with disabilities, promotion of a healthy lifestyle, physical education, and sports, protection of flora and fauna, and promotion of charity and volunteerism, cannot be defined as political activities in terms of foreign agent legislation, even if the organisation aims at influencing decisions and policies by public authorities, provided that these goals do not extend beyond the framework of the said activities.

4.4 Reactions From the NGOs and Individuals

When only introduced as a proposal in 2012, these amendments faced public resistance from NGOs and academicians, notably the Presidential Council for Human Rights and the Development of Civil Society. That resistance proved, however, to be unsuccessful and was instead followed by a massive, unannounced, and invasive inspection of NGOs, starting from October 2012, marking the enactment of legal amendments (Flikke, 2016). Naturally, enacting foreign agent legislation faced international criticism, including from the Venice Commission, which found it to be a violation of the freedom of association (Venice Commission, 2014). After the campaign against independent media and journalists as foreign agents intensified in 2021, the OSCE Representative on Freedom of the Media expressed concerns with these practices (OSCE, 2021). Commenting on actions taken against the Moscow-based independent television channel "*Dozhd*" (TV Rain) and the Latvia-registered investigative media portal "*Vazhniye Istorii*" (iStories), the Representative observed that "a lack of legal certainty and proportionality on the matter" is distressing.

When it comes to individual attempts to protect their right to freedom of expression from the restrictions associated with being declared a foreign agent, it is daunting to verify how many individuals and organisations have attempted to argue against the Ministry of Justice's decision to include them in the registry. We can examine the Registry of Foreign Agents (2023), the press releases, and the available national case law to learn how individuals and organisations protest these decisions and the officials' stance in response to these protests.

The Register of Foreign Agents (2023), available on the Ministry of Justice web page, shows 167 dates when individuals and organisations were removed from the registry (as of January 2023). Unenlisting, unfortunately, does not mean that the person or organisation was granted redress since, under the 2022 Federal Law on the control over the activities of foreign agents, termination of a legal person is grounds for unenlisting (RF Federal Law No. 255-FZ, 2022, Art. 8). Unenlisting, thus, often means that the organisation no longer exists as a legal person (e.g. the case with the organisation memorial, which had been dissolved based on a court decision for not complying with the foreign agent legislation. Another example is the organisation "Golos," which had been listed as a foreign agent between 2014 and 2020 (RF The Register of Foreign Agents, 2023, entry 2). In 2016, the court dissolved it, but it was restructured in 2018. The new "Golos" had been listed in the Registry in 2021 (The Register of Foreign Agents, 2023, entry 241). It is also possible that the foreign agent status is deactivated in the Registry. For example, on 29 April 2022, two members of "Golos," Arkady Lebedev, an expert on elections, and Liudimila Kuzmina, a regional human rights activist, were unlisted from the register (RBC, 2022). That created the first precedent of unenlisting individuals acting as mass media entities (2022).[1]

A fresh listing can follow the unenlisting of physical persons from the Registry of Foreign Agents. Thus, Vladimir Voronov, a coordinator of "Golos," had been unlisted in 2022. He and a journalist, Vitalii Kovin, received no foreign aid for one year before applying for unenlisting (Rossiiskaia Gazeta, 2021). Surprisingly,

20 days after the unenlisting, the entry on Mr. Kovin, a political scientist, appeared in the register again. Mr. Kovin commented that he was first listed as a foreign agent in September 2021 because of three payments to his account from the citizens of the Kyrgyz Republic, Ukraine, and Uzbekistan, varying from 69 to 500 Rub and what the Ministry of Justice called "participation in producing the materials of mass media foreign agents" (Kommersant, 2022a). In early October 2022, he was unlisted, yet listed again, allegedly for political activity in favour of Ukraine, which he claims he did not participate in, as he had not produced any publications on this issue (2022a).

The available case law, where citizens initiate a legal process against their inclusion in the foreign agent registry, provides material for analysing how the authorities employ the existing legal framework to create new norms. This task is otherwise not vested in the courts of law. Although limited by the availability of information, the following review of the available full-text decisions illustrates how the courts apply the rules that evolved into para-constitutional institutions. Even if we assume that the courts still publish online all decisions, as required by the Federal Law of 9 February 2009 No. 8-FZ "On Access to information about the activities of state bodies and local self-government," access to the courts' websites from abroad is restricted in the interests of ensuring information security (RF Federal Law No. 8-FZ, 2009). Below, we analyse two full-text decisions: The Memorial Case (RF Supreme Court, 2021) and the case of the Institute of Law and Public Policy (RF Zamoskvoretsky District Court, 2021). These decisions can be retrieved through an online database, sudact.ru,[2] using the search word "foreign agent."

The analysis of the cases, as mentioned earlier, differentiates the following issues of concern resulting from the application of foreign agent legislation:

- The concept of "political activity," the pursuit linked with receiving foreign aid, is the decisive factor in recognising a person as a foreign agent.
- The concept of "receiving funds and (or) other property from foreign sources" is applied as such, with no information as to the purpose of the funding or the regularity of its acceptance. Receiving funds from another entity recognised as a foreign agent is also considered foreign funding.
- No minimum amount of foreign funding from a foreign source is necessary since the amount of funding is insignificant when enacting foreign agent legislation.

The following three issues are analysed below:

1. The problem of mixing scientific and political activity is revealed in the Institute of Law and Public Policy (from now on referred to as the Institute).[3] According to the Ministry of Justice, the political activities of the Institute are as follows:

> Publication of reports with proposals and recommendations for improving the regulation of the legal profession and human rights protection mechanisms, as well as extrajudicial mechanisms for establishing and publishing facts about the unlawful appropriation and retention of power, torture, and enforced disappearances.

Elaboration of the text of the draft law "On Amendments to the Law of the Russian Federation of 18 October 1991 No. 1761-1 "On the Rehabilitation of Victims of Political Repressions"" and distributing information about this draft law in the media and within the framework of petitions to public authorities.

Submitting amicus curiae opinions with the Constitutional Court. Signing petitions to amend the regulations on the Constitution of the Russian Federation. Addressing the Ministry of Justice by conveying information about the draft law proposals related to implementing general measures within the meaning of the ECHR judgment in the Lashmankin case vis-a-vis the proposals related to implementing freedom of peaceful assembly in Russia.

In addition, the Ministry of Justice introduced a novel qualifying requirement for such activity, that is, its systemic nature. In particular, the political activities of the Institute were found to be systemic because the latter arranges public debates, discussions, seminars, and round tables on issues related to the functioning of the state, the constitutional system, and human rights implementation. In conjunction with the fact that such activities tend to result in proposals for legislative amendments subsequently sent to the authorities, the purpose of such activities is, according to the Ministry, rooted in influencing the legislative process and the judiciary.

The Zamoskvoretsky District Court not only upheld the said arguments of the Ministry by concluding that the draft legislation relates to the sphere of law-making, irrespective of the theme of the draft law, but should also be considered a political activity under par. 3 p. 2 Art. 6 of the Federal Law "On Public Associations." It also devised two more criteria, which show that the activity engaged in by persons is political and prohibited under foreign agent legislation:

> comprehensive coverage in the media and appeals to state authorities. According to the court, these two criteria fall under one of the forms of political activity stipulated in par. 3 p. 2 of Article 6 of the Federal Law "On Public Associations," referencing public appeals to state bodies to influence their activities, including adopting, amending, repealing laws, or other regulatory legal acts. In doing so, the court, at its discretion, supplemented the criterion of the public circulation of information with two more criteria not provided for by law.

In the case of the Memorial Organisation, the political activities providing grounds for enacting foreign agent legislation were found to be "dissemination, including the use of modern information technologies, of opinions on the decisions made by state bodies and their policies, as well as by authoring socio-political views and beliefs in order to influence the development and implementation of state policy" (RF Zamoskvoretsky District Court, 2021).

2. As for the lack of connection between receiving foreign funding and the purpose of this funding, the Memorial Case is an example of when human rights

awards and prizes, received over the long period between 2005 and 2016, were considered by the Supreme Court as foreign funding.[4] Funding from another entity recognised as a foreign agent is considered foreign funding to enact foreign agent legislation (RF Supreme Court, 2019).

3. Regarding a lack of a minimum requirement for foreign funding, Russian legislation does not regulate this issue, unlike the 2017 foreign agent legislation introduced in Hungary, which establishes the minimum amount of funding received from abroad among the conditions of labelling organisations as foreign agents. Although the legislation in Russia does not comment on the minimum amount of funding, the courts stipulated that failing to mention the minimum amount implies that any sum received from foreign sources can be regarded as foreign funding.

4.5 Communicating Data Analysis Findings Back to the Theory

The analysis of the aforementioned legal amendments, read in conjunction with their interpretations by the RF Constitutional Court and their application in cases of two organisations by the RF Supreme Court and Zamoskvoretsky district court, reveals that the authorities resort to the so-called taxonomising technique, as suggested by the LCT theory. The national authorities, whose decisions are portrayed as just, are juxtaposed with other entities attempting to undermine those decisions (including domestic NGOs, whom the state considers to be under foreign influence merely because of receiving even minimal non-recurring payments and especially foreign organisations, foreign states, and their agencies). The government-controlled media transmit such sentiments embedded in public speeches to create a negative image of criticism of the state. For instance, Malkova (2020) reports the results of her analysis of multiple sources where citizens shared their opinions about foreign agent NGOs, concluding that while there is a poor understanding of foreign agent legislation, individuals taking part in surveys reveal strong disapproval of the idea that Russian NGOs receive aid from abroad, and the phrase 'foreign agent' evokes negative associations (2020, p. 205).

Foreign influence had always been something commonly known and condemned in the Soviet Union, as shown in Chapter 2 of this book, explaining the context of the Soviet Union's treatment of the idea of the free flow of information. The amendments in question run parallel with the Soviet campaigns in the press regularly invoked to condition citizens and the police and judiciary against unwanted persons or groups (Kramer, 2019, p. 607; Lokshina, 2012). The Iron Curtain, ensuring that citizens on both sides were not exposed to the adversarial ideologies of East and West, became a "symbol of Russia's prevention of the free flow of ideas and information" (Feuerlicht, 1995, pp. 187, 189). A special commission for travel abroad, established in the 1920s under the Central Committee of the All-Union Communist Party, functioned with various modifications until 1991, when trips abroad were liberalised (Orlov, 2019). The Commission approved certain candidates for travelling abroad, and the rules were strictly regulated to ensure, among other things, that only "credible" citizens with a Soviet-oriented worldview would travel abroad. The "thaw"/"*ottepel*" period under Khrushchev eased the clearance procedure for visiting the socialist states. Still, a strict pre-selection of travellers was in place, as were strict rules for conducting oneself abroad, such as prohibiting solo trips to cafes and similar places (Orlov, 2019). Information related to foreign influences and matters of public significance was controlled in the Soviet Union, and it also included information related to citizens as physical beings.[5]

Now, when many EU and North American states sanctioned Russia, among other things, by not issuing travel visas to its citizens, Russia's leadership keeps the borders open. However, the authorities deem it essential to ensure that Western ideas do not reach Russian citizens. With foreign agent legislation, those Russians who received funding from abroad and who pursue (vaguely defined in law) political activities are not allowed to participate in public debate, and access to leading world news media outlets is banned in Russia. At the same time, the president introduced an inventory of traditional values that Russians should share.

The legal amendments under review, ordinary laws and special subordinate decrees, and the courts' interpretative practices create a para-constitutional institution labelling as a foreign agent any individual sharing foreign values and publicly protesting the war. This is probably best illustrated with the publication of a comprehensive 60-item list of topics by the FSB, the Russian intelligence and law enforcement agency, which posits that individuals can be included in the registry of foreign agents after sharing reports on social media, (e.g. physical abuse of individuals by the authorities or of incidents of corruption) (Roth, 2023). Interestingly, this list also mentions "collecting information on military procurements, reporting on financial troubles at the Russian space agency, revealing information about soldiers' morale and past military experience, as well as the results of investigations into abuses in the military and security and intelligence services" (2023). It also includes comments on the financial assets of public officials, which used to be public information until winter 2023, when amendments were enacted, keeping the incomes of public officials confidential. To limit the risk of scandal (2023), the FSB topic list contributes to information asymmetry by creating a more positive image of the state.

By applying the theories of the dual state (Ledeneva, 2011, 2013; Sakwa, 2010, 2011) to an analysis of how the aforementioned legal amendments impact freedom of expression, access to information, and the possibilities of taking part in public affairs, we noted that these theories were less relevant to the current legal realities. Earlier, the regime was duplicitous, adopting laws yet at the same time relying on direct administrative orders for constricting civil society "by threats of dissolution and reducing the quality of civil control over state organs" (Salamon et al., 2015), a scenario that is hardly applicable to the current Russian realities. The foreign agent legislation eliminated duality by encrypting the administration's wishes to counteract opposition to the laws, which is illegitimate from the perspective of freedom of thought and expression. These amendments exclude any influence on public affairs other than those within the regime.

The possibility of foreign agent legislation keeping unwanted persons outside the public domain means that the state no longer relies on extra-legal mechanisms to deprive unwanted individuals of their rights. The goal of eliminating everyone who follows a foreign ideology is nowadays reinforced by the power of the law (allowing the conclusion that the duality between acting under the law and acting under administrative orders no longer applies to silencing those who receive foreign aid). An idea of duality between acting under the law and acting under the orders of the administrative leaders (what Ledeneva (2013) calls "telephone justice") was also applied to characterising the ways of controlling NGOs by Daucé (2015) and Salamon et al. (2015). These authors assert that the control of NGOs in Russia relies on repression (of the unwanted organisations) by law enforcement, on the one hand, and favouring (a posture adopted by the state) NGOs by public subsidy, on the other. This argument is also no longer valid at the current stage of applying foreign agent legislation. One could conclude that the economic management of NGOs via subsidies gave way to repression. To avoid sanctions, the NGOs must comply with foreign agent legislation, which limits cooperation with any foreign entity or individual.

Such is a situation where an authoritarian regime openly silences its critics while not concealing rules which it easily circumscribes. The legal amendments under consideration demonstrate a clear shift from "paternalism" to those organisations and persons who openly support the regime to "combatting the enemy," as embodied by "the whole of the third sector" (Flikke, 2016, p. 110). The Venice Commission calls the latter a chilling effect (the Venice Commission, 2014) of the foreign agent legislation on exercising political freedoms. It also shows how controlling information flow by creating a negative image of organisations and persons under the alleged foreign influence, as well as by restricting foreign ideas and values from influencing domestic NGOs and persons, leaves those organisations, which are dependent on public funding, compelled to comply with the state at the expense of their own opinions and ideas. This is a way of controlling NGOs, which Plantan (2022) calls selective policies to adjudicate among risks and benefits in the third sector."

As for (Daucé's) argument, imposing restrictions on various NGOs weakens the groups' ability "to work together to contest oppressive policies" (Daucé, 2015). As mentioned earlier, the results of the analysis concur with this thesis. Three scenarios of how the recognition of a person as a foreign agent affects the individual.

1. Some individuals opt to comply with the requirements of the foreign agent legislation, for example, sending activity reports and using the foreign agent tag when releasing publications to clear their status after one year of not receiving any foreign aid, as the legislation prescribes. However, an entry in the official registry of foreign agents is not removed, albeit a mark indicates that the status of the foreign agent was cancelled. In other words, one cannot be released entirely from foreign agent status.
2. Some individuals attempt to argue against the inclusion in the registry before a court of law. No known attempt has so far been successful in this respect. At the same time, citizens risk being exposed to added sanctions for violating foreign

Table 4.1 Analysing Legal Tightening of Foreign Agent Legislation

New Rule	*Impact on Access to Information and Participation*	*Legal Basis*	*Reactions*
Tightening Foreign Agent Legislation	Imposing activity labelling requirements on individuals Introducing a set of prohibitions for individuals recognised as foreign agents: On appointment to positions in public authorities, including filling positions in the state civil service and municipal service, for example, a member of an election commission or a referendum commission. Participating in the activities of commissions, committees, consultative, advisory groups, experts, and other bodies formed under public authorities. On nominating candidates for the Public Monitoring Commission. Public associations are included in the registry. On activities that facilitate or hinder the nomination of candidates, lists of candidates, the election of registered candidates, the initiative to hold a referendum and the conduct of a referendum, the achievement of a particular result in elections, and a referendum, as well as other forms, for example, election campaigns, referendum campaigns, etc. On organising public events. On donations to a political party and its regional branches. On educational activities about minors and (or) pedagogical activities in state and municipal educational organisations. On producing educational products for minors. On receiving state financial support, including the implementation of creative activities. On operating significant objects of critical information infrastructure and carrying out activities to ensure the security of significant objects. On participating as an expert in the state environmental review, participating in the organisation and conducting the public environmental review. Violation of the Russian Federation's legislation on foreign agents entails administrative, criminal, and other liabilities by established procedures.	Federal law of 14 July 2022 No. 255-FZ. On the control of the activities of the persons influenced by foreign entities	Three scenarios: 1. Some opt to comply with the requirements of foreign agent legislation to reinstate their status after one year of not receiving any foreign aid. 2. Some argue against their inclusion in the registry before a court of law. 3. Some combine the said two strategies: Attempts to challenge the inclusion in the register in courts with rare stories of success. Not all argue against these decisions; some prefer to comply with the requirements. When ruling against the applicants, the courts create tighter rules and interpretations than those stipulated in the law.

agent-related restrictions when the courts pronounce new rules for applying foreign agent legislation. It is also possible that the status of legal persons may be annulled for violating regulations on foreign agents.
3. Some individuals combine the said two strategies, that is, attempt to argue against inclusion in the foreign agent registry while waiting out the one year without receiving foreign funding to apply for unenlisting from the registry. However, in all three cases, a person may participate in public activities for a year while significant developments unfold.

Restrictions on political activities are, nevertheless, relevant for the functioning of the regime as such. When the critics of the administration are silenced, there is nobody to lead groups that would follow up, for example, systemic abuse of governmental power or corruption. This conclusion aligns well with the postulates of the asymmetric information theory, whereby the government, no longer exposed to public criticism, is inclined to engage in more risky actions, further increasing political instability. The aforementioned dissenting opinion by Justice Yaroslavtsev in the Ruling of the RF Constitutional Court No. 10-P aptly illustrates the previous point (RF Constitutional Court, 2014a). Yaroslavstev remarks that the fact that many non-commercial organisations, which, for example, fought corruption, are now facing "foreign agent" restrictions implies that the state punishes those who oppose corruption as a critical threat to the state itself.

Implementing human rights, especially in the public sphere, must provide the conditions for achieving social goals and interests effectively and allow people to correlate their behaviours with normatively established rules, allowing them to predict the consequences of their actions to a reasonable extent. Consequently, arbitrariness is accompanied by uncertainty and inconsistency of law, which violates not only equality and the rule of law but also legal guarantees, including judicial protection of citizens' rights, freedoms, and legitimate interests. Legal uncertainty, inconsistency, incompleteness, and gaps in laws may lead to a conflict between legal norms and constitutional rights based on them (RF Constitutional Court, 2014a, 2014b). The summary of these legal amendments is in Table 4.1.

Notes

1 Polina Kostyleva, also associated with the Golos movement, has been unlisted in August 2022 because of receiving no foreign aid for a one-year period (Kommersant, 2022a, 2022b). Later, the unenlisting of Vladimir Zhilkin, Aleksandr Liutov, Aleksandr Grezev, and Iliia Pigalkin (registries numbers 267, 279, 261, and 281) followed, based on their own applications and the documents received from the public authorities (Lenta.ru, 2022).

2 Sudact.ru is still operating as an open, free-of-charge resource of legal information, despite attempts to close it down in 2019.

3 The Institute is an organization known for its expertise in the field of constitutional and international law, which was entered by the Ministry of Justice of the Russian Federation into the registry of NGOs-foreign agents.

4 The Hrant Dink Prize for consistent efforts to preserve the memory of state terror, drawing public attention to new cases of human rights violations, 2012; Pierre Prize Simone,

France, 2005; an award from the American Holocaust Museum in Washington, 2016 (RF Supreme Court, 2021).

5 Confidential medical records are a salient example. Records handwritten by doctors' assistants during each patient's visit were kept in the archives of medical centres and not handed out to individuals but transported straight to the archive and then delivered to the doctors' offices before each new appointment. Empowering doctors to reveal only the information that the doctor considered worth revealing to the patient, the state controlled the entire information flow. Soviet ideology put common interests above private interests (Lichterman, 2005).

References

Brikul'skii, I. (2022). *Spory o priznanii "inostrannym agentom" v zerkale sudebnyh reshenij za 2020–2022 gg* [Disputes on recognition as a "foreign agent" in the mirror of court decisions for 2020–2022]. https://academia.ilpp.ru/blog/spory-o-priznanii-inostrannym-agentom-v-zerkale-sudebnyh-reshenij-za-2020–2022-gg/?ysclid=lbot6e8mxv7265693

Daucé, F. (2015). The duality of coercion in Russia: Cracking down on foreign agents. *Demokratizatsiya*, *23*(1), 57–75.

Explanatory Note. (2022, July 14). *Poiasnitel'naia zapiska k zakonu No. 255-FZ* [To the draft federal law no. 255-FZ]. https://sozd.duma.gov.ru/bill/113045-8

Feuerlicht, I. (1995). A new look at the Iron Curtain. *American Speech*. *30*(3), 186–189.

Flikke, G. (2016). Resurgent authoritarianism: The case of Russia's new NGO legislation. *Post-Soviet Affairs*, *32*(2), 103–131.

Kommersant. (2022a). *Permskij politolog vnov' vkljuchen v reestr inoagentov* [Political scientist from Perm is listed in the registry of foreign agents]. www.kommersant.ru/doc/5692390?ysclid=lubc92cy25748549581

Kommersant. (2022b). *Koordinator "Golosa" Polina Kostyleva iskliuchena iz reestra SMI-inoagentov* [Coordinator of Golos Polina Kostyleva was unlisted from the registry of mass media foreign agents]. www.kommersant.ru/doc/5525336

Kramer, M. (2019). The Soviet legacy in Russian foreign policy. *Political Science Quarterly*, *134*(4), 585–609.

Ledeneva, A. (2011). Can Medvedev change sistema? Informal networks and public administration in Russia. In V. Kononenko & A. Moshes (Eds.), *Russia as a network state. What works in Russia when state institutions do not?* (pp. 39–61). Springer.

Ledeneva, A. (2013). *Can Russia modernize? Sistema, power networks, and informal governance*. Cambridge University Press.

Lenta.ru. (2022). *Miniust iskliuchil eshche neskol'ko chelovek iz reestra SMI-inoagentov* [The ministry of justice unlisted several more individuals from the registry of mass media foreign agents]. https://lenta.ru/news/2022/05/06/inoagents/?ysclid=ldoldp5wfp336367547

Lichterman, B. L. (2005). Basic problems of medical ethics in Russia in a historical context. *Journal International de Bioethique*, *16*(3–4), 43–53.

Lokshina, T. (2012, December 5). Back to the (Soviet) future, foreign policy. *Foreign Policy*. https://foreignpolicy.com/2012/12/06/back-to-the-soviet-future/

Malkova, P. (2020). Images and perceptions of human rights defenders in Russia: An examination of public opinion in the age of the foreign agent law. *Journal of Human Rights*, *19*(2), 201–219.

Orlov, I. (2019). "Otklonit' bez ob''iasnenil": partiinyi kontrol' nad vyezdom sovetskikh grazhdan za granitsu [Reject without explanation: The party control over the departure of Soviet citizens abroad]. *Rossiiskaia Istoriia*, *5*, 92–107.

OSCE. (2021). OSCE Media freedom representative expresses grave concern about the dangerous effects of 'foreign agent' legislation on media freedom in Russia. *Gale Academic OneFile*. link.gale.com/apps/doc/A673051515/AONE?u=aboacad&sid=bookmark-AONE&xid=9ebdbae2

Plantan, E. (2022). Not all NGOs are treated equally: Selectivity in civil society management in China and Russia. *Comparative Politics*, *54*(3), 501–524.
RBC. (2022). *Miniust vpervye iskliuchil iz reestra SMI-inoagentov dvukh chelovek* [The ministry of justice had for the first time unlisted two persons from the registry of foreign agents]. www.rbc.ru/politics/29/04/2022/626bf26d9a794704d96ab027?ysclid=lbowd32zqg311686945
RF Constitutional Court, Postanovlenie No. 14-P. (2014b, May 13). *Po delu o proverke konstitutsionnosti chasti 1 stat'i 7 Federal'nogo zakona "O sobraniiakh, mitingakh, demonstratsiiakh, shestviiakh i piketirovaniiakh" v sviazi s zhaloboi grazhdanina A.N. Iakimova* [On checking the constitutionality of part 1 of article 7 of the federal law "on meetings, meetings, demonstrations, processions and picketing" in connection with the complaint of citizen A.N. Iakimov]. Sobranie zakonodatel'stva Rossiiskoi Federatsii, 2014, No. 21 item 2764.
RF Constitutional Court, Ruling No. 4-P. (2019, January 17). *Po delu o proverke konstitutsionnosti stat'i 19.1 Zakona Rossiiskoi Federatsii "O sredstvakh massovoi informatsii" v sviazi s zhaloboi grazhdanina E.G. Finkel'shteina* [On constitutionality check of article 19.1 of the law of the Russian Federation "on the mass media" in connection with the complaint of citizen E.G. Finkelstein]. https://legalacts.ru/doc/postanovlenie-konstitutsionnogo-suda-rf-ot-17012019-n-4-p-po/
RF Constitutional Court, Ruling No. 10-P. (2014a, April 8). *Po delu o proverke konstitutsionnosti polozhenii punkta 6 stat'i 2 i punkta 7 stat'i 32 Federal'nogo zakona "O nekommercheskikh organizatsiiakh", chasti shestoi stat'i 29 Federal'nogo zakona "Ob obshchestvennykh ob"edineniiakh" i chasti 1 stat'i 19.34 Kodeksa Rossiiskoi Federatsii ob administrativnykh pravonarusheniiakh v sviazi s zhalobami Upolnomochennogo po pravam cheloveka v Rossiiskoi Federatsii, fonda "Kostromskoi tsentr podderzhki obshchestvennykh initsiativ", grazhdan L.G. Kuz'minoi, S.M. Smirenskogo i V.P. Iukecheva* [On constitutionality check of the provisions of paragraph 6 of article 2 and paragraph 7 of article 32 of the federal law "on non-commercial organizations," part six of article 29 of the federal law "on public associations" and part 1 articles 19.34 of the code of the administrative offenses in connection with the address of the Ombudsman, the "Kostroma center for the support of public initiatives," citizens L.G. Kuzmin, S.M. Smirenskogo and V.P. Yukecheva]. Sobranie zakonodatel'stva Rossiiskoi Federatsii, 2014, No. 4 item 359.
RF Federal Law No. 7-FZ. (1996, January 12). *O nekommercheskikh organizatsiiakh* [On non-commercial organizations]. Sobranie zakonodatel'stva Rossiiskoi Federatsii, 1996, No. 3 item 145.
RF Federal Law No. 8-FZ. (2009, February 9). *Ob obespechenii dostupa k informatsii o dejatel'nosti gosudarstvennykh organov i organov mestnogo samoupravleniia* [On access to information about the activities of state bodies and local self-government]. Sobranie zakonodatel'stva Rossiiskoi Federatsii, 2009, No. 7 item 776.
RF Federal Law No. 19-FZ. (2003, January 10). *O vyborakh Prezidenta Rossiiskoi Federatsii* [On the election of the president of the Russian Federation]. Sobranie zakonodatel'stva Rossiiskoi Federatsii, 2003, No. 2 item 171.
RF Federal Law No. 20-FZ. (2014, July 14). *O vyborakh deputatov Gosudarstvennoi Dumy Federal'nogo Sobraniia Rossiiskoi Federatsii* [On the election of the members of the State Duma of the federal assembly of the Russian Federation]. Sobranie zakonodatel'stva Rossiiskoi Federatsii, 2014, No. 29 (part II) item 5222.
RF Federal Law No. 272-FZ. (2012, December 28). *O merakh vozdeistviia na lits, prichastnykh k narusheniiam osnovopolagaiushchikh prav i svobod cheloveka, prav i svobod grazhdan Rossiiskoi Federatsii* [On sanctions for persons involved in violations of fundamental human rights and freedoms, rights and freedoms of citizens of the Russian Federation]. Sobranie zakonodatel'stva Rossiiskoi Federatsii, 2012, No. 53 (part I) item 7597.
RF Federal Law No. 67-FZ. (2002, June 12). *Ob osnovnykh garantiiakh izbiratel'nykh prav i prava na uchastie v referendume grazhdan Rossiiskoi Federatsii* [On the basic guarantees of the electoral rights and the right to take part in the referendum of the citizens of

the Russian Federation]. Sobranie zakonodatel'stva Rossiiskoi Federatsii, 2002, No. 24 st. 2253.

RF Federal Law No. 82-FZ. (1995, May 19). *Ob obshchestvennykh ob"edineniiakh* [On public associations]. Sobranie zakonodatel'stva Rossiiskoi Federatsii, 1995, No. 21 item 1930.

RF Federal Law No. 195-FZ. (2001, December 30). *Kodeks Rossiiskoi Federatsii ob administrativnykh pravonarusheniiakh* [The code of administrative offenses of the Russian Federation]. Sobranie zakonodatel'stva Rossiiskoi Federatsii, 2002, No. 1 (part I) item 1.

RF Federal Law No. 255-FZ. (2022, July 14). *O kontrole za deiatel'nost'iu lits, nahodiashchihsia pod inostrannym vliianiem* [On the control over persons under foreign influence]. Sobranie zakonodatel'stva Rossiiskoi Federatsii, 2022, No. 29 item 5222.

RF Federal Law No. 270-FZ. (2022, July 14). *O vnesenii izmenenii v Federal'nyi zakon "Ob obespechenii dostupa k informatsii o deiatel'nosti gosudarstvennykh organov i organov mestnogo samoupravleniia" i stat'iu 10 Federal'nogo zakona "Ob obespechenii dostupa k informatsii o deiatel'nosti sudov v Rossiiskoi Federatsii* [On amending the federal law "on providing access to information on the activities of state bodies and local self-government bodies" and article 10 of the federal law "on providing access to information on the activities of courts in the Russian Federation"]. https://rg.ru/documents/2022/07/19/document-soceti.html?ysclid=lefgfo791d629768595

RF Federal Law No. 272-FZ. (2012, December 28). *O merakh vozdeistviia na lits, prichastnykh k narusheniiam osnovopolagaiushchikh prav i svobod cheloveka, prav i svobod grazhdan Rossiiskoi Federatsii* [On sanctions for persons involved in violations of fundamental human rights and freedoms, rights and freedoms of citizens of the Russian Federation]. Sobranie zakonodatel'stva Rossiiskoi Federatsii, 2012, No. 53 (part I) item 7597.

RF Government, Rasporiazhenie No. 3417-r. (2022, November 2022). *Ob ustanovlenii ob"ema soderzhashchikhsia v reestre inostrannykh agentov svedenii, podlezhashchikh razmeshcheniiu na ofitsial'nom saite Miniusta Rossii v informatsionno-telekommunikatsionnoi seti "Internet"* [On establishing the volume of information contained in the register of foreign agents, to be placed on the official website of the ministry of justice of Russia in the Internet]. Sobranie zakonodatel'stva Rossiiskoi Federatsii, 2022, No. 47 item 8242.

RF Law of the Russian Federation No. 2124-I. (1991, December 27). *O sredstvakh massovoi informatsii* [On the mass media]. Sobranie zakonodatel'stva Rossiiskoi Federatsii, 1992, No. 7 item 300.

RF Ministry of Justice. (2022, November 29). Order no. 307. *Ob utverzhdenii Poriadka vedeniia reestra inostrannykh agentov i razmeshcheniia soderzhashchikhsia v nem svedenii na ofitsial'nom saite Ministerstva iustitsii Rossiiskoi Federatsii v informatsionno-telekommunikatsionnoi seti "Internet", Poriadka priniatiia resheniia ob iskliuchenii fizicheskogo litsa, vpervye vkliuchennogo v reestr inostrannykh agentov, iz reestra inostrannykh agentov, formy zaiavleniia inostrannogo agenta ob iskliuchenii iz reestra inostrannyih agentov* [Approving the procedure for maintaining the register of foreign agents and posting the information contained therein on the official website of the ministry of justice of the Russian Federation on the Internet, procedure for making a decision on exclusion of an individual included in the register of foreign agents for the first time from the register of foreign agents, and forms for requesting exclusion from the register of foreign agents]. Registered with the Ministry of Justice of Russia on 30 November 2022, No. 71228. https://docs.cntd.ru/document/1300079883?ysclid=lubabj5lzp233515218

RF Registry of Foreign Agents. (2023). minjust.gov.ru

RF Supreme Court. (2019, May 13). *Postanovlenie po delu No. 5-AD19-23* [Ruling on the case no. 5-AD19-23]. https://legalacts.ru/sud/postanovlenie-verkhovnogo-suda-rf-ot-13052019-n-5-ad19-23/?ysclid=lubbkxcrf0734671037

RF Supreme Court. (2021, December 28). *Decision po delu No. AKPI21-969* [On case no. AKPI21-969]. https://legalacts.ru/sud/reshenie-verkhovnogo-suda-rf-ot-28122021-po-delu-n-akpi21-969/?ysclid=lefs2kmjpx326762172

RF Zamoskvoretsky District Court. (2021, October 4). *Decision po delu No. 02a-1258/2021* [On the case no. 02a-1258/2021]. https://mos-gorsud.ru/rs/zamoskvoreckij/services/cases/kas/details/48c53da1-04f4-11ec-9970-116f0cba48c9?ysclid=lubbqet0gs241794157

RFERL. (2017a). *Lawmaker says Russia working on legislation to label media outlets 'foreign agents.' Radio free Europe documents and publications*. http://ww1w.rferl.org/author/19023.html

RFERL. (2017b). *Russia's RT registers under U.S. foreign-agents law*. www.rferl.org/a/russia-duma-working-on-law-to-label-media-foreign-agents/28851482.html

Robinson, N. (2020). "Foreign agents" in an interconnected world: FARA and the weaponization of transparency. *Duke Law Journal*, *69*(5).

Rossiiskaia gazeta. (2021). *Miniust iskliuchil zhurnalista Voronova i sotrudnika "Golosa" Kovina iz reestra SMI-inoagentov* [Ministry of justice unlisted journalist Voronov and Mr. Kovin of "Golos" from the registry of the mass media as foreign agents]. https://rg.ru/2022/10/07/miniust-iskliuchil-zhurnalista-voronova-i-sotrudnika-golosa-kovina-iz-reestra-smi-inoagentov.html?ysclid=ldojxouznt107940947

Roth, A. (2023). Russia extends 'foreign agents' law to critics of military and security; Legislation now covers citizens who study and report on those agencies and people working within them. *Guardian*. https://go.gale.com/ps/i.do?p=AONE&u=aboacad&id=GALE|A677573643&v=2.1&it=r&sid=bookmark-AONE&asid=b0f41ddf. (Original work published October 1, 2021)

Sakwa, R. (2010). The dual state in Russia. *Post-Soviet Affairs*, *26*(3), 185–206.

Sakwa, R. (2011). *The crisis of Russian democracy: The dual state, factionalism and the Medvedev succession*. Cambridge University Press.

Salamon, L. M., Benevolenski, V. B., & Jakobson, L. I. (2015). Penetrating the dual realities of government-nonprofit relations in Russia. *Voluntas*, *26*, 2178–2214.

Venice Commission. (2014). *Opinion on federal law no. 121-FZ on non-commercial organisations ("law of foreign agents") on federal laws no. 18-FZ and no. 147-FZ and on federal law no. 190-FZ on making amendments to the criminal code ("law on treason") of the Russian Federation 14 (June 13–14, 2014)*. www.venice.coe.int/webforms/documents/default.aspx?pdffile=cdl-ad(2014)025-e.the

5 Analysing Legal Amendments Since 2012

Legal Amendments Tightening Requirements for Conducting Public Assemblies

5.1 Introduction

5.1.1 General Notes on Legal Regulation of Public Assemblies

Russia took its "new authoritarian" turn in 2012 with the rule stipulating a compulsory notification procedure about upcoming protests and demonstrations. Notifications must be submitted ten days before the planned public assembly, based on the 2004 Federal Law "On Assemblies, Meetings, Demos, Marches, and Picketing" (from now on referred to as the Federal Law on Public Assemblies). This law stipulates (RF Federal Law 54-FZ, 2004) that when and where protests are to take place should be negotiated with authorities rather than simply notifying the public bodies that the protest will be held (RF Federal Law 54-FZ, 2004, Art. 12). Non-pre-agreed assemblies are, hence, to be dispersed. Those who refuse to cease such demonstrations face enforcement measures (RF Federal Law 54-FZ, 2004, Art. 17), to which belongs, for instance, administrative detention of up to 48 hours (RF Code of Administrative Offences, 2001, Art. 14). The executive authorities have always had the option of rejecting notifications of the forthcoming assemblies based on the alleged violation of the arranging procedures (RF The Code on Administrative Offences, 2011, Art. 12). The authorities have dismissed many requests for public gatherings (Council of Europe, 2017).

The Venice Commission considered the model of pre-agreeing public events sketched above too restrictive (Venice Commission, OSCE/ODIHR, 2019, par. 82, 112). Even assuming that authorities are always acting in good faith, the rigid notification timeline prevents citizens from expressing an immediate response to significant events. However, the Constitutional Court has ruled that such a procedure does not violate fundamental rights (RF Constitutional Court, 2011). According to the Court, the legal regulation of the notification period was intended to prevent assemblies from going violent and misuse of the right to assemble. At the same time, the Court points out that choosing the date of a public event carefully is crucial to its success, especially if the assembly is linked to an anniversary or a specific date. The Court argues that excluding the event on the designated day may violate the Constitution and deprive the right to peaceful assembly (RF Constitutional Court, 2014). Nevertheless, the Court does not see any contradiction between a

DOI: 10.4324/9781032613383-5

10-day notification requirement and the possibility that a designated day could be any day when an unforeseen decision or event occurs that the citizenry wishes to respond to. The Constitutional Court had only softened these restrictive provisions by extending the notification period if notification is to be submitted on a bank holiday (RF Constitutional Court, 2014).

5.1.2 The Spontaneity of Protests and the Visibility of Alexei Navalny

A spontaneous attempt to change Russia's political agenda was made in late December 2011, following the federal parliamentary elections and preceding Putin's third election. Thanks to modern technology, voters could record infractions during those elections. For example, ballots filled out in advance for "*Edinaya Rossiya*," which still holds most parliamentary seats, could be recorded (Riekkinen, 2016). The word about these and other discoveries spread quickly through social media, causing rallies of citizens advocating for free and fair elections. On Bolotnaya Square and the Avenue of Academician Sakharov, two prominent protest meetings took place in Moscow, attracting thousands of protesters to oppose unfair electoral practices. On 6 May 2012, Bolotnaya Square witnessed the culmination of the "*Marsh Millionov*" (the March of Millions) demonstration (RF Constitutional Court, 2014). It is estimated that 80,000 to 120,000 people were involved. According to a commentator for a major Russian media outlet, this projection would have been written off as science fiction if it had been created a year earlier (Kirian, 2011). This achievement is impressive, especially following the prolonged political stagnation and since many citizens had already gone on much-anticipated holidays.

As much as citizens were dissatisfied with the results of the parliamentary elections, Putin's declaration of his intention to run for president again may also have been motivated by this political activity (Medvedev & Putin, 2011). Putin was then the Prime Minister. Simultaneously, then-President Dmitry Medvedev announced he would run for Prime Minister. Those developments enabled power-holders to consolidate control by reorganising the key state executive nominations. And, of course, they revealed the behind-the-scenes deals that shaped the regime's authorisation. The acting Prime Minister was supposed to become a President, and the acting President was supposed to become a Prime Minister. So, despite overall stagnation and no major internal crisis, this double political swap (Nuzov, 2012, p. 314) signalled a critical turn, preventing Russia from returning to its path of transition to democracy (Lewis, 2020). A robust organising force led the citizens: prominent bloggers, Russian celebrities, and opposition leaders, with Alexei Navalny still alive and speaking against the "*Edinaya Rossiya*"'s overwhelming victory (Dress, 2024).

In stifling authoritarian tendencies, citizens have protested on the streets without agreement with public authorities but without being bothered by heavy fines and administrative detention. Protests broke out in response to Navalny's Anti-Corruption Foundation's "Don't Call Him Dimon" video released in 2017

(Dollbaum, 2020, p. 194). The *New York Times* dubbed Mr. Navalny's coordinated display of public dissatisfaction in Moscow and other cities throughout Russia on 26 March 2017, "the largest coordinated display of public dissatisfaction since anti-Kremlin demonstrations in 2011 and 2012" (Higgins & Kramer, 2017). These rallies entitled "*On vam ne Dimon*" (He is not your Dimon) were a response to an unofficial investigation conducted by the anti-corruption foundation led by Mr. Navalny into Prime Minister Dmitry Medvedev's property assets (Mortensen et al., 2017).

As a result of the local electoral commissions preventing opposition candidates, including Liubov Sobol and Ivan Zhdanov, both of Navalny's Anti-Corruption Foundation and Dmitry Gudkov, from running for the Moscow parliament in 2019, there was another intense protest wave (FIDH, 2019).

There was, however, no increase in protest activities following the harsh suppression of protests against the invasion in Ukraine, the introduction of cumulative criminal responsibility for several minor violations of the procedure for participation in assemblies (discussed below), and the exile of many oppositionists.

Public protests can thus bring spontaneity into the political calendar (Izquierdo, 2013, p. 49; Leonard, 2017, p. 9), which might explain the existence of strict protest regulations. As discussed above, starting in 2011, the protesters exposed the authorities to the risk of losing control over the information flow. A protest can, at least in the ideal world, prevent the government from denying the legitimacy of contrasting views and attempting to suppress dissenting voices. The post-2012 legal amendments tightening the freedom of assembly reveal how things turned out in non-ideal Russia.

5.2 Legislative Amendments

5.2.1 Amendments of 2012: Prohibitions on Covering Faces, Widening Authority Over Protest Locations, Banning Series of One-Person Pickets, and Introducing More Prohibitions for Organisers

In June 2012, the Federal Law on Public Assemblies was substantively amended to include a prohibition against the wearing of masks at public events, a harsher penalty for violating the rules for gathering protests, including higher fines (up to ₽20,000 (£167) and community service (from 20 to 200 hours), wider restrictions for organisers of assemblies, and a ban on assembling one-person pickets (which would not require authorisation) that share a common agenda (RF Federal Law No. 65-FZ, 2012). The protest authorisation procedure was also tightened in the amendments.

The Explanatory Note for the 2012 draft law, which followed Medvedev's claim about protesters embodying extremists and provocateurs, states that Russian laws governing public events "primarily safeguard the rights and interests of event planners" (Explanatory Note to the Federal Law No. 65-FZ). However, the authors of the amendments believe that the law should also include more significant sanctions and preventive measures to promote civility and adherence to citizens' lawful interests. Public protests are cited as violating lawful interests by limiting access to residences, workplaces, leisure areas, business premises, public transportation, and pedestrian passage. Moreover, due to public protests, landscaping is damaged, and sanitary and epidemiological conditions are deteriorating. The Explanatory Note claims that administrative sanctions and stringent restrictions for infractions are insufficient to punish violators of established procedures effectively. The Explanatory Note positions fines and community service as humanistic punishments because they use predominantly mild punishments in place of administrative arrests.

In particular, the amendments stipulate that participants in public assembly events are not allowed to hide their faces, including not wearing masks, disguises, and other items especially "designed to make it difficult to establish the identity of a participant" (Explanatory Note to Federal Law No. 65-FZ). Those who hide their faces during protests to make determining their identity more difficult can receive up to 40 community service hours for infringing on the established procedure for holding public meetings (RF Code of Administrative Offences, 2001, Article 20.2, par. 5). Furthermore, the amendments tightened the process for gaining a permit to organise public protests and expanded the power of regional authorities to determine where protests could be held.[1] In effect, the law we examine now requires coordination with the executive authority of a constituent entity of the Russian Federation or a local government body regarding the place and time of the forthcoming event instead of submitting a notice of the forthcoming event.

Lastly, a new prohibition was introduced for one-person pickets that did not need preliminary authorisation. With these amendments, courts can now recognise as one protest event actions carried out by one participant and involving several protesters acting in turn, as long as a common purpose of the protests is established.[2] In this case, all participants of one-person demonstrations with a common goal without authorisation to hold a public assembly would thus be recognised as violating picket rules. As discussed in the following paragraph, the Constitutional Court of the Russian Federation declared the raising of fines as penalties for infringing on the procedure for the conduct of public events unconstitutional less than a year after they were introduced. Lastly, persons convicted of a breach of public peace and security or who have been subject to administrative penalties for rally violations twice or more within a year are also prohibited from organising public assemblies.[3] Due to the tendency to penalise various procedural violations during assemblies, this rule targets those who actively express their dissent (Amnesty International, 2015).

A constitutional challenge was filed against these amendments. The Constitutional Court delivered Ruling No. 4-P on the constitutionality of the 2012 amendments, tightening the right to assembly on 14 February 2013 (RF Constitutional Court, 2013). Overall, the Court upheld the amendments but stated that fines for unlawful public events should be reduced. In addition, the Court argued that community service can only be mandated as a penalty in cases where unlawful assemblies harm another person's property or health.

A remark worth noting is that the Constitutional Court emphasised back in 2013 that Russia is a democratic state based on the rule of law. Notably, it stressed that the right to assemble peacefully, hold meetings, rallies, and demonstrations, and participate in processions and picketing is inextricably bound to one's legal status in Russia as a democratic state governed by the rule of law. Further, the Court noted that the right to assembly allows citizens to influence the activities of public authorities and contribute to a peaceful dialogue between civil society and government while criticising state and local government actions. According to Section 7 on prohibitions of discrediting the military and the authorities, by May 2023, the Constitutional Court had interpreted the freedom of expression vis-à-vis public authorities and the military as not allowing criticism. Moreover, the Court stressed the importance of public authorities responding neutrally to public events. Regardless of the political views of the protesters, the Court continued, the authorities should ensure conditions for citizens and associations to exercise their right to assembly, including clear rules for organisation and conduct, within permissible restrictions in a democratic state.

As part of this ruling, the Court also commented on the procedure of preliminary notification of upcoming public events. According to the comment, public event organisers must notify the authorities of the event's nature, format, location, start and end times, attendees, and strategies for maintaining public order as soon as possible. As a result, the authorities will comprehensively understand the event's nature and scope, enabling them to uphold and safeguard human rights and liberties as per their constitutional duty. By balancing both public and private interests, this legislative requirement does not compromise peaceful assembly rights.

According to the Court, restrictions on the right to assemble are necessary and permissible since state protection of peaceful public gatherings can be limited by Federal Law. The Court cites international law as a source of justification for its position, particularly the Universal Declaration of Human Rights, the International Covcnant on Civil and Political Rights, and the Convention for the Protection of Human Rights and Fundamental Freedoms. In addition to the ruling under review, 11 European Court of Human Rights judgments mention that freedom of assembly is subject to limitations, including those against Armenia, Greece, Moldova, Russia, Turkey, and the UK.

5.2.2 Amendments of 2016: Prohibiting One-Person Pickets Using Construction Structures

2016 brought further restrictions to the regulations for arranging a one-person protest. As a result of the amendments, the rule of no authorisation has been narrowed to require authorisation only if the participant in a forthcoming one-person picket intends to use a prefabricated structure (RF Federal Law No. 61-FZ, 2016), meaning an easily assembled and disassembled construction like stairs or stages. Using such structures is likely to make the protest more visible, thereby increasing the chances of attracting public support and attention. That seemed a valid reason to limit the number of solo protesters using them.

5.2.3 Amendments From 2014 to 2020: Regarding Limitations for Journalists

In 2014, legislators began restricting journalists' professional activities during protests. In the beginning, journalists were required to wear a sign that would allow them to be distinguished from the protesters. As part of the amendment, journalists at public events must have an editorial certificate or other document verifying their authority and professional credentials. The amendments further state that a journalist attending a public event must wear a distinguishing sign of a mass media representative (RF Federal Law No. 258-FZ, 2014). To safeguard their health and ensure their ability to perform their duties, it is imperative to identify journalists in the crowd immediately, as explained in the Explanatory Note. There was further tightening of the requirements for distinguishing journalistic signs by 2020. Journalists today must display a mass media sign when covering public events, and this sign must meet a complex regulatory standard. In particular, the standards are set by the federal executive body that controls and supervises mass media, mass communications, information technology, and communications. Federal executive bodies with jurisdiction over internal affairs, national guards, arms trafficking, and private security are required to collaborate with relevant state departments to develop these standards (RF Federal Law, No. 497-FZ, 2020).

The Explanatory Note to the 2020 amendments requiring journalists to display a sign during public events sheds light on the legislator's motivations (Explanatory Note to the draft law introducing limitations for journalists). It clarified the procedure for media representatives' participation in public events to create additional conditions for ensuring their rights. During professional activities at a public event, a journalist is not allowed to take part directly in its conduct, including completing several actions that are the responsibility of organisers and participants in the event (e.g. administrative functions, collecting signatures, participating in decision-making, and using visual propaganda). The Explanatory Note also explains that multiple one-person pickets cannot be held simultaneously to improve legal certainty and ensure consistency in their preparation and execution (Explanatory Note to the draft law introducing limitations for journalists). This necessitates the introduction of a provision that allows a court to recognise various types of picketing, including single-participant pickets, alternate participation, and mass movements of citizens expressing opinions and demands on political, economic, social, and cultural topics.

5.2.4 2014 Amendments: Tightening the Penalties for Non-Pre-Agreed Assemblies, Riots, and Introducing a Cumulative Criminal Liability for a Series of Minor Offences

Due to new legislative amendments passed in May 2014, riots, or mass disorder during public assemblies, will now be punishable by a maximum of 15 years in prison instead of ten (RF Federal Law No. 130-FZ, 2014). As a means of preventing mass disorders, these amendments also operationalised citizen snitching by adding an amendment to Article 212 of the Criminal Code (i.e. on liability for organising and participating in mass riots) that relieves the individual of criminal liability for passing the training for organising mass riots if the individual informs the authorities of their involvement in such training (2014). Three State Duma deputies, including Alexander Sidiakin, who wrote the 2012 law on foreign agents, proposed the amendments (Human Rights Watch, 2014).

The legislative amendments adopted in July 2014 introduced a maximum penalty of 10 days of administrative arrest for organising or holding a public event without submitting the required notice of the public event (RF Federal Law No. 258-FZ, 2014). One can be arrested for up to 15 days for participating in non-pre-agreed public events that interfered with life support facilities, transport or social infrastructure, communications, pedestrian and vehicle movement, or citizens' access to residential properties or transportation or social infrastructure facilities.

Also included in the amendments is a new Article 212.1 in the Criminal Code that penalises repeated violations of public assembly procedures (RF Criminal Code, 1996). Criminal sanctions for repeated violations include fines of ₽600,000 to ₽1,000,000 (approximately £5,000 to £8,400) or the number of the employee's wages for two to three years, community service (up to 480 hours), corrective labour (up to two years), forced labour (up to five years), or imprisonment for the same term (up to five years). In this context, repeated means committing a violation more than twice within 180 days if the individual was previously brought to administrative responsibility for an administrative offence, as defined in Article 20.2 of the Russian Federation Code on Administrative Offences (RF Code on Administrative Offences, 2001).

The 2014 legal revisions restricting those with prior criminal convictions from organising public events are also based on the assumption that the penalties for violating the procedure are so mild they endanger the health and safety of citizens. Even after receiving multiple fines for violating public event regulations, many people still participate in unapproved gatherings, say the authors of the revisions in the Explanatory Note (Explanatory Note to the draft law on improving regulation on public assemblies). To support the requirement for criminal penalties of up to five years for persistently violating the public events protocol, the Explanatory Note attempts to use statistical evidence. As a result, the statistics are based on three single demonstrations in Moscow in February 2014. Out of the dozens detained for participating in non-agreed protests, two or three individuals were found guilty more than ten times under Article 20.2 of the Code of Administrative Offences prohibiting violations of the procedure for holding public events. These figures prompted parliamentarians to consider criminalising non-agreed rallies to strengthen liability.

In its 2017 Ruling No. 2-P, the Constitutional Court interpreted Article 212.1 of the Criminal Code relating to criminal liability for repeated violations of the procedure for holding public assemblies (RF Constitutional Court, 2017). Citizens Iakimov, who initiated this case, claims that imposing liability on him under Article 212.1 of the Criminal Code is unconstitutional as it provides the legal framework for the imposition of criminal penalties for violations of public events held in peace as well as punishments for actions that do not harm people or property.

As a matter of constitutional law, Article 50 prohibits convicting someone twice for the same crime. The Court remains mindful of the importance of adhering to this. At the same time, it also stated that the authorities should protect the right to peaceful assembly without exerting excessive control over those who participate in and organise. As well as supporting legitimate civil initiatives, the authorities should oppose unjustified restrictions on meetings, rallies, demonstrations, processions, and picketing. The Court, nevertheless, determined that such repeated violations are constitutional grounds for additional punishment and restrictions on freedom of assembly. To protect rights and values from public danger, criminal liability is necessary for violations of assembly rules.

Once again, the Court declared at the outset that the right to freedom of assembly is an essential component of an individual's legal status in Russia, which is a democratic state governed by the rule of law that recognises political and ideological diversity as well as multiparty systems and is responsible for defending its citizens' rights and freedoms. Again, the Court cited international law and decisions of the European Court of Human Rights to support its claim that limitations to freedom of assembly are permissible.

While breaking the law by organisers and participants of assemblies may not always result in property or health damages, the Court clarified that procedural infractions are inherently harmful. This manifestation should, therefore, be stopped and repressed by the state using "all legal means." In one sense, the Constitutional Court defines criminal law as an exceptional tool for the state to protect public relations and respond to illegal behaviour. On the other hand, the federal legislature can enforce criminal coercive measures against individuals who violate public assembly rules, ensuring the right to freedom of assembly is protected.

Furthermore, the Court concluded that administrative law and criminal law share identical duties, guiding principles, and the objective of defending human and civil rights. Thus, it is possible to prosecute offences using administrative liability as a basis for criminal liability, therefore using a dualistic approach. Referring to the European Court of Human Rights as the authority, the Constitutional Court defends the said approach. It is claimed that the Strasbourg Court differentiates administrative offences from crimes, finding that certain administrative offences are criminal due to their severity.

In conclusion, criminal liability for repeated violations of established procedures for organising public assemblies does not involve excessive coercion, deviation from equality, proportionality, or fairness. It does not exceed the federal legislator's discretionary powers. The Constitutional Court concludes that the repeated commission of administrative offences indicates insufficient administrative and legal mechanisms for combating them. The close nature of relevant actions and the potential harm they can do to social relations under criminal law make them constitutionally significant. This is the rationale cited in the Explanatory Note to the legal revisions that introduced the rule under review.

5.2.5 2016 Amendments Regarding the Powers of the National Guard During Protests

In 2016, National Guard troops, recently introduced by Putin (see Section 2), were tasked with supervising order in public protests based on the Federal Law on Public

Assemblies amendments (RF Federal Law, No. 227-FZ, 2016). The amendments stipulate that public event participants must comply with all legal requirements of the organiser, persons authorised by them, representatives of executive bodies, and employees of internal affairs (including military and National Guard troops). Only two paragraphs long, the Explanatory Note to the legislative changes is brief unless the file containing it is corrupted or damaged (Explanatory Note to the draft law on powers of the national guards). Improving state and public security and protecting human rights and freedoms are the stated objectives of the draft legislation. The Note concludes that legislative changes in Russian law will be required to ensure that the tasks and functions assigned to the Russian National Guard troops are fulfilled.

5.2.6 2018 Amendments Penalising Minors Involved in Unauthorised Protests

A further amendment to the Federal Law on Public Assemblies was made in 2018, regulating participation by underage individuals in non-authorised public meetings (RF Federal Law No. 557-FZ, 2018). As mentioned, Aleksei Navalny organised anti-corruption protests across Russia in March 2017, which led to the prohibitions, as discussed below. Thus, an amendment to Article 20.2 of the Code of Administrative Offences prohibits involving a minor in an unauthorised meeting, demonstration, procession, or picketing if the action does not constitute a criminal offence. Under these actions, citizens are subject to administrative fines ranging from ₽30,000 to ₽50,000 (£260 – 445), community service of 20 to 100 hours, or administrative arrest for 15 days. A higher fine may be imposed on officials, and a tenfold increase may be imposed on legal entities should they be responsible for such actions.

5.2.7 Stricter Protest Location Limits in 2020 Amendments

A new set of stricter rules was implemented in 2020 to regulate protests with more participants. An (obligatory) notification of a forthcoming public event with an estimated number of participants exceeding 500 people should now include details of the organiser's bank account used to collect funds for arranging a public event. All funds for arranging a public event, with the estimated number of participants exceeding 500 people, are transferred only by bank transfer to the bank account specified in the notice of the public event and opened with a Russian bank. The use of other bank accounts for these purposes, as well as the acceptance of cash, is not allowed (RF Federal Law No. 541-FZ, 2020).

5.2.8 2022 Amendments: Foreign Agent Prohibitions and Stricter Fiscal Requirements

By 2022, prohibitions for foreign agents to organise public events followed (RF Federal Law No. 498-FZ, 2022). In the same law on amendments, new prohibitions were introduced on places where public events could be held, including:

- Educational, medical, and welfare organisations' buildings and territories, and children's and sports grounds.

- Buildings, adjacent territories, and infrastructure, and network and support facilities of public authorities.
- Territories directly adjacent to: (a) the residences of the president, (b) the buildings occupied by courts and emergency operational services, and (c) the territories and buildings of institutions executing punishment in the form of deprivation of liberty (RF Federal Law No. 498-FZ, 2022).

The following phrase provides a concise explanation of these 2022 legal adjustments (Explanatory Note to prohibitions related to foreign agents). A draft law "On amending separate legislative acts of the Russian Federation" is part of a package of federal laws designed to optimise foreign agent regulation. The rationale for introducing more restrictions on protest sites was not explained.

5.3 Discussion

5.3.1 Legal Amendments as Means of Asymmetric Information: Communication of the Findings Back to Theories

The legal amendments outlined above demonstrate how asymmetrised information attempts to limit mass mobilisation's determinants in non-democracies: political opportunity structures or "dimensions of the political environment," grievances that breed social unrest, and formal, informal social networks (Nikolayenko, 2023, p. 207). We can use Niklas Luhmann's categories to understand how these determinants are limited. Therefore, a legal system based on asymmetrical information would not accept spontaneous changes in political agenda via protests as they would interfere with its autopoiesis or ability to correct itself. In the context of the legal system, autopoiesis refers to the ability of the system to maintain its identity and integrity by resisting external influences and changes. Therefore, an asymmetrical information-based legal system will strive to limit the right to assemble since unrestricted freedom of assembly can threaten its stability. After Alexei Navalny's imprisonment and death, mass assemblies were replaced by other forms of protest. At ad hoc memorials throughout Russia and even abroad, thousands of people paid tribute to Navalny, probably not believing in active assemblies, at least for the time being. On occasions, even those silent and sad mourning demonstrations led to police detentions in Russia (Reuters, 2024).

In addition to restricting the freedom of assembly, an asymmetrical information-based system would thus not welcome any significant driving force behind the protests, such as past Boris Nemtsov and Alexei Navalny. As a result of Alexei Navalny's support and motivation for citizens to speak out against the restrictive governance style, he was hailed as the "Hope for Russia." This hope died on 16 February 2024 (Faulconbridge & Light, 2024). Developments on the structural level, when the laws are rewritten to tighten the freedom of expression further, require not only legitimation and explanations, as those which we have seen in the Explanatory notes to amendments, but also action against individuals who are strong enough to voice their own story that challenges the official narrative loudly.

This also suggests that it is not enough to neutralise the known descendants; it is imperative to detect other potential challengers. Ensuring that faces are not covered during public assemblies also aligns with the rationale of asymmetrical information systems to detect potential opponents early on. A symmetrical legal system would have raised ethical issues concerning this prohibition in parliament, rather than applause for the respective 2012 amendments. These amendments are particularly relevant considering the following events. In 2017, Moscow opened one of the largest video surveillance networks in the world. By 2023, face recognition technology will be integrated into the surveillance network to track political activists enlisted by the authorities, particularly those involved in extremism (Masri, 2023). In the absence of adequate privacy protection and accountability regarding the collection, storage, and use of data, these practices could, and have, led to mass surveillance.

Consequently, it becomes clearer why additional avenues for citizen snitching were introduced in 2014. People who reported coaches for mass riot arrangements were promised rehabilitative relief through these avenues. Here, we can find another vital technique and feature an asymmetrical information-based system by increasing the divide between "us" (those who are loyal to the system) and "them" (those who are disloyal by sharing the international human rights and values of the unfriendly West). Luhmann called it a binary division, while Akrelof explained a similar idea with the category of social distance.

5.3.1.1 Interventions at the Individual Level: The Bolotnoe Affair

Legal amendments tightening the freedom to assemble, which we will examine above, were supported by individual efforts to punish most active protest organisers and participants. Thus, with the efficient application of the legislation, the most vocal series of cases within the Bolotnoe Affair (Riekkinen, 2016) were designed to suppress protesters' freedom of expression via judicial prosecution. The term *Bolotnoe* is derived from Moscow's Bolotnaya Square, often used for political demonstrations and meetings due to its size and location. The dispersal of public assemblies on the spot was not the only disproportionate action the security forces took (European Parliament Resolution on Russia, 2014, par. E). Those who went on the streets were subjected to disproportionate verdicts and politically motivated charges (2014, par. E). Many protesters were penalised under the Code of Administrative Offences for failing to comply with lawful orders to cease illegitimate rallies (Riekkinen, 2016).

Additionally, as we discuss the current use of the law to suppress protests, it is essential to note that the Bolotnoe Affair paved the way for invoking Article 212 of the Criminal Code (prohibiting riots) when sanctioning protesters. Despite being pre-arranged with Moscow authorities, the May 2012 assembly turned violent as demonstrators clashed with police, resulting in mass detentions, administrative arrests, trials, and prosecutions, followed by a series of pilot decisions by the European Court of Human Rights against Russia. Some of the Bolotnoe protesters were sentenced to life imprisonment for participating in *riots*, even though during the

"March of the Millions," protesters organised sit-in strikes during the assemblies in question, resulting in the disarray that ensued (Riekkinen, 2016). Put another way, the idea of turning a minor violation into a criminal verdict followed, if not the result, the practices found in the Bolotnoe case.

The courts sentenced several of the most vocal protesters, including Alexei Navalny and Boris Nemtsov, who would later lose their lives under the regime, to prison sentences for disobeying police during non-pre-agreed demonstrations (European Parliament Resolution on Russia, 2014, par. I). These events led to Navalny being placed under house arrest for violating his travel restrictions and committing an administrative offence, eventually resulting in his death in prison.

Detentions and prosecutions within the Bolotnoe Affair are once again being sided with asymmetrical information strategies that utilise the media under widespread government control to discredit the protesters. A slight valorisation of the word *bolotnyi*, which is an adjective derived from the noun "boloto" (i.e. swamp), was displayed by the media when the events of the mass prosecution of protesters were named the Bolotnoe Affair. In Russian folklore, a swamp symbolises dark forces,[4] representing dishonesty and violations of the law by the opposition. While there were reports of police violence and unfair trials in international and foreign media, Russian media referred to the Bolotnoe case as a mass disorder in Moscow, transmitting information regarding the protesters' violations of the law (Interfax, 2014).

5.3.1.2 *Interventions at the Structural Level: Discrediting the Sincerity of Protest Views*

In his 2011 annual address to the Federal Assembly, then-President Dmitry Medvedev warned against attempting to manipulate the will of the citizens in response to the Bolotnoe protests, which was a reaction to the protests. He said that these protests were instigated by extremists and provocateurs who should not interfere with the internal affairs of the state (RF President, 2011). In this way, asymmetricing information can discredit dissenting views to minimise the number of possible other protesters by accusing those who protest the ruling power of interference with public affairs. If the authorities ignore the actual opinions of the people about elections, they can dismiss their objections to dubious electoral practices as unreasonable and ill-intentioned. Based on the assumption that criticising the government is tantamount to provoking the authorities, Medvedev's speech has little to do with symmetrical citizen-government communication. By presenting only those who agree with the state (and are not willing to understand its inner affairs) as law-abiding welcomed voters, the state artificially widens what Akerlof called social distance and Luhmann designated as a binary division between us (obedient citizens) and them" (provocative protesters). Denial of the sincerity of protesting views could lead to the perception that protesters are outsiders, extremists, and ultimately to the undermined legitimacy of their concerns. In this context, asymmetrical information refers to an attempt to create a disparity of knowledge between those who recognise the truth and those who prefer to ignore it, seeing only the picture presented to them by the authorities. Therefore, suppressing protests as a means of asymmetrical information allows unequal information distribution between the state and its obedient electorate, which can erase biased perceptions of decision-making.

Annual presidential addresses to the Federal Assembly, as the one by Dmitry Medvedev quoted above, served as a precursor to future legislative action addressing the priorities raised. As we can see, there was no delay in implementing the amendments that tied up the requirements for public protests in this case. In June 2012, a series of legislative amendments increased punishments for violating laws in public assemblies and legal possibilities for criminal prosecution of people who commit a series of minor offences (RF Federal Law No. 65-FZ, 2012).

5.3.2 Dividing to Self-Correct: Early Allusions to Russia as a Democratic Rule-of-Law State and to the Now-Unfriendly West

The "unfriendly" West was not yet discussed when Russia was a member of the Council of Europe in 2012. By analysing the Explanatory Note to the 2012 legal amendments (Explanatory Note to amending the Code of Administrative Offences) with an eye on how they treated the now-unfriendly West, the asymmetrical binary division of "us" and "them" becomes evident. In 2012, legislators sought to tighten public protest legislation, citing the example of now-declared unfriendly Western states, including the United States, the critical official non-friend of Russia. According to the Explanatory Note, the National Foreign Policy Laboratory examined foreign legislation regulating public meetings and processions of citizens at the request of the Public Chamber. This, however, could not be verified due to a lack of publication information. The report indicates that Western legislation regulates demonstrations and marches more strictly and specifically than Russian law, with longer application periods in major U.S. cities, bans in Germany, blacklists in Sweden, and other restrictions. There is a special mention of the recent referendum in Geneva, where a canton allegedly approved a law tightening street demonstration rules, imposing fines of up to €110,000 or five years of depriving participants of their rights to participate in street demonstrations. All developed democracies are also cited as examples. The authors of the legal amendments under review quoted the report as stating that citizens of developed democratic countries are criminally liable for abusing their freedom of assembly, with distinctions made between different types of public events, allowing swift enforcement methods and severity of punishment.

In Chapter 5 of this book, the West, which provided an example previously, and liberal democracy were almost overnight branded as malicious. As a result of the new amendments, those recognised as foreign agents for pursuing allegedly political activities and receiving funding from abroad will not be permitted to organise public assemblies. Taking a more authoritarian turn is, in a sense, understandable: becoming an authoritarian does not presuppose that there exists dissent. Righteous leadership that is strong, authoritarian, and perfect does not look good to itself if it produces leaders like Alexei Navalny. To make sense of internal issues, it is necessary to reference external enemies, and this external enemy was declared to be the unfriendly West, which fed the opposition.

5.3.3 Struggling for the Audience: Asymmetrical Feeding for Minors

As discussed in Chapter 2 of this book explaining the context, Russia spent much effort on military-patriotic upbringing to create a loyal army of construction bricks that composed the system's environment. Alexei Navalny's strategy of sending messages to young people via internet channels ran contrary to the official course of monopolising the younger generation's attention. The 2018 legal amendments reviewed above, which introduce liability for involving minors in unauthorised public assemblies, illustrate a conflict between Navalny's conscious policy of appealing to younger generations with addresses against corruption and political stagnation in Russia and the official course on indoctrinating minor minds with ideas of patriotism. As a result of underage persons participating in non-preagreed assemblies in 2017, the president's spokesman, Dmitry Peskov, stated that the children were lured into the event by monetary compensation promises (MKRU, 2017a). Under such an official course, the upbringing of children was later named by the 2020 constitutional amendments as the primary objective of the state (Riekkinen et al., 2019). We discussed how the policy of holding the next generation of Russians for the state's benefit moved from 2020 to the Constitution in Chapter 2 of this book, explaining the context.

A single non-authorised anti-corruption protest organised by Navalny's team in the spring of 2017 drew around 1000 participants, most of them young (Higgins & Kramer, 2017). It is not known exactly how many underage demonstrators exactly attended that event. Yet according to the information service of the Ministry of Internal Affairs of Russia, "there were a lot of students and minors" who participated (2017). Russian law permits minors to be detained for identification verification and to draw a protocol for administrative offences, provided that parents or legal guardians are informed and the detention must not exceed three hours (The Code of Administrative Offences, 2001). Scores of schoolchildren stood with adults in a non-authorised gathering and were also detained by police. According to Russian media reports, 46 minors were arrested on 27 March 2017 (MKRU, 2017b).

Video footage of underage protesters being taken away by the police, sometimes violently, and detained in police vans for hours before being taken to a station for paperwork has been widely circulated. There was a solid public reaction when teenagers were held in these circumstances. Valentina Matvienko, a close ally of Putin, proposes that parents be held responsible for their children's protest participation and refrain from participating (Mislivskaya, 2017). However, the proposal had not advanced. Researchers in Russia (Chirun, 2013; Tsiunik, 2017, p. 149), and outside it interpreted Navalny's actions as deliberate attempts to appeal to young people as supporters (Judah, 2013, p. 223). For instance, it is reported in the media that Mr. Navalny has appealed to the youth to boycott the school referendums scheduled by the Moscow region on 18 March 2018, the day after the election of the new president. The authorities intended to offer children the opportunity to vote on school-related issues to train their skills and become active participants in the political process (TASS, 2008). It was Navalny's view that this move was intended to use the children as a way of attracting the attention of the children's families to the presidential elections by involving those children. During the run-up to these referendums, the oppositionist warned youth via his "YouTube" channel: "Don't let them fool you, and don't be fooled by their messages."[5] Children thus were attracted to participate in demonstrations by Navalny's appeals through social media; some did not inform their parents (Higgins & Kramer, 2017).

When the 2018 amendments were adopted, the 2001 Code of Administrative Offences was in force, and those involved in administrative misconduct, including those who organised illegal assemblies, were subject to special liability for the involvement of minors as aggravating circumstances (RF Code of Administrative Offences, 2001). Since the legislation in force at the time already provided legal liability for those who intentionally included underage people in illegal activities, it seems likely that the 2018 amendments were introduced for no other reason than to regulate what kind of information is available to young people, symmetrised or free-flowing.

The introduction of special liability for the involvement of minors in public assemblies in 2018 thus further demonstrates a motivation to deter and prevent underage persons' participation in activities that could challenge the government's authority. This aligns with the policy of holding the next generation of Russians for the state's benefit, where the goal is to shape their thinking and behaviour to align with the government's agenda. Chapter 6 of this book on codifying traditional values further explores how the free flow of information is symmetrised with the view of fostering information for children, especially when authorities prevent children from accessing LGBTQ+ resources or other information they may find, as well as harmful content, such as violence, pornography, and misinformation, that may adversely impact their mental health and development. Such intentions are good intentions unless they are used to limit freedom of expression, including through assemblies, and ban undesirable associations.

5.3.4 Increasing Reliance on Power Structures to Control Dissent

To control dissent, a repressive apparatus was widely deployed to track the existing and potential dissent following the 2011 protests of the electoral breaches to quell the growing protest opposition. The newly introduced National Guards troops (headed by Viktor Zolotov, a former bodyguard of Putin) have been given the authority to prevent mass disorder and to issue orders to citizens when law and order is alleged to have been violated in public gatherings. Police thus appear untrustworthy in such a way that elite military units with special anti-terrorism duties and guarding federal and regional leaders were chosen to reinforce their presence during protest demonstrations. Therefore, failure to comply with the instructions issued by the National Guard of the Russian Federation to terminate a public event incurs liability under the Act on Public Assemblies.

Trusting power ministries and structures to handle dissent became a topic again, as evidenced by the above discourse (see Chapter 1 for a description of our framework for the legal system based on asymmetrical information). By appointing National Guard squads with authority to intervene in protests, the issue of regulating free expression is further symmetrised with bias and favouritism towards governmental structures. On the one hand, this further exacerbates the gap between the government and the people, which aligns with Akerlof's social distance and Luhmann's binary division between the system and the environment. Those who do not protest are further segmented from those who do by the system's involvement of elite military units, which handle only the most severe offences.

Table 5.1 Summary of Legal Amendments Tightening Protest Regulations

Year	*Amendment*	*New Penalty*
2012	Prohibitions on covering faces, widening authority over protest locations, banning series of one-person pickets, and introducing more prohibitions for organisers.	Community service 20–200 hours Administrative fine of up to ₽ 20,000 (£167)
2016	Prohibiting one-person pickets using construction structures.	
2014–2020	To be distinguished among protesters, journalists must wear a sign, and journalists must carry editorial certificates.	
2014	Cumulative criminal liability follows minor protest law violations. A promise of liability relief if citizens snitch on mass riot training organisers.	Up to 15 days of administrative arrest for holding an unauthorised assembly Fines of ₽ 600,000 to ₽ 1,000,000 (£ 5,000 to £ 8,400) or the number of the employee's wages for two to three years, community service (up to 480 hours), corrective labour (up to two years), forced labour (up to five years), or imprisonment for the same term (up to five years)
2016	Supervising public assemblies becomes the role of National Guard troops.	
2018	Prohibition for involving a minor in an unauthorised assembly.	Fines of ₽ 30,000 to ₽ 50,000 (£ 260 –£ 445), community service (20–100 hours), or administrative arrest for up to 15 days
2020	Over 500-person assemblies are under stricter control. All funds for organising the assemblies must be transferred via banks, not cash.	
2022	Foreign agents cannot organise public assemblies. Assembly places are more restricted.	

5.5 Concluding Remarks

The gradual but steady tightening of the right to assembly has resulted in citizens protesting government policies and facing heavy fines and prison sentences of decades, if not more. Table 5.1 illustrates the heavy financial burden of protesting in the streets and the seriousness of the chances of arrest or imprisonment.

Notes

1 Currently, Article 8, para. 1.1 of the Federal Law on Public Assemblies.
2 Currently, Article 7, para. 1.1 of the Federal Law on Public Assemblies.
3 Current Article 5, para. 2.1.1. of the Federal Law on Public Assemblies.
4 Here is how basic Russian interpretive dictionaries, such as Vladimir Dahl's, define the term "boloto." In his description of the swamp, Dahl quotes the Russian proverb, "Vtikhom bolote (omute) cherty vodiatsia" (literally, "There are demons in quiet swamps" in the sense of assuming caution when dealing with a silent dog and still water). Dahl, 2008.
5 Youtube.com, The video entitled "Ne daite sebia obmanut'" (Don't let them fool you) is available at www.youtube.com/watch?v=VETOQ6BTTTQ

References

Amnesty International. (2015, December 7). *Russia: Peaceful activist sentenced under the repressive new law must be released.* www.amnesty.org/en/latest/press-release/2015/12/russia-peaceful-activist-sentenced-under-repressive-new-law-must-be-released/

Chirun, S. N. (2013, August 8–August 14). New youth policy of Aleksei Navalny. In V. V. Pavlov (Ed.), *Biosocial characteristics of the modern human psychology/social and political aspects of the post-industrial life activity of states* (pp. 60–61). Materials Digest of the LIX International Research and Practice Conference and II Stage of the Championship in Psychological Sciences.

Council of Europe. (2017, September 29). *Memorandum: The law on freedom of assembly in the Russian Federation needs thorough revision.* www.coe.int/fi/web/commissioner/-/the-law-on-freedom-of-assembly-in-the-russian-federation-needs-thorough-revision

Dahl, V. (2008). *Tolkovyi slovar' zhivogo velikorusskogo iazyka* [Explanatory dictionary of Russian language]. Ripol Klassik.

Dollbaum, J. M. (2020). Protest trajectories in electoral authoritarianism: From Russia's "for fair elections" movement to Alexei Navalny's presidential campaign. *Post-Soviet Affairs*, *36*(3), 192–210.

Dress, B. (2024, December 16). Alexei Navalny's rise from blogger to Putin's chief rival: Timeline. *The Hill.* https://thehill.com/policy/international/4473313-alexei-navalny-life-death-timeline/

Explanatory note to amending the code of administrative offences, *Poiiasnitel'naia zapiska k proektu federal'nogo zakona "O vnesenii izmenenii v Kodeks Rossiiskoi Federatsii ob administrativnykh pravonarusheniiakh".* https://sozd.duma.gov.ru/bill/70631-6

Explanatory note to the draft law introducing limitations for journalists, *Explanatory Note to the Draft Law "O vnesenii izmenenii v nekotorye zakonodatel'nye akty Rossiiskoi Federatsii" (v chasti sovershenstvovaniia zakonodatel'stva o publichnykh meropriiatiiakh).* https://sozd.duma.gov.ru/bill/485729-6

Explanatory note to the draft law on improving regulation on public assemblies, *Poiiasnitel'naia zapiska k proektu federal'nogo zakona "O vnesenii izmenenii v nekotorye zakonodatel'nye akty Rossiiskoi Federatsii" (v chasti sovershenstvovaniia zakonodatel' stva o publichnykh meropriiatiiakh).* https://sozd.duma.gov.ru/bill/485729-6

Explanatory note to the draft law on powers of the national guards, *Poiiasnitel'naiia zapiska k proektu federal'nogo zakona "O vnesenii izmenenii v otdel'nye zakonodatel'nye akty Rossiiskoi Federatsii i priznanii utrativshimi silu otdel'nykh zakonodatel'nykh aktov (polozhenii zakonodatel'nykh aktov) Rossiiskoi Federatsii v sviazi s priniatiem Federal'nogo zakona "O voiskakh natsional'noi gvardii Rossiiskoi Federatsii*". https://sozd.duma.gov.ru/bill/1037366-6

Explanatory note to the federal law no. 65-FZ, *Poiiasnitel'naia zapiska k proektu federal'nogo zakona "O vnesenii izmenenii v Kodeks Rossiiskoi Federatsii ob administrativnykh pravonarusheniiakh"*. https://sozd.duma.gov.ru/bill/70631-6

Explanatory note to prohibitions related to foreign agents, *Poiasnitel'naia zaposka k proektu federal'nogo zakona "O vnesenii izmenenii v otdel'nye zakonodatel'nye akty Rossiiskoi Federatsii"*. https://sozd.duma.gov.ru/bill/140449-8

Falaleev, M. (2017, October 17). *Parents may be punished for their children's participation in unauthorized actions*. RGRU. https://rg.ru/2017/10/17/roditelej-mogut-nakazat-za-uchastie-detej-v-nesoglasovannyh-akciiah.html

Faulconbridge, G., & Light, F. (2024, February 16). Navalny's death deprives Russia's opposition of a leader and hope. *Reuters*. www.reuters.com/world/europe/navalnys-death-deprives-russias-opposition-leader-hope-2024-02-16

FIDH. (2019). *Brutal repression of protests in Moscow: A complete account of violations*. www.fidh.org/IMG/pdf/russiemoscow738aweb.pdf

Higgins, A., & Kramer, A. E. (2017, March 27). In protests, Kremlin fears a young generation stirring. *New York Times*. www.nytimes.com/2017/03/27/world/europe/in-protests-kremlin-fears-a-young-generation-stirring.html

Human Rights Watch. (2014, April 1). *Russia: New attack on freedom of assembly*. www.hrw.org/news/2014/04/01/russia-new-attack-freedom-assembly

Interfax. (2014, June 3). *"Pred"iavleno obvinenie novomu figurantu "bolotnogo dela"* [Charges were brought against a new player in the Bolotnoe case]. www.interfax.ru/russia/379422

Izquierdo, F. (2013). *Political regimes in the Arab World: Society and the exercise of power*. Routledge.

Judah, B. (2013). *Fragile Empire: How Russia fell in and out of love with Vladimir Putin*. Yale University Press.

Kirian, P. (2011). On the eve of the New Year Vladimir Putin and the country learned a lot of news about each other. *RBC Daily*. www.rbcdailyru/2011/12/28/focus/562949982408179

Leonard, L. (2017). *The sustainable nation: Politics, economy and justice*. Emerald Publishing Limited.

Lewis, D. G. (2020). *Russia's new authoritarianism. Putin and the politics of order*. Edinburgh University Press.

Masri, L. (2023, March 28). *Facial recognition is helping Putin curb dissent with the aid of U.S. tech*. www.reuters.com/investigates/special-report/ukraine-crisis-russia-detentions/

Medvedev, D., & Putin, V. (2011, September 24). *The speech on the XII session of the Edinaya Rossiya party*. www.президент.рф/news/12802

Mislivskaya, G. (2017, December 11). *Matvienko did not rule out punishing parents for their children's participation in rallies*. RGRU. https://rg.ru/2017/12/11/matvienko-ne-iskliuchila-nakazanie-roditelej-za-uchastie-detej-v-mitingah.html

MKRU. (2017a, March 27). *Kreml' otreagiroval na protestnuiu aktsiiu v Mosve: "Provokatsii i lozh"* [The Kremlin reacted on the protest event in Moscow: "Provocation and lie"]. www.mk.ru/politics/2017/03/27/kreml-otreagiroval-na-protestnuyu-akciyu-v-moskve-provokacii-i-lozh.html

MKRU. (2017b, March 27). *Schoolboy detained at Navalny's rally: I attached a yellow duck to my backpack*. www.mk.ru/social/2017/03/27/shkolnik-zaderzhannyy-na-akcii-navalnogo-zheltuyu-utochku-pricepil-na-ryukzak.html

Mortensen, A., Pleitgen, F., Rehbein, M., & Prior, R. (2017, March 27). *Report: Hundreds arrested at anti-corruption protests in Russia*. https://edition.cnn.com/2017/03/26/world/russia-corruption-protests/index.html

Nikolayenko, O. (2023). Anti-corruption protests and university students: Evidence from Russian cities. *Government and Opposition*, *58*, 207–226.

Nuzov, I. (2012). The Role of political elite in transitional justice in Russia: From false "nurembergs" to failed desovietization. *U.C. Davis Journal of International Law and Policy*, *20*.

Official Journal of the European Union. (2014, March 11). *European Parliament resolution on Russia: Sentencing of demonstrators involved in Bolotnaya Square events*. https://eur-lex.europa.eu/legal-content/EN/TXT/PDF/?uri=CELEX:52014IP0253

Reuters. (2024, February 17). *Navalny's death deprives Russia's opposition of a leader and hope*. www.reuters.com/world/europe/navalnys-death-deprives-russias-opposition-leader-hope-2024-02-16/

RF Code of Administrative Offences No. 195-FZ. (2001, December 30). *Kodeks Rossiiskoi Federatsii ob administrativnykh pravonarusheniiakh*. Sobranie zakonodatel'stva Rossiiskoi Federatsii, 2001, No. 1 (part I) item 1.

RF Constitutional Court, Opredelenie No. 1320-O-O. (2011, September 29). *Ob otkaze v priniatii k rassmotreniiu zhaloby Administratsii goroda N'iagan' Khanty-Mansiiskogo Avtonomnogo okruga na narushenie konstitutsionnykh prav i svobod chast'iu 1 stat'i 7 Federal'nogo Zakona "O sobraniiakh, mitingakh, demonstratsiiakh, shestviiakh i piketirovaniiakh* [On the refusal to accept for consideration the complaint of the administration of the city of N'iagan of the Khanty-Mansi autonomous Okrug for violation of constitutional rights and freedoms, article 7 of the federal law "on assemblies, rallies, demonstrations, processions and picketing]. https://base.garant.ru/58204220/?ysclid=lrlwgrjyc5654665405

RF Constitutional Court, Postanovlenie No. 2-P. (2017, February 10). *Po delu o proverke konstitutsionnosti polozhenii stat'i 212.1 Ugolovnogo kodeksa Rossiiskoi Federatsii v sviazi s zhaloboi grazhdanina I.I. Dadina* [On checking the constitutionality of article 212.1 of the criminal code of the Russian Federation concerning citizen I.I. Dadina]. Sobranie zakonodatel'stva Rossiiskoi Federatsi*i*, 2017, No. 9 item 1422.

RF Constitutional Court, Postanovlenie No. 4-P. (2013, February 14). *Po delu o proverke konstitutsionnosti Federal'nogo zakona "O vnesenii izmenenij v Kodeks Rossijskoj Federatsii ob administrativnykh pravonarusheniyakh i Federal'nyj zakon "O sobraniiakh, mitingakh, demonstratsiiakh, shestviiakh i piketirovaniiakh" v sviazi s zaprosom gruppy deputatov Gosudarstvennoi Dumy i zhaloboi grazhdanina E.V. Savenko* [On checking the constitutionality of the federal law "on amendments to the code of the Russian Federation on administrative offenses" and the federal law "on assemblies, meetings, demonstrations, processions and picketing" in connection with a request from a group of deputies of the State Duma and a complaint from citizen E. I. Savenko]. Sobranie zakonodatel'stva Rossiiskoi Federatsii, 2013, No. 8 item 868.

RF Constitutional Court, Postanovlenie No. 14-P. (2014, May 13). *Po delu o proverke konstitutsionnosti chasti 1 stat'i 7 Federal'nogo zakona "O sobraniiakh, mitingakh, demonstratsiiakh, shestviiakh i piketirovaniiakh" v sviazi s zhaloboi grazhdanina A.N. Iakimova* [On checking the constitutionality of part 1 of article 7 of the federal law "on assemblies, rallies, demonstrations, processions, and picketing upon a complaint from citizen A.N. Iakimov]. Rossiiskaia gazeta, 20.05.2014, No. 112 (6384).

RF Criminal Code No. 63-FZ. (1996, June 13). *Ugolovnyi kodeks Rossiiskoi Federatsii*. Sobranie zakonodatel'stva Rossiiskoi Federatsii, 1996, No. 25 item 2954.

RF Federal Law No. 54-FZ. (2004, June 19). *O sobraniiakh, mitingakh, demonstratsiiakh, shestviiakh i piketirovaniiakh* [On meetings, rallies, demonstrations, processions, and picketing]. Sobranie zakonodatel'stva Rossiiskoi Federatsii, 2004, No. 25 item 2485.

RF Federal Law No. 61-FZ. (2016, March 9). *O vnesenii izmenenii v stat'i 2 i 7 Federal'nogo zakona "O sobraniiakh, mitingakh, demonstratsiiakh, shestviiakh i piketirovaniiakh"* [Amendments to articles 2 and 7 of the federal law "on assemblies, rallies, demonstrations, processions, and picketing"]. Sobranie zakonodatel'stva Rossiiskoi Federatsii, 2016, No. 11 item 1488.

RF Federal Law No. 65-FZ. (2012, June 8). *O vnesenii izmenenii v Kodeks Rossiiskoi Federatsii ob administrativnykh pravonarusheniiakh i Federal'nyi zakon "O sobraniiakh, mitingakh, demonstraciiakh, shestviiakh i piketirovaniiakh"* [On amending the code of the Russian Federation on administrative offenses and the federal law on meetings, rallies, demonstrations, processions, and picketing]. Sobranie zakonodatel'stva Rossiiskoi Federatsii, 2012, No. 24 item 3082.

RF Federal Law No. 130-FZ. (2014, May 5). *O vnesenii izmenenii v otdel'nye zakonodatel'nye akty Rossiiskoi Federatsii* [On amending the federal law "on assemblies, rallies, demonstrations, processions, and picketing]. Sobranie zakonodatel'stva Rossiiskoi Federatsii, 2014, No. 19 item 2335.

RF Federal Law No. 227-FZ. (2016, July 3). *O vnesenii izmenenii v otdel'nye zakonodatel'nye akty Rossiiskoi Federatsii i priznanii utrativshimi silu otdel'nykh zakonodatel'nykh aktov (polozhenii zakonodatel'nykh aktov) Rossiiskoi Federatsii v sviazi s priniatiem Federal'nogo zakona "O voiskakh natsional'noi gvardii Rossiiskoi Federatsii"* [Amendments to certain Russian Federation legislative acts and recognition of certain Russian Federation legislative acts (provisions of legislative acts) as invalid in connection with the adoption of federal law "on the military national guard of the Russian Federation"]. Sobranie zakonodatel'stva Rossiiskoi Federatsii, 2016, No. 27 (part I) item 4160.

RF Federal Law No. 258-FZ. (2014, July 21). *O vnesenii izmenenii v otdel'nye zakonodatel'nye akty Rossiiskoi Federatsii v chasti sovershenstvovaniia zakonodatel'stva o publichnykh meropriiatiiakh*. Sobranie zakonodatel'stva Rossiiskoi Federatsii, 28.07.2014, No. 30 (part I) item 4259.

RF Federal Law No. 497-FZ. (2020, December 30). *O vnesenii izmenenij v Federal'nyi zakon "O sobraniiakh, mitingakh, demonstratsiiakh, shestviiakh i piketirovaniiakh"* [On amending the federal law "on assemblies, rallies, demonstrations, processions, and picketing"]. Sobranie zakonodatel'stva Rossiiskoi Federatsii, 2021, No. 1 (part 1) item 36.

RF Federal Law No. 498-FZ. (2022, December 5). *O vnesenii izmenenii v otdel'nye zakonodatel'nye akty Rossiiskoi Federatsii* [On amending the federal law "on assemblies, rallies, demonstrations, processions, and picketing]. Sobranie zakonodatel'stva Rossiiskoi Federatsii, 2022, No. 50 (part III) item 8792.

RF Federal Law No. 541-FZ. (2020, December 30). *O vnesenii izmenenii v Federal'nyi zakon "O sobraniiakh, mitingakh, demonstratsiiakh, shestviiakh i piketirovaniiakh*". Sobranie zakonodatel'stva Rossiiskoi Federatsii, 04.12.2021, No. 1 (part I) item 80.

RF Federal Law No. 557-FZ. (2018, December 27). *O vnesenii izmeneniia v stat'iu 20.2 Kodeksa Rossiiskoi Federatsii ob administrativnykh pravonarusheniiakh* [On amendments to article 20.2 of the code of administrative offenses of the Russian Federation]. Sobranie zakonodatel'stva Rossiiskoi Federatsii, 2018, No. 53 (part I) item 8483.

RF President. (2011, December 22). *Poslanie Prezidenta RF Federal'nomu Sobraniiu. Annual address of president Medvedev to the federal assembly of the Russian Federation.* www.consultant.ru/document/cons_doc_LAW_123798/?ysclid=lubeayrtk3853474906

Riekkinen, M. (2016). The "Bolotnoe affair" and the implementation of the right to freedom of assembly in the Russian Federation. *Review of Central and East European Law*, *41*(3–4), 396–426.

Riekkinen, M., Adilghazy, S., & Tasbulatova, A. (2019). Protected or neglected? Analysing legislation governing minors' participation in protest rallies in Russia against the background of international law. *International Journal of Children's Rights*, *27*(3), 482–516.

TASS. (2008, February 8). CIK otmenil shkol'nyj referendum v Podmoskov'e i sdelal preduprezhdenie glave izbirkoma/The Central Election Commission canceled the school referendum in the Moscow region and issued a warning to the head of the election commission. *TASS*. http://tass.ru/politika/4940392

Tsiunik, D. A. (2017). *Oppositsionnaia deiatel'nost' molodogo pokoleniia v postsovetskikh gosudarstvakh* [Opposition activity of the young generation in post-Soviet states]. PolitBook.

Venice Commission, OSCE/ODIHR. (2019). *European commission for democracy through law (Venice commission), OSCE office for democratic institutions and human rights (OSCE/ODIHR) guidelines on freedom of peaceful assembly, CDL-AD(2019)017-e* (3rd ed.). www.venice.coe.int/webforms/documents/default.aspx?pdffile=CDL-AD(2019)017-e

Youtube.com. *The video entitled "Ne daite sebia obmanut" (Don't let them fool you).* www.youtube.com/watch?v=VETOQ6BTTTQ

6 Analysing Legal Amendments Since 2012

Codifying Traditional Societal Values

6.1 Legal Amendments

As a result of the 2020 Constitutional Amendment, the concept of traditional values was introduced into the Constitution. In particular, the government received the power to ensure the implementation in the Russian Federation of an integrated socially oriented state policy in the fields of culture, science, education, healthcare, social security, support, strengthening, and protection of the family, preservation of traditional family values, and environmental protection (RF, Federal Constitutional Law No. 1-FKZ, 2020). In July 2021, Putin approved Russia's Strategy for National Security, which included a section on preserving traditional Russian moral and spiritual values, culture, and history (The Strategy for National Security, 2021). This strategy contends that enduring moral principles and traditional spiritual guidelines are under threat in the modern world (2021, par. 84). Moreover, personal freedom is being absolutised, and violence, consumption, and pleasure are being ingrained (2021, par. 85). Implementing reforms in science, education, culture, religion, language, and information without considering previous generations' historical traditions and experiences in science and education exacerbates polarisation and undermines cultural sovereignty. Multinational companies, foreign organisations, and the U.S. attack traditional Russian spiritual, moral, cultural, and historical values (2021, par. 87).

As a result of such informational and psychological warfare and "Westernization," Russia is more likely to lose its cultural sovereignty (2021, par. 88). However, Russia will maintain and strengthen its sovereignty by observing its fundamental moral, spiritual, and cultural-historical values. The traditional Russian spiritual and moral values are listed: putting the spiritual above the material, promoting high moral ideals, a strong family, creative work, historical memory and generational continuity, humanism, mercy, justice, collectivism, mutual assistance and respect, life, dignity, human rights and freedoms, patriotism, citizenship, service to the Fatherland and responsibility for its fate, as well as unity among the Russian people (2021, par. 91). Traditional Russian spiritual and moral values unite Russia's multi-ethnic and multireligious nation (2021, par. 90).

On 9 November 2022, Putin issued another decree approving state policy fundamentals for preserving and strengthening traditional Russian spiritual and moral

DOI: 10.4324/9781032613383-6

values (RF President, 2022). Several sections make up the document: (a) general provisions, (b) risk assessment, (c) state policy goals to uphold and preserve traditional values, (d) tools to implement the policy, and (e) anticipated outcomes. Since it outlines a set of goals, objectives, and instruments for implementing the strategic protection of traditional Russian spiritual and moral values, culture, and historical memory, the decree is referred to as a component of strategic planning to ensure national security. In other words, it is intended to preserve traditional Russian moral and spiritual values. As per paragraph six of this decree, Orthodoxy plays an essential role in forming traditional values, which are influenced by Buddhist, Islamic, Christian, and Jewish religious beliefs (2022, par. 6).

The decree under consideration defined traditional values as moral principles inherited from their ancestors and shaping the outlook of Russian citizens. In the spiritual, historical, and cultural advancement of Russia's diverse population, these principles are the foundation for the nation's cohesive cultural space and all-Russian civic identity, strengthening civil unity and promoting civic unity. It specifies that Russia views traditional values as the cornerstone of Russian society, allowing the nation to safeguard and strengthen its sovereignty, maintain its unity as a multinational and multireligious nation, preserve its citizens, and realise human potential. Compared to paragraph 91 of the aforementioned 2021 Strategy of National Security, the value inventory in paragraph five is identical. Values have been assigned to respond timely and effectively to new challenges and threats while preserving Russian civic identity (2022, par. 8).

Section 2 of the decree outlines the threats to traditional values and scenarios for developing the situation. Russia views the current situation as a global civilisational and value crisis that is leading to the loss of spiritual and moral guidelines. Russia's social cohesiveness and spiritual growth should be enhanced to prevent humanity from losing moral principles (2022, par. 11).

According to this decree, several threats to traditional values are being reinstituted. These include extremist and terrorist organisations, certain media outlets, the actions of the United States and other unfriendly foreign countries, as well as transnational corporations and international non-profits, along with some Russian organisations and individuals (2022, pars. 12, 13). A destructive ideology that promotes immorality, permissiveness, and selfishness. These values alienate Russians, jeopardising their demographic stability and allegedly exerting ideological and psychological influence on citizens, as stated in paragraphs 14 and 15 of the documents under review (2022).

Consequently, this ideology juxtaposes family values, patriotism, and the natural continuation of life with non-traditional values. As a result of the destructive ideology proposed, self-destruction conditions can arise, socio-cultural stratification will grow, moral health will suffer, antisocial stereotypes will emerge, an immoral lifestyle will develop, spiritual and ethical values will be neglected, historical truths will be distorted, Russian identity will be denied, civic identity will be weakened, trust in state institutions will be undermined, and military and public service will be negatively viewed (2022, par. 17).

Suggestions for avoiding them follow a list of potential hazards. State support for culture and education projects will be improved, strategic planning documents will be adjusted, interdepartmental coordination will be ensured, destructive ideology will be countered, children and youth will be raised and educated better, and science, education, and cultural organisations will be strengthened. Law enforcement agencies will be strengthened to prevent and suppress illegal actions that spread destructive ideology. Two possible implementation scenarios are presented for enhancing traditional values: negative and positive. In an optimistic scenario, state policy is implemented methodically, emphasising safeguarding Russian society from external threats and cultivating morally upright individuals (RF Strategy for National Security, 2021, par. 21). An adverse scenario can arise if counteraction against harmful ideologies is not taken (2022, par. 22).

Implementing the state policy requires the creation of strategic planning documents, the participation of civil society organisations, and the enhancement of the regulatory framework. When determining whether state support is appropriate, action plans, project assessments (including information and other materials), programs, and activities aimed at ensuring traditional values are upheld, monitoring goal achievement, controlling budget compliance, and inviting civil society organisations to participate in the implementation of state policies to strengthen and uphold traditional values are examples of organisational tools. According to paragraph 27 of the decree, scientific and analytical tools include conducting research, developing methodological guidelines, and communicating with the media. Goals can be tracked using indicators derived from official statistics, sociological studies, and problematic data (2022).

In no way are these ideas novel. A speech by Putin in December 2012 cited spiritual and traditional values as counterbalances to the decline of Russia and denounced foreign influences (Barry, 2012). Rather than referring to democracy as the realisation of standards imposed from outside, he described it as the strength of the Russian people and their traditions. However, there is no doubt that the Russian Federation has taken action to safeguard these ideals. These actions include limiting foreign ownership of Russian media and restricting website access. Systematically, it ensured that these ideals became the foundation of society. Corresponding amendments were introduced to the 1991 Law on Mass Media on December 5th, 2022 (RF Federal Law No. 2124-I, 1991). Article 4 of this law, which stipulates the inadmissibility of abuse of freedom of the media, was amended to prohibit the use of media to spread content that encourages non-traditional sexual relationships and preferences, paedophilia, gender reassignment, pornography, violence, cruelty, and material with obscene language (RF Federal Law No. 478-FZ, 2022).

Previously, there was a list of prohibitions, including the illegal use of media, revealing state secrets, disseminating material that incites terrorism, and publicly defending terrorism. Under the amended Federal Law on Information, Information Technologies, and Protection of Information (RF Federal Law No. 149-FZ, 2006, Art. 10.6), owners of websites and pages have an additional responsibility. As part of the obligation, it is required to monitor material promoting non-traditional sexual relationships and preferences, paedophilia, gender reassignment, and pornographic, violent, or cruel content (RF Federal Law No. 478-FZ, 2022).

Based on the Explanatory Note accompanying the amendments to these federal laws (Explanatory Note, 2022), they are intended to shield society from misinformation regarding non-traditional sexual relationships and preferences, as well as shield kids from damaging information. In the amendments, the authors contend that the LGBT community is consolidating worldwide along with more straightforward gender reassignment procedures and that compulsive propaganda is depathologising these phenomena. Due to the internet, media, advertising, literature, and films actively disseminating information and distorting social equivalence of traditional and non-traditional sexual relationships, these phenomena have become more prevalent in the Russian Federation. The explanation note describes this kind of dissemination as aggressive, intrusive, and offensive, causing widespread public outrage. Non-traditional values, propagating non-traditional sexual orientation as an individualising factor, exaggerating the advantages of gender reassignment, and justifying paedophilia pose a particular threat to children and adolescents who are fragile, according to the draft law's authors.

Thus, the first claim made in these *travaux préparatoires* is that media and information flow intentionally distort the balance and promote same-sex relationships and gender identity transformation over traditional forms of relationships and gender identity. Nevertheless, the Explanatory Note later states that the current laws do not limit such phenomena; they refer to the distortion of social equivalence rather than the information itself.

The Federal Law on Information was amended again on 31 July 2023, targeting the dissemination of information regarding gender reassignment, paedophilia, and non-traditional relationships. This amendment could include websites spreading such information in the special prohibition inventory.[1] This provision was added to Article 15 of the previously mentioned Federal Law, implying that websites that distribute these materials will be blocked.

6.2 Interpretations of the Constitutional Court

The Constitutional Court rendered an interpretation of the significance of traditional values as part of its 2020 evaluation of the constitutionality of the constitutional amendments that introduced the Government's power to ensure that a state policy aimed at preserving traditional family values was implemented (RF Constitution, Article 114, para. c). The Court considered that the power reflects social norms intended to safeguard and develop humanity. According to the Court, this strategy complies with international law and the Russian Constitution, and respects individual autonomy (RF Constitutional Court, 2020). Since marriage is a union of a man and a woman (Article 72, par. g. 1 of the Constitution), the state is not required to encourage, support, or acknowledge same-sex relationships but to respect traditional values. Through this power, the Russian government can carry out a cohesive, socially conscious state policy that supports, strengthens, and defends traditional family values. Based on traditional values, the Court ruled that the state has the right to control individual relationships and sexual relations:

> *It is based on traditional values and the ethnic and religious makeup of Russia's population that the country has the right to resolve certain issues of legislative regulation in areas affecting sexuality and related interpersonal relationships.*
>
> (RF Constitutional Court, 2020)

The Constitutional Court's interpretation aligns with a list of traditional values and a National Security Strategy that followed later; these all assert that individual rights and autonomy must give way to immaterial values and collective interests rather than being used solely for pleasure. Thus, personal freedom, including liberties associated with intimacy, should be restricted using these values.

6.3 Communicating the Findings Back to Theory

As mentioned above, in defence of traditional values, the Constitutional Court cites international law as a basis for limiting individual liberties. When ordering everyone to adhere to the codified values, the 2022 Presidential decree and the 2020 Constitutional Court interpretation refer to universally recognised standards and principles. Allusions like these, however, do not sit well with the ideas of Aleksander Dugin, who described it as the cornerstone of Russian sovereignty in a commentary on the 2022 decree in enshrining traditional values (Mirtesen, 2022). Dugin sees these values as the core of Russia's sovereign ideology.

Dugin asserted in his commentary that in Russia, we are currently discussing the creation of a socio-political model that will replace liberal democracy, which will be the foundation for the next phase of our civilisation war. He continued, "[t]he most important conceptual weapon for Russia during the Northeast Military District, which turned into a full-fledged conflict of civilisations, is Decree No. 809 (Mirtesen, 2022). In contrast to the sovereign internet, the notion of sovereign ideology may not seem novel when viewed through the 2020 constitutional amendments that define Russia as the continuator of the Soviet Union (RF Constitution, Article 67.1). This sovereignty thus echoes socialist views by shifting the focus from individual rights to community interests and controlling information flows.

As a result of misreadings between the international dimension of values and their essence as a basis for Russia's sovereignty, we find ourselves back at the notions of a controlled society and managed democracy that international research suggests Russia consciously and consistently attempts to impose (Ledeneva, 2013; Petrov et al., 2010; Richter, 2009). Society is controlled not just by limiting freedoms and suppressing critical thinking but also by giving citizens the illusion of being in control. For example, certain advisory bodies can be established and revoked (Petrov et al., 2010, p. 3). The codification of traditional values by the president, who is portrayed as a defender of historical tradition, does not only serve to conceal the establishment of a lifetime presidency (Zorin, 2022). It is also intended to create a bond between the president and the people by giving them the things they genuinely want, not to mention ensuring stability (Sakwa, 2021, pp. 222–241).

However, with Akerlof's social distance model in mind, codifying traditional values reveals an additional dimension. More particularly, Akerlof (1970) provides two examples of social interventions to illustrate the concept of social distance (Akerlof, 1997). As a result of Eugene Lang's college scholarship program in New York, most students who received this aid could secure scholarships on their initiative without Lang's help. A dedicated social worker involved in the project and the support of parents were essential to this intervention's success, but the students' cohesiveness was equally important. Participants formed a cohesive group through this scholarship program and received peer support on a similar academic path. Based on the social distance model, Akerlof explains that students would expect to be more isolated from their peers if they dropped out. A similar explanation can also be applied to codifying traditional values in Russia as a way of symmetrising information, only in reverse order. The commitment to values can bring people together, and this vow is what Akerlof implied and what Russia's authorities expect. In contrast to Lang's faithful intentions, the Russian authorities assume a unified position around their narrative, or, in the words of Luhmann, around the alternative reality created by the system, emphasised by a new presidential decree.

Akerlof's model suggests individuals will maintain values if they value and benefit from being part of a group rather than if their thinking is restricted (Akerlof, 1997, p. 1006). In Luhmann's view of values in communication, implication and assumption are significant means of enacting them (Luhmann, 1992, p. 256). A value bonus is provided to those who communicate in the name of good by assuming their values are valid. As Luhmann points out, nobody directly declares, "I support peace because I value my health" (and do not wish to be killed in war), since that could lead to rejection (1992, p. 256). Similarly, it is simpler to state that we are fighting for a higher purpose than to state that we started the war merely. A key observation of Luhmann is that values are volatile and can thus be applied at one time and possibly not at another.

An example of self-correcting the narrative using values is the switch between three official explanations justifying Ukraine's invasion. Denazification of Ukraine (Troianovski, 2022), fighting NATO (Moskowitz, 2022), and preserving the Slavic people's unity against assimilating with European values were all among the critical narratives. These three explanations employ values in a way that strengthens the system's core: Ukraine is neo-Nazi because it opposes Russian-speaking regions supported by NATO, thereby helping the United States impose its beliefs on Russian-speaking people in Ukraine via Europe, where Ukraine seeks to join. Considering a military-rooted process such as Nazification, a soft-power diffusion strategy through soft means would not be necessary. Despite the system's apparent ease of communicating with citizens despite contradictions like these, these contradictions reinforce the system's recursive nature, which remains self-referential by repeating that Russia's values are superior to NATO's and European values.

Likewise, urging citizens to unite around values leads to citizen snitching, as is evident on an increasing number of Russian websites displaying lists of national traitors compiled by those who probably adhere most to official narratives (Soldatov, 2015). The psychologist Liudmila Petranovskaia, who lives in exile after being declared a foreign agent, argues such behaviour makes sense given the history of repressions, in which neighbours reported one another to the authorities (Poligon. Media, 2022). She continues that such behaviour illustrates generations' agony, which calls for action. Being with abusers is easier than being abused, so identity as the aggressor is common. Victimisation and waiting for the worst to come are also standard practices, according to Petranovskaya. She, however, contends that these tactics lack specific values and convictions that could make them self-sufficient (Poligon.Media, 2022).

Instead of empathy, conformism or snitching on others shows a lack of ideas and forces for change. Considering Luhmann's view of values within the system, it would be as if the individual is blatantly declaring: I am for peace because I chose my health, thereby rejecting any superior value. Such individuals do not get the social benefit of holding good values, yet they feel more secure in their well-being. As a result, managing and governing values suggests there are no values, only enforcement. While it can serve as a mechanism for the system's self-reference, it cannot prevent it from collapsing. Petranovskaia, for instance, uses the historical example of the Black Hundred. This reactionary ultra-nationalist movement supported the Romanov family and opposed any change from the ruling monarchy during the early 20th century (Savino, 2018). One day, the Black Hundred, a watchdog everyone should fear, vanished. Even though these groups can harm separate individuals, they are not a guarantee for the system.

True, it is supposed to cause a value-split when individuals are forced to choose which side of the value system they believe in. The invasion of Ukraine ruined a long-term historical narrative of Russia as a protector who never attacked anyone. The system could hold on to this argument for some time, but now it had to re-adjust its argument and self-correct. By reinforcing the idea of traditional values, the asymmetrical information could remind us that NATO now endangers these values, which is the cause of the current conflict. True, as if to confirm Luhmann's assumptions, the system attempts to self-preserve by erasing misreadings in historical memory, moving from an old narrative to a new one. As a result of this shift, the nation's identity and history books must be rewritten and redefined. For those who already have identified some values, it means a break from the system; for others, it means nothing. The narrative about Russia as a protector is no longer relevant, but many people still hold onto their child-parent image of power, following Petranovskaia. Due to this, criticism of the state's power has been forbidden (see Chapter 7 on discrediting the military and the authorities in this book). At the same time, people have been encouraged to unite for their motherland. This unification would combine a moral argument appealing to the love of the motherland and a legal argument reminding them there are penalties for criticising public power.

The possible social distance between those who have values and those who do is not, however, sufficient to testify to any possibility of a civil war capable of collapsing the system. All groups in the system environment have been affected recently almost equally, so there was no conflict of interest. As Petranovskaya points out, no group in society would be untouched by this development since, regardless of whose interests are most adversely affected, regardless of how differently philosophically and otherwise these groups are, everyone is now at risk.

Additionally, civil wars require a significant number of young people, which is currently lacking due to long-term civil-patriotic indoctrination and otherwise unfavourable demographics. Moreover, no pathos or passion is necessary for social change. In addition to demographics, no one will brave death for an idea or value worth dying for when there is nothing worth dying for. Again, the system and the environment evolved together (Luhmann, 1995, p. 60). While everyone does not need to become more aware, economic decline and political instability may lead to a regression into primitive and archaic. It is difficult to predict what will happen, as the system has already invented a new argument to maintain its autopoietic closure, so even the current circumstances are probably not testifying for the system to be pathological.

Note

1 The inventory is referred to as the "Unified Register of domain names, indexes of pages of sites on the internet, and network addresses that allow the identification of sites on the Internet containing information the distribution of which is prohibited in the Russian Federation."

References

Akerlof, G. A. (1970). The market for "lemons": Quality uncertainty and the market mechanism. *The Quarterly Journal of Economics*, *84*(3), 488–500.

Akerlof, G. A. (1997). Social distance and social decisions. *Econometrica*, *65*(5), 1005–1027.

Barry, E. (2012, December 12). Putin says Russia's history should guide its future. *The New York Times*. www.nytimes.com/2012/12/13/world/europe/putin-tells-russia-to-seek-clues-from-its-past.html

Explanatory Note to the Draft Federal Law. (2022). *O vnesenii izmenenii v Federal'nyi zakon "Ob informatsii, informatsionnykh tehnologiiakh i o zashchite informatsii"* [On amending the federal Law "on information, information technologies and information protection"]. https://sozd.duma.gov.ru/bill/217471-8

Ledeneva, A. (2013). *Can Russia modernize? Sistema, power networks, and informal governance*. Cambridge University Press.

Luhmann, N. (1992). What is communication? *Communication Theory*, *2*(3), 251–259.

Luhmann, N. (1995). *Social systems*. Stanford University Press.

Mirtesen, UKAZ Decree No. 809. (2022, November 29). *Osnovanie suverennoi ideologii polozheno* [The foundation of sovereign ideology has been laid]. https://vmestevselegche.mirtesen.ru/blog/43201812394/UKAZ-809-osnovanie-suverennoy-ideologii-polozheno?utm_referrer=mirtesen.ru

Moskowitz, K. (2022, October). Did NATO expansion really cause Putin's invasion? *The Foreign Service Journal*. https://afsa.org/did-nato-expansion-really-cause-putins-invasion

Petrov, N., Lipman, M., & Hale, H. E. (2010). *Overmanaged democracy in Russia: Governance implications of hybrid regimes*. Carnegie Endowment for International Peace.

Poligon.Media. (2022, March 30). *Real'nost' ne zavisit ot VPN. Liudmila Petranovskaia o tom, kak govorit' s temi, kto verit v propagandu* [The reality does not depend on VPN.

Liudmila Petranovskaia told us how to talk to those who believe propaganda]. https://poligon.media/lyudmila-petranovskaya/

RF Constitutional Court, Zakliuchenie No. 1-Z. (2020, March 16). *O sootvetstvii polozheniiam glav 1, 2 i 9 Konstitutsii Rossiiskoi Federatsii ne vstupivshikh v silu polozhenii Zakona Rossiiskoi Federatsii o popravke k Konstitutsii Rossiiskoi Federatsii "O sovershenstvovanii regulirovaniia otdel'nykh voprosov organizatsii i funktsionirovaniia publichnoi vlasti", a takzhe o sootvetstvii Konstitutsii Rossiiskoi Federatsii poriadka vstupleniia v silu stat'i 1 dannogo Zakona v sviazi s zaprosom Prezidenta Rossiiskoi Federatsii* [On the compliance with chapters 1, 2 and 9 of the Russian constitution of the provisions on the law "on improving the regulation of certain issues of public power organization and functioning" that have not entered into force, and on the compliance with the constitution of the procedure for entering into force article 1 of this law, upon the Russian president's request]. http://publication.pravo.gov.ru/Document/View/0001202003160037?ysclid=lt4jc2wazx507880896

RF Federal Constitutional Law No. 1-FKZ. (2020, March 14). *O sovershenstvovanii regulirovaniia otdel'nykh voprosov organizatsii i funktsionirovaniia publichnoi vlasti* [On improving the regulation of separate issues of public power organization and functioning]. Rossiiskaia Gazeta, March 16.

RF Federal Law No. 149-FZ. (2006. July 27). *Ob informatsii, informatsionnykh tekhnologiiakh i o zashchite informatsii* [On information, information technologies and information protection]. Sobranie zakonodatelstva Rossiiskoi Federatsii, 2006, No. 31 (part I) item 3448.

RF Federal Law No. 478-FZ. (2022, December 5). *O vnesenii izmenenii v Federalnyi zakon "Ob informatsii, informatsionnykh tekhnologiiakh i o zashchite informatsii" i otdelnye zakonodatelnye akty Rossiiskoi Federatsii* [On amendment to the federal law "on information, information technologies and information protection" and certain legislative acts of the Russian Federation]. Sobranie zakonodatelstva Rossiiskoi Federatsii, 2022, No. 50 (part III) item 8772.

RF Federal Law No. 2124-I. (1991, December 27). *O sredstvakh massovoi informatsii* [On mass media]. Rossiiskaia gazeta, 1992, No. 32.

RF President, Decree No. 809. (2022, November 9). *Ob utverzhdenii Osnov gosudarstvennoi politiki po sokhraneniiu i ukrepleniiu traditsionnykh rossiiskikh duhovno-nravstvennykh tsennostei* [On upholding the foundations of state policy for preservation and strengthening of the traditional Russia's spiritual and moral values]. www.kremlin.ru/acts/bank/48502

RF Strategy for National Security, Upheld by Decree of Decree of the President of the Russian Federation No. 400. (2021, July 2). *O Strategii natsionalnoi bezopasnosti Rossiiskoi Federatsii* [On the strategy for national security of the Russian Federation]. www.kremlin.ru/acts/bank/47046

Richter, J. (2009). Putin and the public chamber. *Post-Soviet Affairs*, *25*(1), 39–65.

Sakwa, R. (2021). Heterarchy: Russian politics between chaos and control. *Post-Soviet Affairs*, *37*(3), 222–241.

Savino, G. (2018). A reactionary utopia: Russian black hundreds from autocracy to fascism. In M. Laruelle (Ed.), *Entangled far rights: A Russian-European intellectual romance in the twentieth century* (pp. 31–44). University of Pittsburgh Press.

Soldatov, A. (2015). The taming of the internet. *Russian Politics & Law*, *53*(5–6), 63–83.

Troianovski, A. (2022, March 17). Why Vladimir Putin invokes Nazis to justify his invasion of Ukraine. *The New York Times*. www.nytimes.com/2022/03/17/world/europe/ukraine-putin-nazis.html

Zorin, A. (2022, September 22). *The crusade and the Ferris wheel. How the ideology of Putin's regime has changed over the past twenty years*. RE: Russia. https://re-russia.net/en/expertise/022/

7 Analysing Legal Amendments Since 2012

Prohibitions on Discrediting the Military and the Authorities

7.1 General Remarks

One of the most significant steps towards restricting freedom of expression was revising legislation banning critical remarks about the Russian military. On the one hand, the amendments prohibiting criticism of the armed forces are in many ways expected, especially since the Constitution emphasises the significance of Russia's performance defending its territory and prohibits any belittling of the importance of the people's feat in defence of the Fatherland (RF Constitution, Article 67.1, par. 3). On the other hand, the new aspect was how the amendments were adopted. When it became apparent that the "special military operation" would continue beyond March 2022, the amendments were adopted through the legislative process concerning different matters, initiated much earlier but put on hold by the parliament. Trying to determine the length of the law adoption process, we found a study by Borzenko (2019) that showed that government drafts of laws typically take 172 days; state Duma drafts take 217 days.

Given the long process of adopting a law, this explains why such a method was used. Therefore, the halted process serves as a "winter preservative" or "canned food," as Petranovskaya described excessive legislative restrictions on LGBTQ+ individuals (Petranovskaia, 2023). As Petranovskaya noted, the limits may appear dramatic from afar, but they have little impact on the status quo inside Russia. Just like canned food, these restrictions can be easily lifted when the time comes to end the sanctions. If the time comes to talk about lifting sanctions, removing these restrictions can serve as a bargaining chip. A similar situation occurs with the legislative process that is currently on hold, and, despite it relating to a different issue, it is used at just the right time to further one's objectives.

Rather than the amendments themselves, the Constitutional Court's interpretation of those amendments is at issue with asymmetrising information. The Court ruled on legislation banning critical remarks about Russian special military operations and the military. The Court clarified that the state is a constitutional value that citizens should respect and protect, even in combat zones, and should not be openly criticised.

DOI: 10.4324/9781032613383-7

7.2 Legislative Amendments

As of March 2022, criticism of the military, public authorities, and volunteers, as they act to protect the interests of the Russian Federation and maintain international peace and security, was prohibited (RF Federal Law No. 31-FZ, 2022). A new article, 20.3.3, has been added to the 2001 Code of the Russian Federation on Administrative Offences as part of this round of legislative revisions. Initially, this article stated that:

- Public actions aimed at discrediting the use of the Armed Forces of the Russian Federation to protect the interests of the Russian Federation and its citizens to maintain international peace and security, including public calls to prevent the use of the Armed Forces of the Russian Federation for these purposes, provided these actions do not contain signs of criminal activity, will entail imposing an administrative fine on citizens ranging from ₽30,000–₽50,000, officials ranging from ₽100,000–₽200,000, and legal entities ranging from ₽300,000–₽500,000.
- In addition to the same actions, calls for unauthorised public gatherings, as well as threats to property, lives, and health, a threat of widespread disturbances in public order and safety, or a threat of interfering with or stopping critical infrastructure, energy, industrial, and communications facilities, transportation, or social infrastructure, provided these actions do not constitute criminal activity, may result in administrative fines of ₽30,000–₽50,000 for citizens, ₽100,000–₽200,000 for officials, and ₽300,000–₽500,000 for legal entities. If these actions are not criminal, fines may be imposed.

Thus, the newly introduced Article 20.3.3 of the 2001 RF Code of Administrative Offences first permitted the prosecution of individuals, authorities, and legal entities who engage in public acts that undermine the legitimacy of the Russian Federation's military in defending its territory and people, maintaining international peace and security. A fine between ₽30,000–₽50,000 will be imposed on civilians, ₽100,000–₽200,000 on officials, and ₽300,000–₽5000,000 on legal entities. More severe penalties apply if the actions are related to unauthorised gatherings, mass disturbances, damage to property or health, or disruption of critical infrastructure. As we have already discussed in earlier chapters of this book review, authorities are not interested in mass protests that could significantly impact society, as criticisms of the military can be amplified in mass events – which can have a more significant impact if amplified.

The provisions of Article 20.3.3 of the Code of the Administrative Offences were further amended in March 2023 (RF Federal Law No. 57-FZ, 2023) to include a prohibition on discrediting state authorities and volunteer organisations in connection with protecting Russia's interests and international peace and security.

From that point on, the total wrongdoing, as prohibited by the amended Article 20.3.3, includes the following:

- Public actions aimed at discrediting the use of the Armed Forces of the Russian Federation to protect the interests of the Russian Federation and its citizens to maintain international peace and security. This includes public calls to prevent the use of the Armed Forces of the Russian Federation for these purposes, provided these actions do not contain signs of criminal activity, or discredit the exercise of Russian Federation state powers outside the territory for the specified purposes by state bodies, or discredit the provision of assistance to the Russian Armed Forces by volunteer formations, organisations or individuals in the performance of those tasks, provided these actions do not constitute criminal activity.

Discrediting the military or public authorities may also be considered criminal, as we noted when analysing Article 20.3.3. Additionally, a new Article 280.3 was added to the Criminal Code on the same day administrative sanctions for such discrediting were adopted. As initially drafted, this article prohibited the public from discrediting the military for its role in maintaining national security and interests.

Public actions aimed at discrediting the use of the Russian Federation's armed forces to protect their interests and its citizens, maintaining international peace and security, including public calls to prevent the Russian Federation's armed forces from being used in such a way, committed by a person after they have been brought to administrative responsibility for a similar act within a year, shall be punishable by (a) a fine between ₽100,000–₽300,000, (b) forfeiting the convicted person's wages or other income for one to two years, (c) by forced labour for up to three years, (d) by arrest for up to six months, or (e) by imprisonment for up to five years without the right to hold certain positions or engage in certain activities.

If the same act causes death by negligence, harm to property, public order, or safety, or interferes with life support facilities, transport, infrastructure, credit institutions, energy, or communications facilities, harsher penalties are imposed. In addition to the amendments made by Federal Law No. 58-FZ dated 18 March 2023, this article prohibits discrediting the exercise of state power by Russian Federation state bodies and assisting volunteer formations, organisations, or individuals in fulfilling military tasks.

In the same move, the 1996 Criminal Code of the Russian Federation was amended to include another new Article 207.3 (RF Federal Law No. 32-FZ, 2022). Initially, it prohibited the public dissemination of knowingly false information regarding the use of the Russian Armed Forces:

- Public dissemination of false information under the guise of reliable messages containing information on the use of the Russian Armed Forces to protect Russian interests and its citizens, to maintain international peace and security,

- shall be punished by a fine of between 700 and 1.5 million rubles, or in the amount equal to the wages or other income of the convicted person for 1 year to 18 months, or by correctional labour for 1 year, or by forced labour for up to 3 years, or by imprisonment for the same period.

A more severe penalty was imposed on these offences if they had been committed by an official or by a group, including a previous conspiracy, by an organised group, or by fabricating evidence out of self-interest or hate toward any social group, or out of hatred for political, ideological, racial, national, or religious beliefs, or if they entailed grave consequences. Article 207.3 of the Criminal Code was further amended in March 2023 (RF Federal Law No. 58-FZ, 2023), as with the grounds for administrative liability, to prohibit discrediting state authorities and voluntary formations.

The search for the Explanatory note that goes with these amendments to the Code of Administrative Offences and the Criminal Code leads to an unconventional circumstance and the outcome of not finding an official justification for penalising citizens for discrediting actions. The Explanatory note on the State Duma's website related to adopting the aforementioned legal amendments contains information justifying revised penalties for illegal external economic activity during the outer sanction pressure.[1] Similarly, the Criminal Code amendments under review remain unexplained: the Speaker of the State Duma, Vyacheslav Volodin, introduced in 2018 a draft law No. 464757-7 that stressed the need to amend the Criminal Code to increase penalties for crimes against constitutional order and state security, especially those that refuse to cooperate in the implementation of restrictive measures imposed in response to international sanctions.[2] There was no progress on either of the draft legislations in 2018, so the process was put on hold. Thus, the amendments discussed against discrediting the military were adopted as part of a legislative process that had been started but paused to consider another set of amendments.

The procedure can have a variety of possible explanations that one can only speculate upon. The 2018 idea of toughening penalties for not cooperating with authorities in the face of foreign sanctions may have been operationally revived. It could have been presented to parliament to undergo significant changes geared toward prohibiting criticism of the military in the heat of the moment. In February through March of 2022, when the amendments were adopted, the situation surrounding the Ukraine invasion worsened, and it became evident that a special military operation would be prolonged. There was not enough time to consider a credible update for the Explanatory note. A human error could also be the cause of the Explanatory Notes for the Criminal Code and Code of Administrative Offences amendments lacking a valid reason for forbidding criticism of the military – the documents cannot be attached to the system in their actual form. To be clear, all of these are just conjectures. What is not speculated is that the legislative processes that were previously initiated, then put on hold, were used as "winter preservatives." Petranovskaya coined this phrase to describe unnecessary legal restrictions that could be lifted later if negotiations to lift the economic sanctions between Russia and the countries imposing them manage to resume.

However, the provision that was initially intended to be introduced during the winter preservative legislative process, initiated in 2018, was also adopted. As part of the Criminal Code, Article 284.2 prohibits calls for restrictive measures against Russia, its citizens, and entities. A Russian citizen accountable for a similar act within a year may not call for implementing restrictive measures, specifically political or economic sanctions against the country. These calls should be addressed to interstate and state associations and unions. There is a maximum fine of ₽500,000, three years of forced labour, six months of arrest, or three years of imprisonment, and a fine of up to ₽ 200,000 or one year's worth of wages.

7.3 Interpretations by the Constitutional Court

In order to bring anti-war activists facing prosecution for discrediting the Russian army before the Constitutional Court, the Russian human rights organisations OVD-Info, Memorial, and Russia Behind Bars, along with private attorneys who collaborated with OVD-Info, formed a coalition (OVD-Info, 2023). Nearly 20 cases were filed, urging the Constitutional Court to strike down Article 20.3.3 of the Code of Administrative Offences. As reported by Richter, the Constitutional Court rejected the admissibility of individual applications against violations of their constitutional rights by Article 20.3.3 of the Code on Administrative Offences with 13 inadmissibility decisions on 30 May 2023 (Richter, 2023). The reasons and text of those resolutions and later ones published in June 2023 are nearly identical. We obtained the full text of Kristina Markus' decision, which is examined below.

The Constitutional Court of the Russian Federation rejected the application of Ms. Markus, a citizen who challenged the constitutionality of the prohibition against discrediting the Armed Forces but managed nonetheless to announce several significant principles regarding the evaluation of citizens' actions that may be construed as disparaging public authorities and the Armed Forces (RF Constitutional Court of the Russian Federation, 2023). This application was rejected for consideration on merits by the Russian Constitutional Court.

The applicant challenged as unconstitutional Part 1 of Article 20.3.3 of the Russian Code of Administrative Offences, under which a citizen, official, or legal entity can be held accountable for actions that discredit the armed forces or the execution of state authority outside of Russia. Ms. Markus alleged that this provision violates the rights to freedom of conscience, thought, speech, assembly, and the principle of equality and prohibition of discrimination. As a result of an administrative offence committed in violation of Article 20.3.3 of the Russian Federation Code, a district court judge fined the applicant ₽ 50,000 .

According to the applicant, the legal provision under review violates the freedoms of conscience, thought, expression, and assembly, as well as the freedom not to be compelled to adhere to any ideology because it penalises criticism of government authority and the use of Russian military force. The applicant contends that administrative sanctions apply only to views and convictions critical of the Russian Armed Forces and how they exercise their authority outside the Russian Federation. Thus, both the equality principle and the prohibition of discrimination are violated.

According to the Constitutional Court of the Russian Federation, the information provided does not justify a review of the constitutionality of this case. The Court states that the Russian Constitution, from the Preamble onwards, gives state bodies authority to take actions and decisions, including those involving the armed forces, to maintain international peace and security and to protect the interests of the Russian Federation and its citizens. Federal legislation outlines constitutional parameters for such actions.

Under the Constitution, state authorities are authorised to decide whether to use their armed forces to accomplish their goals. Under the Constitution, human rights and freedoms cannot be used to justify rejecting the constitutionally established state system. In addition to the system in which the state guarantees human rights, such rejection can also apply to how such rights are implemented and protected. Hence, according to the Constitutional Court, the state is a constitutional value everyone must defend and uphold. Additionally, the rejection implies a denial of both a moral and constitutional duty to defend the Fatherland. If citizens violate the rights of others while exercising their freedom of speech or thought, they may be held accountable. The form of expression of one's beliefs and the content of the information disseminated are essential here. A federal legislator is responsible for setting legal penalties for law and order, security, and public safety violations.

According to Article 20.3.3 of the Code of Administrative Offences, actions of a public nature intended to discredit the activities are prohibited. Considering the variety of forms in which actions acquire a public character in the modern information society, the court affirms that the concept of public nature is subjective. Despite this, specific actions can still be qualified in this capacity. The term discrediting is not defined precisely in the article, but it is generally understood as undermining the confidence that individuals and society have in a person. Therefore, discrediting implies undermining people's confidence in an individual and their actions. Considering the variety of actions (e.g. verbal and visual) that may be intended to undermine trust, the legislator may not have defined discrediting. Accordingly, the circumstances must always be specified to determine whether publicly acting to discredit qualifies as an administrative offence.

Further, the disputed legal provision does not connect discrediting actions to any specific special military operation. Federal legislators have mandated administrative responsibility for actions undermining military operations based on their circumstances. The Constitutional Court defended the validity of the provision under consideration by citing its earlier decisions regarding the legality of international treaties between the Russian Federation and the four Eastern Ukrainian regions it had occupied (i.e. Donetsk, Lugansk, Zaporizhzhia, and Kherson). The Court concluded that there would be no constitutional challenges during the special military operations since it had already investigated the constitutionality of Russia, accepting four currently occupied regions in Eastern Ukraine onto its territory (RF Constitutional Court of the Russian Federation, No. 36-P, 37-P, 38-P, and 39-P, 2022). In this regard, evaluating the contested provision outside the specified circumstances would effectively exercise abstract normative control. Abstract normative control would be a completely different procedure for the present application.

Additionally, moral obligations and constitutional principles were invoked to defend the disputed provision of the administrative code. Keeping global peace and security and protecting Russia's interests and its citizens are primary objectives for state authorities, so their decisions cannot be contested solely based on subjective assessment. If citizens challenged public authorities' decisions, it would be implied that Russia is not a rule-of-law state, that the Constitution is not supreme, and that people do not abide by it.

The Constitutional Court agreed that safeguarding Russia's interests often entails risks to life and health. People who carry out official, military, or civil duties determine the effectiveness of these actions primarily based on their moral and psychological states. Consequently, society should support those who make relevant decisions and those who carry them out. As a result, constitutional values such as mutual trust between state and society,[3] upholding citizens' dignity, honouring Fatherland defenders, striking a balance between citizen rights and responsibilities, and promoting social and political solidarity can only be achieved. Negative assessments of these activities can harm their implementation, reduce their effectiveness and decisiveness, and even assist forces that oppose the interests of the Russian Federation.

By calling for an end to the use of the armed forces, the public prevents the government from enacting policies to safeguard the interests of the Russian Federation and its citizens and protect them. These are, therefore, distinct offences governed by the disputed legal provision. The Administrative Code's Article 20.3.3 does not advocate war, impose mandatory ideologies, or treat people differently based on their beliefs. The Constitutional Court examined the applicant's claim of imposing ideology. There is no violation of anyone's right to choose and maintain their beliefs since such a right does not suggest committing offences. Expressing opinions about the armed forces and state bodies, including pointing out shortcomings, is acceptable if it is based on open, trustworthy information and does not entail an arbitrary rejection of the constitutionally mandated administration system. A court must determine whether specific public actions are genuine expressions of one's position or a cover-up for undermining the armed forces, the state, or their functions. Courts should, therefore, consider the circumstances of disputed actions, including their location, timing, recipients, and contents. It is also essential to consider whether the facts supporting the actions are objective or based on arbitrary opinions, value judgments, or doubtful information. As a result, Article 20.3.3 does not violate any of the applicant's constitutional rights.

7.4 What Exactly Is Penalised

7.4.1 General Notes

There is much to be encouraged about the fact that some citizens were not deterred by the relevant legal amendments in many ways. Many people continued to express their critical opinions, even when fines and imprisonment threatened them for doing so. In the months following the enactment of the legislative modification, thousands of court cases have been filed in Russia.

The majority of these cases occurred in the following regions: Samara Region (79), Komi Republic (77), Karelia Republic (73), Krasnodar Territory (164), Crimea (140), Kaliningrad Region (123), Perm Territory (82), Moscow (632), and Arkhangelsk Region (70) (RBC, 2022). Although current Russian broadcasts should be viewed with caution since they support the legal system's effectiveness, there is no way to completely discount this information, as the publication we are citing supports this idea. Alexey Gorinov, the deputy and chairman of the Krasnoselsky municipal district council, became the first person sentenced under Article 207.3 of the Criminal Code (to seven years in prison) for expressing his opposition to war during a children's drawing competition discussion (BBC, 2022).

Not only did Gorinov and other critics face consequences, but many also argued against the imposition of these penalties. A minimal number of cases were successful in court, as can be seen from the results of our case analysis. Attempting to conduct our investigations of court cases, we realised we would only be able to find a few of the court cases for this study due to blocked access to the Russian courts' website and the tight publication schedule for this book. However, we attempted to retrieve full texts of decisions available in publicly accessible Russian law databases, including from abroad. In the sudact.ru database, searches for Article 207.3 of the Criminal Code of the Russian Federation, Article 280.3 of the Criminal Code of the Russian Federation, and Article 284.1 of the Criminal Code of the Russian Federation did not yield any results.

Nevertheless, we retrieved 24 cases from the same *sudact.ru* legal database using the search words "Article 20.3.3 of the Code of the Russian Federation on Administrative Offences," which allowed us to examine and view instances of public actions that the courts determined were violations causing administrative liability. All 24 cases were decided between 14 April 2022 and 27 February 2023. The recovered cases are all appeals that regional courts decided. We were able to retrieve several cases from the Yaroslavl Region Court, as well as from the Dagestan Republic, Kurgan Region, and Tula Region. In the cases reviewed below, the courts in four of Russia's regions found all citizens guilty of the offence under Article 20.3.3, except for two instances where the cases were dismissed for procedural reasons.

Based on substantive criteria, such as the type of actions deemed offensive by the court, and procedural criteria, such as whether the decision text discloses details about the messages disseminated and whether grave procedural omissions were allowed during the trials against citizens, these cases can be divided into the following 11 groups.

7.4.2 Penalties for Social Network Calls to Stop Using the Armed Forces

Mr. Andrey Broy was punished for publishing his comments on social media and sharing them within a social media community (Yaroslavl Regional Court No. 30-1-289, 2022). The court found that the publication aimed to undermine the military's use of force for national security and peace. Mr. Broy expressed his desire to prevent using the Armed Forces, thereby "distorting the goals of a special military operation."

7.4.3 Penalties for Demonstrating With Posters Bearing (Undisclosed) Slogans

In five different cases, Citizens B, C, D, E, F, and G were found guilty of "using means of visual propaganda" to discredit the military, the contents of which were not made public. Citizen B "publicly demonstrated for an indefinite circle of people" his homemade poster, which displayed an unidentified slogan. According to the court, the slogan undermined the Armed Forces' role in protecting Russia's and its citizens' interests (Yaroslavl Regional Court, No. 30-1-185, 2022). In similar circumstances, citizen C came near the regional government building to undermine the legitimacy of the Armed forces. He held an image-filled poster for 45 minutes and displayed it to onlookers. However, nothing was disclosed about what was displayed in the image (Yaroslavl Regional Court, No. 30-1-216, 2022).

Citizen D was also found guilty of disparaging the military at a shopping centre. He held the poster (no information on the contents is given) as he displayed it to onlookers (Yaroslavl Regional Court No. 30-1-187, 2022). In front of onlookers near a house, E displayed a poster with a slogan for ten minutes. Even though the slogan's content is undisclosed, the court determined that he engaged in public actions to undermine the military's use (Yaroslavl Regional Court No. 30-1-244, 2022). Similarly, citizen F went to the shopping centre to discredit the use of the armed forces. He displayed a poster with a slogan for 20 minutes to passers-by. Although the content of the slogan was not made public, the court found that he was engaging in public activities intended to undermine the use of the armed forces (Yaroslavl Regional Court No. 30-1-244, 2022). Citizen G displayed a poster with a slogan in front of a house for ten minutes. Even though the content of his slogan was not disclosed, the court determined that his actions were intended to discredit the use of the military (Yaroslavl Regional Court No. 30-1-159, 2022).

7.4.4 Penalties for Posting on Social Networks (Undisclosed Contents)

H, I, and J were punished for spreading content (which was not disclosed in the decisions). Citizen H uploaded to the public domain of his social media page a publication and commentary "intended to attract the attention of wide audiences" and "indicating discrediting of the use of the Armed Forces." The decision does not reveal the contents of the publication (Yaroslavl Regional Court (Yaroslavl Region), 2023, 2022). Citizen I released publications "intended to attract the attention of an indefinite circle of people" on her social network page, thus undermining the use of armed forces and promoting their prohibition (Yaroslavl Regional Court Similarly, No. 30-1-16, 2022). It is unknown what the social media posts contain (Yaroslavl Regional Court No. 30-1-367, 2022). The circumstances are similar to those of Citizen J, who posted information on his social media page, including photographic material with overlaid text. An undisclosed text of the comment was intended to discredit the Armed Forces by drawing the attention of an indefinite circle of people (Yaroslavl Regional Court No. 30-1-393, 2022).

7.4.5 Penalties for Posting on Social Networks on Military Exceeding the Authority

In a case from the Kurgan Region of Russia, social network member citizen K was found to have defamed the military by authorising and posting information on it, criticising it, and claiming that its leadership had exceeded its authority (Shadrinsky District Court No. 5-116, 2023).

7.4.6 Penalties for Demonstrating with Posters Saying "No to War"

Citizens L and M were found guilty of using posters as a "means of visual propaganda." The poster of L read "No to war." It included black text that read: "This is real, even though it's difficult to believe. No to dictatorship" (Yaroslavl Regional Court No. 30-1-227, 2022). Similarly, citizen M demonstrated a poster. In the bottom line of his poster were five black squares with a tick above the middle square; in the top line, there were three black squares with a tick above the last square. The well-known group "TaTu" used this image to protest the war. While holding the poster, he demonstrated it to passing citizens (Yaroslavl Regional Court No. 30-1-188, 2022).

7.4.7 Penalties for Demonstrating with (Undisclosed) Inscriptions on Clothes

Citizens N and O were found guilty of discrediting the armed forces when walking in public places with inscriptions on their clothes. Citizen N participated in a 10-minute public demonstration in Yaroslavl, wearing an inscription-adorned jacket, which was visible to passers-by (Yaroslavl Regional Court No. 30-1-203, 2022). In a public place, citizen O held a picket with two posters in A4 format, made at home, printed with a printer, one attached to the chest and the other to the back of his backpack. He was found to conduct a public action discrediting the military for 17 minutes by moving from a point within a radius of no more than 10 meters, displaying these posters with the inscription "Stop the war" (Yaroslavl Regional Court No. 30-1-243, 2022).

7.4.8 Penalties for Making (Undisclosed) Inscriptions on the Walls of a Prison Cell

Accused of calling for extremism in public, Citizen P spent three days in a cell at the temporary detention facility. He made five inscriptions on the prison cells' walls. The court found that these inscriptions were "addressed to an indefinite number of persons" and intended to discredit the use of military force during a special military operation in Ukraine (Yaroslavl Regional Court No. 30-1-2/2023, 2023).

7.4.9 Penalties for Making Inscriptions on the School Fence

Two cases from the Republic of Dagestan reveal that citizens Q and R were found guilty of disrespecting the armed forces by spray-painting inscriptions on school fences with black aerosol paint. Citizen Q painted two phrases: "[name extracted] is a *** – (obscene word)" and "Z + Z = (Nazi symbols)" (Leninsky District Court of Makhachkala No. 5-7142, 2022). Additionally, the court has censored Citizen R's (undisclosed) inscription on the school fence (Leninsky District Court of Makhachkala No. 5-7143, 2022).

7.4.10 Penalties for Disseminating Social Media Communication About War-Related Topics

In a case from Tula Region, Citizen S publicly corresponded with an unidentified group of people on social media. A communication he later shared related to the collapse of the Crimean Bridge and the partial mobilisation in Russia claimed, among other things, that "While we are shown something different to justify mobilisation and war while our soldiers blew the bridge . . . We don't understand . . . Once this bridge is repaired, no one will be able to cross it again and spend a vacation there because so many people lost their lives in these battles for nothing." As a result of his post receiving 6,700 views, 59 likes, 14 comments, and 24 reposts, the court found him to be "undermining trust" in the authorities who authorised a special military operation to protect citizens of Donetsk People's Republic and Lugansk People's Republic and who announced the partial mobilisation (Yasnogorsk District Court No. 5-325, 2022).

7.4.11 Penalties for Reposting Publications in Social Media

The prohibition against discrediting the military is also violated by reposting publications on social media, as in the cases of T and U. Citizen T retweeted "Vesna"/The Spring Movement's call for an unapproved public event. In the court's view, T's action undermined the legitimacy of the military intervention (Yaroslavl Regional Court No. 30-1-362, 2022). Furthermore, a citizen U was found guilty under Article 20.3.3 when inviting social media community members to an unauthorised public protest by reposting the internet messenger Telegram (Yaroslavl Regional Court No. 30-1-263, 2022). The post insisted that Google removed the Smart Voting app from Apple Stores due to pressure from Russian authorities. Imagine, the post continued, the government threatens to arrest an employee of a foreign company because there is an app on the Apple Store that lists election candidates. According to the post, people should resist since the government is accustomed to using force and will not stop at anything. U called for everyone to attend a rally that day, emphasising that the conflict in Ukraine was not a sudden event but rather the result of two decades of devastation, elections, legal proceedings, media coverage, economic decline, and imperialism. Even though the Telegram post impacted the removal of the voting application, the citizen was convicted under Article 20.3.3 of discrediting the military and authorities.

7.4.12 Cases Where Citizens Were Convicted Despite Serious Procedural Errors

As a result of the following three cases, citizens V, W, and Vlasova filed appeals with the courts, citing procedural inconsistencies allowed by lower courts as they were found guilty of undermining the military.

On the positive side, the courts overturned the courts' rulings of the first instance in two cases, ruling in favour of the citizens in two cases out of three. Thus, following her appeal, the charge against citizen V was dropped by the Yaroslavl Regional Court. She had 2,529 followers on an open social media website when she was found guilty of discussing open-access articles to cast doubt on using armed forces by a first-instance court. However, when the court ruled, the procedural window for bringing her to administrative accountability was already closed. In other words, the appeals court considered the flagrant procedural deficiencies in the decision V argued against in nullifying the decision (Yaroslavl Regional Court No. 30-1-25, 2023). Likewise, citizen W's appeal against being found guilty of defaming the military in a court trial that involved serious procedural violations was successful in Yaroslavl Regional Court. In a recent trial, W was found guilty of publishing content on her social media page to "attract attention from an indefinite group of people to cast doubt on the use of force by the military." However, an invitation to a trial was sent to W by text message. Even though text message notification is not recognised as a legitimate method of notifying trial participants, the case was tried in her absence. After W appealed, the regional court determined that there was no information in the case demonstrating that she had been appropriately notified of the hearing's time and location. The decision of the first-instance court was thus reversed (Yaroslavl Regional Court No. 30-1-324, 2022).

On the other hand, the Yaroslavl Regional Court did not interpret procedural rules favouring citizen Vlasova, showed no leniency (Yaroslavl Regional Court No. 30-1-403, 2022). Before the legal amendments took effect, citizen Vlasova shared information on an open social media page. Following the court, the information contradicted the notion that the Armed Forces had been called into action to launch a special military operation to protect the interests of Russia and its citizens. The disputed material distorted the goals and objectives of this special military operation, discrediting the use of the military (albeit the court did not reveal what the social media post said). Even though the post was published before the prohibition laws were enacted, the appellate court confirmed citizen Vlasova's guilt because she had not taken the materials down.

7.5 Bringing the Findings Back to the Theory

There can be various theoretical explanations for these legal restrictions. Maintaining the system's status quo when asymmetrical information serves its preservation is the most crucial consideration. A state engaging in aggression is doomed to face challenges in maintaining the notion of being a great nation with a bright future; in such situations, it is vital to eliminate any traces of opposition from public discourse to clear history. As authorities presumably thought, the victory of Russia over Ukraine should be etched in stone as a landmark in history rather than the military being criticised.

These restrictions can be better understood considering views regarding the motivations behind propaganda. The invasion of Ukraine was initially revealed as a "special military operation" within a few days. So, it can be assumed that the authorities were anticipating victory, if not like the 2014 occupation of Crimea, then similar to the 2008 five-day war in Georgia. Small victorious wars describe situations where authorities anticipated an easy victory (Libman, 2010; Wood, 2015). Initially, the concept was conceived to divert (Chubb & Wang, 2023, p. 5) attention from ongoing problems before the Russian-Japanese War, which started in 1904–1905. Due to civil rights violations, corruption, and declining living conditions, Russia experienced political and economic difficulties during the early 20th century. As a distraction from domestic problems, one of Nicholas II's ministers suggested using the current Far Eastern conflict to wage a small victory war against Japan (Libman, 2010). Japan's perceived weakness did not prevent Russia from losing the war, and the Emperor had to negotiate hard for peace.

The war in Ukraine may also contribute to severely restricting freedom of expression by reducing what researchers call audience costs of propaganda by signalling one's military might abroad. In making announcements regarding military deployments (which are proven to help military advancement), they tie the hands of the authorities by raising the "audience cost" at home (Chubb & Wang, 2023, p. 4). A leader will likely be rebuked if he yields on his public promises. Authoritarian regimes thus have lower audience costs as they silence the possible opposition, as was done with the legislative amendments under review. The authorities, therefore, reduced the audience cost by silencing any possible opposition through the legislative amendments under review. Now, it is safer to threaten other countries with nuclear deployments and other measures to prevent them from providing Ukrainian military assistance, just as it might have been during the Soviet prosecution of anti-Afghanistan war expressions.

In analysing the distinction between law and how courts interpret it (even introducing new regulations), Sakwa and others' dual-state theory (Sakwa, 2010) is brought back into focus. The Constitutional Court's interpretations in the Kristina Markus case and the appellate decisions of four regional courts that we could find and examine demonstrated how judicial authorities could use the existing legal framework to create new legal rules (RF Constitutional Court of the Russian Federation, 2023). In Russia's legal system, which is not based on precedent, courts are not supposed to assume such powers. When we discussed the extension of foreign agent legislation to private individuals, we saw a similar process in action – through case adjudication, the courts created rules of application that were absent from federal laws.

Inadmissibility decisions, such as Kristina Markus' case, can show how the Constitutional Court has declared the state as a constitutional value that should be respected and protected:

> *State bodies are responsible for safeguarding a country's and its citizens' interests and upholding global peace and security. Their decisions and*

> *actions cannot be arbitrarily questioned based only on subjective perception. Due to this, Russia's rule-of-law nature, the Constitution's primacy, and the requirement to comply with its regulations would be denied.*
> (RF Constitutional Court of the Russian Federation, 2023)

Suppose we ignore the debate over what a rule-of-law state should entail and let the Russian authorities devise their sovereign ideology and concept of a rule-of-law state. In that case, there will still be contradictions between the Constitutional Court's interpretations and the Russian Constitution. This reasoning would appear to contradict Article 2 of the 1993 Russian Constitution, which states that human and human rights are the most valuable thing. Moreover, the (non-amended) Article 2 stipulates that the state must recognise, respect, and protect human rights, of which free expression is one. This contrasts with the Constitutional Court's explanation that citizens are expected to respect the government without criticism. Banning criticism of the military appears to be against the spirit of the 2020 Constitutional amendments, especially Article 67.1, which presents Russia as a *pravoprodolzhatel* or continuator of the Soviet Union. The contradiction becomes even more apparent when considering that the Soviet Constitution of 1977 (art. 49) guaranteed citizens' rights to criticise and suggest improvements to state institutions without fear of prosecution (Riekkinen, 2013, p. 80).

In this particular case of Markus, the Constitutional Court had a chance to deepen what Niklas Luhmann calls binary distinctions and what LCT calls taxonomisation. According to the Court's earlier 2014 Ruling No. 10-P concerning foreign agents (RF Constitutional Court, 2014), taxonomy regarded those (individuals and entities) upholding Russian values and those upholding other values. Ruling No. 10-P cited international law, and the dissenting opinion quoted classical Russian literature. In Kristina Markus' case, we do not even have a decision on the merits; it is only an inadmissibility decision. Despite this, this decision interprets the Constitution contrary to its original intent by simply introducing new rules coupled with its narration without citing any sources and juxtaposing the Russian state with everything else. Defending restrictions most advantageous to the current administration, the Constitutional Court enacts new regulations without much justification. Still, it cannot avoid drawing contrasts between Russian interests and those of its enemies. Discrediting Russia's interests, authorities, and the military can not only negatively affect the implementation of relevant measures but also decrease the decisiveness, effectiveness, and motivation of military personnel. Still, it can also "assist forces that are hostile to the interests of the Russian Federation and its citizens" – insisted the Court (2014). To justify the shift from "citizens and their welfare are the primary values" to "the state is the primary value, and citizens cannot criticise it," one had to maintain a poker face. This admissibility decision achieved a challenging legal mission by declaring Russia's state the highest value. As Finnish President Sauli Niinistö noted after Russia invaded Ukraine, "Now the masks are off" (YLE, 2022).

In clarifying that terms like public actions and discrediting are approximations that depend on the facts of each case, the Constitutional Court confirmed that the door is open to other courts to find discrediting citizens' words and actions related (or even unrelated, as we could witness (Yaroslavl Regional Court No. 30-1-263, 2022)[4] to military assessment). In any case, the regional courts, acting as appellate instances, were able to create new rules and interpretations that had not been specified in federal legislation even before this ruling of the Constitutional Court by applying the analysed legal amendments in individual cases. For instance, it demonstrated creativity when Yaroslavl Regional Court concluded that Russia's military could be used outside its territory, including repelling or preventing an armed attack on another state that contacted the Russian Federation with a similar request, defending Russian citizens outside the Russian Federation (Yaroslavl Regional Court No. 30-1-289, 2022). While the Constitutional Court will explain in the Markus case that discrediting the military does not end with the current special military operation, the Yaroslavl Court reiterates that the use of the military is legitimate in the current situation when the authorities of LND and DNR asked Moscow for assistance in establishing independence from Ukraine. In another decision, the same regional court found itself authoritative in interpreting the federal code of law provisions when claiming that not having notions like discredit in the Code on Administrative Offences of the Russian Federation does not constitute a violation of "quality of law" (Yaroslavl Regional Court No. 30-1-188, 2022).

As demonstrated by the frequency of cases seeking indictments for defaming the armed forces, authorities are implementing the new laws. In addition, this represents an impressive consumption of resources. Public and law enforcement agencies spend astounding administrative resources on cases involving penalising criticism of the military, as evidenced by the volume of documents they produce to establish a person's guilt. As part of its oversight of social media platforms, Roskomnadzor, the Russian federal communications agency, examines posts and comments that could undermine the government's and military's credibility (Shadrinsky District Court No. 5-116, 2023). There are countless documents to be collected for each case as proof, such as social media inspection reports, the protocol of administrative offences, data from VimpelCom telecommunication company, media articles, and the testimony of several witnesses (Yaroslavl Regional Court No. 30-1-289, 2022). However, these resources are intended for activities similar to those prosecuting anti-war expression during the Soviet campaign in Afghanistan in the 1980s. Those who had been convicted were later rehabilitated, and those actions were acknowledged as "repression" (OVD-Info, 2023).

Notes

1 Currently, documents accompanying draft law No. 1197680-7, titled "On Amendments to the Russian Federation's Code on Administrative Offenses," are available at https://sozd.duma.gov.ru/bill/1197680-7. The package includes an explanation that the amendments are on establishing administrative liability for transactions or financial transactions with property obtained by criminal means in the interests of a legal entity, as well as public actions aimed at discrediting the use of the Armed Forces of the Russian Federation, as well as calls for the introduction of restrictive measures against the Russian Federation.

2 Similarly, documents accompanying draft law No. 464757-7, titled "On amendments to the Criminal Code of the Russian Federation and Articles 31 and 151 of the Criminal

Procedure Code of the Russian Federation," are available at https://sozd.duma.gov.ru/bill/464757-7. The package includes an explanation that the amendments are on establishing criminal liability for actions aimed at discrediting the use of the Armed Forces of the Russian Federation, as well as for disseminating knowingly false information about the use of the Armed Forces of the Russian Federation.

3 A new concept of "mutual trust between society and the state" is introduced in Article 75.1 of the Constitution as a result of the 2019 Constitutional Amendments.

4 Among the cases discussed above is U who, when posting publications about a voting application withdrawn from the foreign-maintained services for download, was found guilty of discrediting the military. https://shorturl.at/bcgiX

References

BBC. (2022, July 8) *Moskovskogo deputata Alekseia Gorinova osudili na sem' let kolonii za "voennye feiki"* [Moscow deputy Alexei Gorinov was sentenced to seven years in prison for "military fakes"]. This is the first real sentence in such a case. www.bbc.com/russian/news-62090629

Borzenko, E. (2019). *So skorostiiu prezidenta: put zakonoproekta v Rossii*. https://pravo.ru/story/212484/?ysclid=lpy2r3y5e910745935

Chubb, A. C., & Wang, F. Y. (2023). Authoritarian propaganda campaigns on foreign Affairs: Four birds, one stone, and the South China Sea arbitration. *International Studies Quarterly*, *67*(3), 1–15.

Documents Accompanying Draft Law No. 1197680-7, titled "On amendments to the Russian Federation's code on administrative offenses". https://sozd.duma.gov.ru/bill/1197680-7

Documents Accompanying Draft Law No. 464757-7, titled "On amendments to the criminal code of the Russian Federation and articles 31 and 151 of the criminal procedure code of the Russian Federation". https://sozd.duma.gov.ru/bill/464757-7

Leninsky District Court of Makhachkala (Republic of Dagestan) Resolution No. 5-7142. (2022, December 27). On case no. 5-7142/2022. https://sudact.ru/regular/doc/QHVwpfZjg7mv/?ysclid=lubh47vsnr63969696

Leninsky District Court of Makhachkala (Republic of Dagestan) Resolution No. 5-7143. (2022, December 27). On case no. 5-7143/2022. https://sudact.ru/regular/doc/KfSPwDJr7m6u/?ysclid=lubh591lle435652164

Libman, A. (2010). A small victorious war: Domestic revolution and international conflict. *Peace Economics, Peace Science, and Public Policy*, *16*(10), 1–25.

OVD-Info. (2023). *Russian civil society demands an end to prosecution of anti-war protests*. Human Rights House Foundation. https://humanrightshouse.org/opinion/ovd-info-russian-civil-society-demands-an-end-to-prosecution-of-anti-war-protests/

Petranovskaia, L. (2023, July 15). *Discussion of the LGBTQ+ restrictions in Russia, on her Facebook page*. www.facebook.com/lv.petranovskaya

RBC. (2022). *Sud peresmotrel delo o "net voble" i oshtrafoval rossiianku za nadpis* [Upon reviewing the case of "net voble", the court fined the Russian woman]. www.rbc.ru/politics/20/12/2022/63a1760e9a794781b8f0b0db?ysclid=lbw56n77wn392269450

RF Constitutional Court. (2014, April 8). *Ruling no. 10-P on constitutionality check of the provisions of paragraph 6 of article 2 and paragraph 7 of article 32 of the federal law "on non-commercial organizations", part six of article 29 of the federal law "on public associations" and part 1 articles 19.34 of the Code of the administrative offenses in connection with the address of the Ombudsman, the "Kostroma center for the support of public initiatives", citizens L.G. Kuzmin, S.M. Smirenskogo and V.P. Yukecheva*. Sobranie zakonodatel'stva Rossiiskoi Federatsii, 2014, No. 16 item 1921.

RF Constitutional Court, Determination No. 1387-O. (2023, May 30). *Ob otkaze v priniatii k rassmotreniiu zhaloby grazhdanki Markus Kristiny na narushenie ee konstitutsionnykh prav chastiiu 1 statii 20.3.3 Kodeksa Rossiiskoi Federatsii of Administrativykh Pravonarusheniialh.*

https://legalacts.ru/sud/opredelenie-konstitutsionnogo-suda-rf-ot-30052023-n-1387-o/?ysclid=lpsf30dclc88103881

RF Constitutional Court No. 36-P, N 37-P, N 38-P i N 39-P. (2022, October 2). *O proverke konstitucionnosti ne vstupivshikh v silu mezhdunarodnykh dogovorov mezhdu Rossiiskoi Federatsiei i Donetskoi Narodnoi Respublikoi, Luganskoi Narodnoi Respublikoi, Zaporozhskoi oblastiiu i Khersonskoi oblastiiu o priniatii ih v Rossiiskuiu Federatsiiu i obrazovanii v sostave Rossiiskoi Federatsii novykh subiektov* [A verification of the constitutionality of international treaties that have not yet been signed between the Russian Federation and the Donetsk people's republic, the Lugansk people's republic, the Zaporozhye region, and the Kherson region, as well as their acceptance into the Russian Federation and the establishment of new entities within the Russian Federation]. https://legalacts.ru/

RF Federal Law No. 31-FZ. (2022, March 4). *O vnesenii izmenenii v Kodeks Rossiiskoi Federatsii ob administrativnykh pravonarusheniiakh* [On amendmending the Code of the Russian Federation on administrative offenses]. Sobranie zakonodatel'stva Rossiiskoi Federatsii, 2022, No. 10 item 1388.

RF Federal Law No. 32-FZ. (2022, March 4). *O vnesenii izmenenii v Ugolovnyi kodeks Rossiiskoi Federatsii i stat'i 31 i 151 Ugolovno-processualnogo kodeksa Rossiiskoi Federatsii* [On amending the criminal code of the Russian Federation and articles 31 and 151 of the criminal procedure code of the Russian Federation]. Sobranie zakonodatel'stva Rossiiskoi Federatsii, 2022, No. 10 item 1389.

RF Federal Law No. 57-FZ. (2023, March 18). *O vnesenii izmenenii v statii 13.15 i 20.3.3 Kodeksa Rossiiskoi Federatsii ob administrativnykh pravonarusheniiakh* [On amendments articles 13.15 and 20.3.3 of the code of the Russian Federation on administrative offenses]. Sobranie zakonodatel'stva Rossiiskoi Federatsii, 2023, No. 12 item 1870.

RF Federal Law No. 58-FZ. (2023, Match 18). *O vnesenii izmenenii v Ugolovnyi kodeks Rossiiskoi Federatsii* [On amending the criminal code of the Russian Federation]. Sobranie zakonodatel'stva Rossiiskoi Federatsii, 2023, No. 12 item 1871.

Richter, A. (2023). Resolution of the constitutional court on the ban on "discrediting the army". *IRIS*, *7*(1). https://merlin.obs.coe.int/article/9814

Riekkinen, M. (2013). *Pursuing substantive participation in Russia: A perspective from international legal obligations and comparative law*. Åbo.

Sakwa, R. (2010). The dual state in Russia. *Post-Soviet Affairs*, *26*(3), 185–206.

Shadrinsky District Court (Kurgan Region) No. 5-116. (2023, May 30). On case no. 5-116/2023. https://sudact.ru/regular/doc/c7Rhc1yqpMhp/?ysclid=lubh8nytm601765525

Wood, E. A. (2015). A small, victorious war? The symbolic politics of Vladimir Putin. In E. A. Wood, W. E. Pomeranz, E. W. Merry, & M. Trudoljubov (Eds.), *Roots of Russia's War in Ukraine* (pp. 97–130). Columbia University Press.

Yaroslavl Regional Court. (2022, July 22). No. 30-1-289/2022 on case no. 30-1-289/2022. https://sudact.ru/regular/doc/ARNAnmmqbMrv/?ysclid=lubhky0m4j316724134

Yaroslavl Regional Court (Yaroslavl Region). (2022, April 14). No. 30-1-159/2022 on case no. 30-1-159/2022. https://sudact.ru/regular/doc/jbVWiV4IhmWJ/?ysclid=lubhs5cq7o337121982

Yaroslavl Regional Court (Yaroslavl Region). (2022, April 29). No. 30-1-187/2022 on case no. 30-1-187/2022. https://sudact.ru/regular/doc/MyqC6Aw6q2dp/?ysclid=lubhsuyk6w163872938

Yaroslavl Regional Court (Yaroslavl Region). (2022, May 6). No. 30-1-216/2022 on case no. 30-1-216/2022. https://sudact.ru/regular/doc/LWk75eACDkYP/?ysclid=lubhri8izr682965839

Yaroslavl Regional Court (Yaroslavl Region). (2022, May 16). No. 30-1-185/2022 on case no. 30-1-185/2022. https://sudact.ru/regular/doc/L4EVTx2oHYVN/?ysclid=lubhmje5th215578994

Yaroslavl Regional Court (Yaroslavl Region). (2022, May 19). No. 30-1-188/2022 on case no. 30-1-188/2022. https://sudact.ru/regular/doc/JAFCMBi5sfQ5/?ysclid=lubhn8vhv5606503915

Yaroslavl Regional Court (Yaroslavl Region). (2022, May 19). No. 30-1-203/2022 on case no. 30-1-203/2022. https://sudact.ru/regular/doc/53jQjzBULUQQ/?ysclid=lubhnya0wp397907454

Yaroslavl Regional Court (Yaroslavl Region). (2022, June 2). No. 30-1-227/2022 on case no. 30-1-227/2022. https://sudact.ru/regular/doc/zfI2WNp85s1m/?ysclid=lubhop5s8n100579902

Yaroslavl Regional Court (Yaroslavl Region). (2022, June 7). No. 30-1-244/2022 on case no. 30-1-244/2022.

Yaroslavl Regional Court (Yaroslavl Region). (2022, June 9). No. 30-1-243/2022 on case no. 30-1-243/2022. https://sudact.ru/regular/doc/6VchsJ9C99oT/?ysclid=lubhqoxmta948969807

Yaroslavl Regional Court (Yaroslavl Region). (2022, June 20). No. 30-1-263/2022 on case no. 30-1-263/2022. https://sudact.ru/regular/doc/Ap4hok2GiJP/?ysclid=lubhtk7o9b307383312

Yaroslavl Regional Court (Yaroslavl Region). (2022, July 29). No. 30-1-324/2022 on case no. 30-1-324/2022. https://sudact.ru/regular/doc/uZ6N3QoVFhdt/?ysclid=lubhub7tj9522029750

Yaroslavl Regional Court (Yaroslavl Region). (2022, September 5). No. 30-1-362/2022 on case no. 30-1-362/2022. https://sudact.ru/regular/doc/ODAoLZlUSlx/?ysclid=lubhfmr829777734029

Yaroslavl Regional Court (Yaroslavl Region). (2022 September 9). No. 30-1-367/2022 on case no. 30-1-367/2022. https://sudact.ru/regular/doc/zR1PJ8WGT8xB/?ysclid=lubhebrto7129805072

Yaroslavl Regional Court (Yaroslavl Region). (2022, October 10). No. 30-1-393/2022 on case no. 30-1-393/2022. https://sudact.ru/regular/doc/JkaYtsPostLC/?ysclid=lubhex0x85661956900

Yaroslavl Regional Court (Yaroslavl Region). (2022, October 17). No. 30-1-403/2022 on case no. 30-1-403/2022. https://sudact.ru/regular/doc/uB1Ems2BcXVJ/?ysclid=lubhk8181q607328776

Yaroslavl Regional Court (Yaroslavl Region). (2023, January 16). No. 30-1-2/2023 on case no. 30-1-2/2023. https://sudact.ru/regular/doc/hbXuKPlaFOWN/?ysclid=lubgcg7qd4651328886;https://sudact.ru/regular/doc/hbXuKPlaFOWN/?ysclid=lubhlroe15943441407

Yaroslavl Regional Court (Yaroslavl Region). (2023, February 16). No. 30-1-25/2023 on case no. 30-1-25/2023.

Yaroslavl Regional Court (Yaroslavl Region). (2023, February 27). No. 30-1-16/2023 on case no. 30-1-16/2023. https://sudact.ru/regular/doc/m0u9mm3c4YQj/?ysclid=lubhdidzg2104549994

Yasnogorsk District Court (Tula Region). (2022, December 21). No. 5-325/2022 on case no. 5-325/2022. https://sudact.ru/regular/doc/5uqlhv0kWMmU/?ysclid=lubhuwzpnf316840165

YLE. (2022, February 24). *Presidentti Sauli Niinistö: "Nyt naamiot on riisuttu, vain sodan kylmät kasvot näkyvät" – näin Suomen johto tuomitsi Venäjän hyökkäyksen*. https://yle.fi/a/3-12331829

8 Russia's Asymmetrical Information-Based Legal System

Concluding Observations

8.1 Our Findings in a Nutshell: The Primary Objective

Considering the analysis of legislative changes that restrict freedom of expression after 2012 based on the framework of asymmetrical information and its interpretation through the analytical lens of systems theory, supportive theories, and the legitimation code theory (LCT), we are now approaching the point where we can conclude our analysis of Russia's asymmetrical information-based legal system. Our primary objective was to determine whether Akerlof's concept of asymmetrical information applies to Russia's legal system, which tightens freedom of expression. Using Luhmann's insights, we could conclude that if the system does not enter a pathological state, Akerlof's ideas are relevant to the critical topic of our inquiry. Hence, we did these studies to assert that the asymmetrical information framework, elucidated by Akerlof, applies to Russia's legal system. Just one paragraph from Niklas Luhmann's *Law as a Social System* illuminates this conclusion:

> For example, in economic transactions, personal preferences, interests, and wishes are not enough in law. Instead, forms of presentation should be sought out and found that suggest a rational, reasonable, or just solution is possible. It's important to treat the system as a decision-maker, no matter how controversial the facts, rules, and principles are.
>
> (Luhmann, 1984, p. 428)

Russia's legal system is controversial because of its asymmetry of information. Russia's human rights situation has dramatically deteriorated due to the adoption of ambiguous laws that further restrict opposition and civil society actors and hinder freedom of expression and assembly (European Parliament resolution on Russia, 2014, par. J). It does appear that the laws after 2012 reflect preferences, interests, and wishes to keep the status quo, no matter what the stakes are. It is hard to develop rational, reasonable, or just solutions when there are no differences of opinion, critical thinking, or free expression. The system is controversial, but it is also a decision-maker. A form of justice must be defined every time. So, the stakes are high, and even if citizens' dissent is taken under control, even fully controlled power is vulnerable to being overtaken or misused on the side of its allies without

DOI: 10.4324/9781032613383-8

the strict rules of the game. Akerlof referred to these features of a system based on asymmetrical information as adverse selection (1970).

8.2 Asymmetrical Information – What Are the Critical Characteristics of Asymmetrical Information in Russia?

As explained in Chapter 1, our framework of asymmetrical information is based on three pillars: (a) information, (b) asymmetrising these data, and (c) communicating the asymmetrised data selectively. As we have used this framework, Figure 8.1 illustrates the structure of asymmetrical information.

Below, we summarise our findings about creating asymmetrical information through legal amendments limiting free expression and communicating this information to the public.

8.2.1 On Creating Asymmetrical Information

It has been found that Russian propaganda and techniques of asymmetrical information fuel intensive self-correction and learning from mistakes (Rodgers & Lanoszka, 2023). The results of the current study could support these claims as well. Utilising the possibilities of the LCT, we could analyse the explanatory notes to introducing new legislation tightening freedom of expression in Russia, also keeping in mind the possibility of resorting merely to stating facts instead of inventive narrating to justify the needed legal outcome.

Additionally, based on the LCT, we can evaluate whether the explanatory notes for this legislation take into account the option of presenting straightforward facts rather than employing narratives to justify the intended legal outcome. We have found two examples of this practice. The process worked smoothly in most cases, with the inventive asymmetrising machine highlighting the specific knowledge and dramatising the threats to Russia while minimising the attributes of actors viewed as using Western influence and as detrimental and dangerous. This reflects the "ER+/SR-" narration style – the LCT methodology is explained in Attachment 1 to Section 1. Table 8.1 summarises our findings on communicating asymmetrical information through legal amendments.

Based on our analysis of the process of asymmetrising information, we discover that most often, legal amendments are explained through thoroughly prepared narratives and legitimation. This process involves invoking alleged threats, supporting

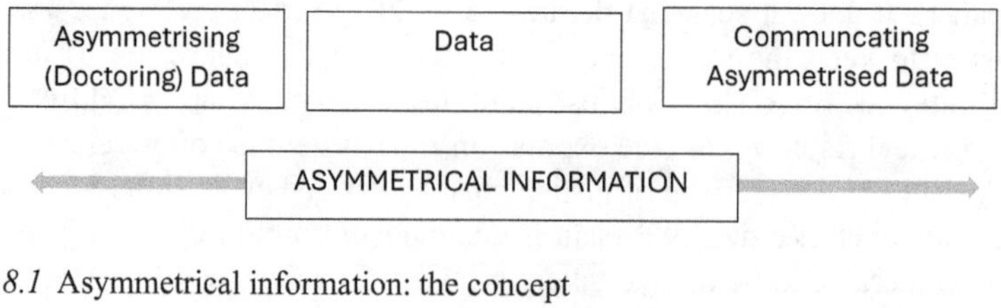

Figure 8.1 Asymmetrical information: the concept

Table 8.1 A Summary of LCT-Based Analysis of Findings on Creating Asymmetrical Information Through Legal Amendments

Amendment(s)	*Document*	*Finding*	*Comment*
Regulating the Enlightenment Activities	Explanatory Note to the Draft Law No. 1057895-7 On Amendments to the Federal Law "On Education in the Russian Federation" (introducing Enlightenment Activities), https://sozd.duma.gov.ru/bill/1057895-7.	Given that there is no legal regulation for these extracurricular activities in Russia, its formalisation was justified (ER+). A negative image of the "West" is presented (SR-), allegedly trying to interfere with Russia's education.	ER+, SR–
Extending the legislation on foreign agents to individuals	*Explanatory Note to the Draft Law of 14 July 2022* No. 255-FZ, https://sozd.duma.gov.ru/bill/113045-8	It was necessary to adopt these amendments based on the knowledge that current legislation contains "disparate provisions" in various federal laws, establishing different approaches to essential elements of the foreign agent status (ER+). A negative image of the "West" is presented (SR-), which interferes with Russia's society and commits "internationally wrongful acts" (SR-).	ER+, SR–
Limiting Protest Activities 2012 prohibitions on covering faces, widening authority over protest locations, banning series of one-person pickets, and introducing more prohibitions for organisers	*Explanatory Note to the Draft Law* "O vnesenii izmenenii v Kodeks Rossiiskoi Federatsii ob administrativnykh pravonarusheniiakh," https://sozd.duma.gov.ru/bill/7063[illegible]-6	As a result of the knowledge that insufficiently regulated protests are a threat to society, new regulations are necessary (ER+). The Western countries can show good examples of high fees for violating protest rules (SR+).	ER+,SR+

(Continued)

Table 8.1 (Continued)

Amendment(s)	*Document*	*Finding*	*Comment*
2014 to 2020 amendments regarding limitations for journalists	*Explanatory Note to the Draft Law* "O vnesenii izmenenii v nekotorye zakonodatel'nye akty Rossiiskoi Federatsii" (v chasti sovershenstvovaniia zakonodatel'stva o publichnykh meropriiatiiakh), https://sozd.duma.gov.ru/bill/485729-6	The journalists should not join the protesters and fulfil their professional duties while remaining easily identifiable in crowds. A statement of fact: ER–, SR–.	Indication of crisis ER–,SR–
2014 amendments tightening the penalties for non-pre-agreed assemblies, riots and introducing a cumulative criminal liability for a series of minor offences	*Explanatory Note to the Draft Law* "O vnesenii izmenenii v nekotorye zakonodatel'nye akty Rossiiskoi Federatsii" (v chasti sovershenstvovaniia zakonodatel'stva o publichnykh meropriiatiiakh), https://sozd.duma.gov.ru/bill/485729-6	"Statistics" were cited to support criminalising protesters who committed several minor offences (ER+). Protesters with ill intentions were criticised (SR–).	ER+,SR–
2016 amendments regarding the powers of the National Guard during protests	*Explanatory Note to the Draft Law* "O vnesenii izmenenii v otdel'nye zakonodatel'nye akty Rossiiskoi Federatsii i priznanii utrativshimi silu otdel'nykh zakonodatel'nykh aktov (polozhenii zakonodatel'nykh aktov) Rossiiskoi Federatsii v sviazi s priniatiem Federal'nogo zakona "O voiskakh natsional'noi gvardii Rossiiskoi Federatsii," https://sozd.duma.gov.ru/bill/1037366-6	In two sentences, a brief statement of facts.	Indication of crisis ER–,SR–
2018 amendments penalising minors involved in unauthorised protests	*Explanatory Note to the Draft of Federal Law* "O vnesenii izmeneniia v stat'iu 20.2 Kodeksa Rossiiskoi Federatsii ob administrativnykh pravonarusheniiakh v chasti ustanovleniia administrativnoi otvetstvennosti za vovlechenie nesovershennoletnego v uchastie v nesanktsionirovannom publichnom meropriiatii," https://sozd.duma.gov.ru/bill/462244-7	The goals of legal amendments are merely reiterated with references to the irrelevant Eurasian Economic Union Treaty.	Indication of crisis ER–,SR–

(*Continued*)

Table 8.1 (Continued)

Amendment(s)	*Document*	*Finding*	*Comment*
2022 amendments: foreign agent prohibitions and stricter fiscal requirements	*Explanatory Note to the Draft Law* "O vnesenii izmenenii v otdel'nye zakonodatel'nye akty Rossiiskoi Federatsii," https://sozd.duma.gov.ru/bill/140449-8	A brief statement of facts in one sentence.	Indication of crisis ER–,SR–
Codifying Societal Values	RF Constitutional Court, Zakliuchenie of 16 March 2020 No. 1-Z "O sootvetstvii polozheniiam glav 1, 2 i 9 Konstitutsii Rossiiskoi Federatsii ne vstupivshikh v silu polozhenii Zakona Rossiiskoi Federatsii o popravke k Konstitutii Rossiiskoi Federatsii "O sovershenstvovanii regulirovaniia otdelnykh voprosov organizatsii i funktsionirovaniia publichnoi vlasti," a takzhe o sootvetstvii Konstitutsii Rossiiskoi Federatsii poriadka vstupleniia v silu stat'i 1 dannogo Zakona v sviazi s zaprosom Prezidenta Rossiiskoi Federatsii," in Sobranie zakonodatel'stva Rossiiskoi Federatsii, 23.03.2020, No. 12 item 1855.	Quoting pre-existing traditional values (ER+) Making allusions to international law (SR–)	ER+,SR–
Prohibiting Discrediting the Military and the Authorities	Using the preparatory materials from another legislative process that was on hold.	No explanation whatsoever ER–, SR–	Indication of crisis ER–,SR–

ER = knowledge framing SR = knower framing
ER+ SR- = knower qualities are downplayed in favour of knowledge
ER–, SR+ = knower attributes are emphasised, and knowledge is downplayed
ER+, SR+ = knower's qualities and knowledge are both important
ER–, SR– = neither knowledge nor knower qualities are important

their significance, and highlighting the negative features of the external enemy (e.g. the West and those citizens who share its values) (ER+, SR-). In 2012, however, the explanatory note used a different technique to create a positive image of the West (SR+) and justify tightening protest rights based on the threat loose regulation poses to society (ER+). During the protests, the system was most alert when dealing with the presence of journalists in demonstrations, the non-admittance of foreign agents in protests and the deployment of the just-created national guards to deal with mass demonstrations. Explanatory notes in these cases limited themselves to statements of fact (ER-, SR-). Moreover, the strategy of late oppositionist Aleksei Navalny, who appealed to young people regarding their appearance at public protests, also appears to be an alert for the system since the 2018 amendments prohibiting minors from participating in unauthorised protests are a mere statement of facts (ER–,SR–). In the end, when things became more serious and Ukraine was able to resist Russia's invasion for longer than expected, there was a need to silence opposing voices, and the legislators said no word about passing new laws to prevent it. A legislative process on hold was taken, we called it "legislation through winter preservatives" (ER-, SR-). As a result, our methodology successfully identified four crisis alerts when the asymmetrising technique deviated from its usual narration and explanation. Three of these involved the suppression of mass protests. In contrast, the fourth involved suppressed criticism of the war in Ukraine. The system is thus likely concerned about the possibility of its narrative being ruined by mass disobedience and by destroying a significant part of the current narrative: the planned and imminent victory in Ukraine. Free expression acquires more meaning for forming Russia's system as it is now. Figure 8.2 summarises our framework of asymmetrical information.

8.2.2 The Process of Communication

Asymmetrised transmission occurs only when there is a difference between utterances and information (Luhmann, 1992). Thus, there is specifically organised communication or transmission of this data to ensure the doctored information is understood in the way it is supposed to be understood. No information self-understands, requiring an independent decision whether to believe it.

The reason is that communication creates redundancy by allowing people to access the memory in different ways. The system thus limits access to memory by creating false memories with new stories and explanations. This is to avoid the risk that eventually, the limits of communication are reached or patience, that is, the burden the psychical environment can tolerate, is exhausted. Finally, an interest in other topics or partners takes precedence (Luhmann, 1992). So, the system silences dissent, sensors the news, and rewrites the history books.

When authorities often amend the law to asymmetrise information, they resort to the so-called taxonomising technique based on the LCT theory we discussed earlier. This taxonomy follows Luhmann's binary coding (1992) of good, just, and right (positive value) and bad, unjust, and wrong (negative value), with constant self-reference to we (national authorities and loyalists) and others (West and

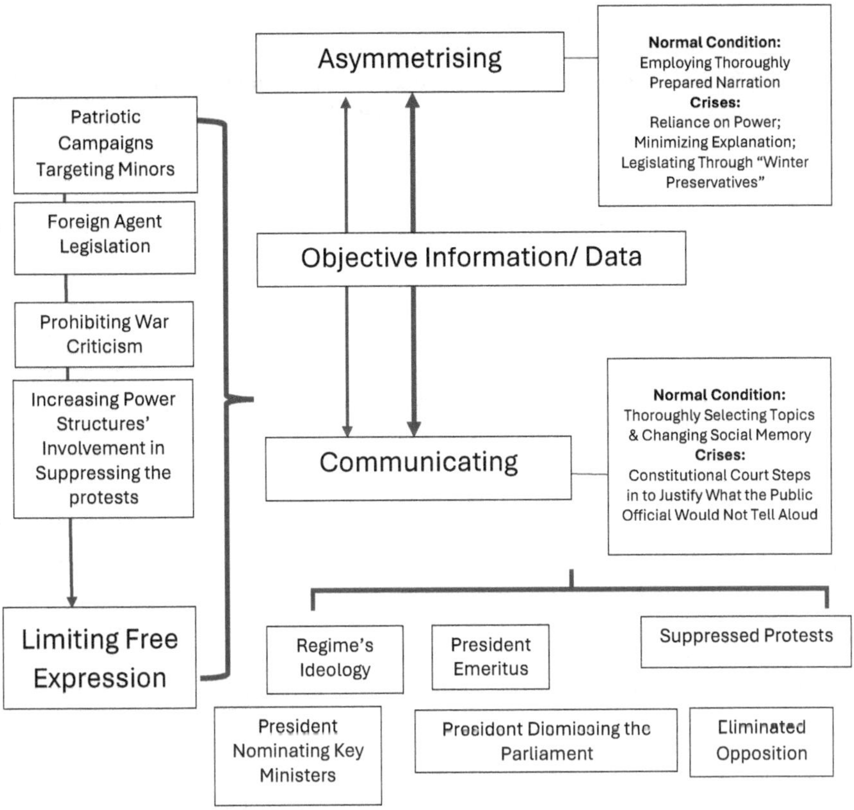

Figure 8.2 Framework for asymmetrical information in Russia's legal system

traitors). The national authorities, whose decisions are portrayed as just with references to traditional values, are juxtaposed with all other individuals and entities who are unjust foreign agents, the mass media calling the war "the war," and individuals appearing on the streets to protest the public narrative. Therefore, following Luhmann, juxtaposition occurs through self-referencing and other-referencing with positive and negative values: the "collective West" (1992, p. 86) and NATO with their unjust and wrong values versus traditional national authorities.

8.3 Self-Correction: Serving the System's Survival

This paragraph summarises how self-correction works and how non-existent free expression fits this process. It also provides answers to the following research questions:

- What role do asymmetrical information techniques play in the system's survival?
- Are there specific asymmetrising information techniques this legal system went through?

This will be done by differentiating the functions of asymmetrical information to ensure its functioning: guaranteeing (i.e. preserving) the system, facilitating its construction, and dealing with uncertainties. We have already mentioned that the reviewed legal amendments strengthen the status quo of the existing regime as it existed before the invasion of Ukraine, which sparked the ongoing crisis.

8.3.1 Self-Correction: Preserving Operative Closure

Defining the system's boundaries by law is among the primary means of preserving the operative closure of the legal system. This defining is done by concentrating on societal issues and through binary coding of what is legal and what is not (Luhmann, 2004). In our case, laws are formulated and implemented based on the principle of information asymmetry. Fierce marketing campaigns for these amendments in media and public speeches support all of this, creating an atmosphere where the official narrative is the only one to be shared. A position such as this deviates from equality; the official narrative is a narrative, and anyone can present one. However, in the current system, no one can speak their narrative aloud without fearing consequences. The legal amendments that we analysed are to make sure everyone is required to articulate the official narrative. Equal treatment should qualify as a reason in itself, whereas unequal treatment must be justified (Luhmann, 2004). However, our asymmetrical legal system justifies dissimilarity between wanted and unwanted actors in similar cases by introducing broad and vague legal formulations that the courts and administrative authorities freely interpret in their favour. Nevertheless, this is not unusual for highly stratified societies that interpret equality in its current form as the norm (2004).

Notably, such forms of equality also emphasise the system's dynamics. This occurs when frequently repeated questions are asked by the system concerning "whether something is equal or unequal" (Luhmann, 2004, p. 133). Thus, the system must "create the criteria" upon request, using narration, inventing (vague) arguments, justification, or propaganda[1] to justify its interpretation (Kenez, 1985). As a result, the legal principle of equality within Russia's legal system ceases to be normative, and the laws adopted in violation of this principle and interpretations that defend these violations become an asymmetrised norm of the current forms of equality. In other words, the legal norms drafted through a technique of asymmetrical information are a legal basis for violating the equality principle. For example, we will see in Chapter 7 of this book on prohibitions of discrediting the military and the authorities how the Constitutional Court defended a new legal ban against criticism of the armed forces: armed forces activities are so vital to national security that criticising them should be prohibited, unlike criticism related to other topics. It may also be found in Chapter 4, revealing how the legislation provides a definition of a foreign agent that is too broad. When we examined how the courts apply such vague definitions, we could see that a lot of discretion is used, so almost any undesirable oppositionist can be excluded from the public sphere as a foreign agent.

8.3.2 Self-Correction: Facilitating the Construction

Self-correction in the frames of asymmetrical information also facilitates the construction of the system. When read against the background of asymmetrical information framework and systems theory, a journey of Russia's freedom of expression legislation from 2012 until 2023, limiting free expression, acquires more meaning for forming Russia's system as it is now. There are voices in research and the media claiming that the system has changed for the worse since the war in Ukraine started (Eltsov, 2019). Yet, we could not confirm this is true by analysing public speeches, interpretations of the Constitutional Court, general courts' decisions, and Explanatory notes to new laws. There used to be all the same old ER+, SR- technique, except the four cases all through introducing legal limitations on free expression.

As it happened when legislation was introduced to tightening protest activities and prohibiting discredit of the military (using the ER-, SR- technique), we are left inferring that the system remained unchanged, despite the changes in the environment allowing opportunities to reveal its inner nature. During the Yeltsin period, Russia liberalised the economy, politics, and human rights, possibly to gain West-European recognition and EU Council of Europe support. Russia ran fiscal reforms to strengthen the ruble with the assistance of the IMF and the World Bank (Boughton, 2012). In 2012, Boughton predicted Russia's potential failures, including impoverishment, return to communism, and political isolation. Post-invasion of Ukraine, Boughton's 2012 scenario parallels what Russia is experiencing now. One thing to note is that the system accumulated significant financial resources to sustain all the implications, resources it acquired by trading natural resources with the West, and resources that enabled it to strengthen and resume familiar countermeasures against NATO (2012).

8.3.3 Managing Uncertainty

According to systems theory, a message communicated to the audience can be believed or rejected. How Russia's system communicates asymmetrical information is to be accepted or rejected. Communication creates the first alternative and, with it, the risk of rejection (Luhmann, 1992). Even such doctored communication involves risk. Information asymmetry in Russia's legal system has also revealed the purpose of managing uncertainty. It confirms Luhmann's argument that every legal communication requires uncertainty (Luhmann, 2004, p. 255). Despite the recent amendments to the Constitution nullifying Putin's acquired presidential terms, there is always uncertainty about the future. This is similar to Luhmann's example of a good advocate entering a court case with a conditional uncertainty about the outcome (2004, p. 255). It remains to be seen how those whose loyalty to the system is crucial will continue "quiet sabotage" (Shulman, 2022) after Putin "won" the Presidency in 2024. However, by asymmetrising information, one can ensure that all possible measures are taken to prevent angry mobs from becoming angry electors.

The system is thus self-correcting to manage uncertainties. As Chapter 2 of this book explains the context, the gradual and steady tightening of freedom of expression strengthened new authoritarianism. It went conceptually through sovereign democracy (akin to Akerlof's sellers leaving for another used car market). During the pre-Ukraine invasion period, the system shifted from sovereign democracy to neo-Eurasianism," altering the Constitution in a way that made Russia a "continuator" of the Soviet Union. The renewed regime again increased restrictions on freedom of expression even more. It arrived at the constitutional guarantees of personal leadership, entrenching the institution of President Emeritus through the decline of international law and the censoring of military criticism. It invented a procedure to adopt a needed law overnight: opening winter preservatives.

The normativity of the law continues to diminish in importance as a result of the adoption of comprehensive legal rules and prohibitions, with the Constitutional Court declaring a regime change in Kristina Markus' case, where the Court declared that the central value of Russia is its Constitution and state, which citizens must protect at all costs, from withdrawing from criticism – playing in favour of Russia's foes – or giving their lives on the battlefields (RF Constitutional Court, 2023). The previous tricks answer our second research question, which is about the symmetrising techniques the system has gone through. Yes, it did go through quite a lot of them. But no, the system had not become worse; it evolved to the level where it can take off the masks, and limiting free expression, with all the tricks outlined above, guaranteed this evolution.

True, instability and failure are attributed to internal tensions by several pundits and scholars (Blank, 2006). It is also what Akerlof predicts will happen to the used car market based on asymmetrical information; it will collapse. A market based on lies is doomed to fail, following Akerlof's "The Market for Lemons" – buyers won't pay fair prices for good second-hand cars since they do not know all the cars' qualities, and sellers will flee and look elsewhere for profits (Akerlof, 1970). In the real estate sector, asymmetrical information also impacts market dynamics. A negotiating power imbalance may result from buyers and sellers having different understandings of a property's state, location, and potential resale value. This could result in unfair dealings or exploitation. To explain why Russia continues to exist as a "new authoritarian" state with tremendous nuclear power after imperialism, socialism, and democracy have fallen, a convincing argument would be needed.

There is a good explanation for this in both Akerlof's and Luhmann's ideas. In Luhmann's view, non-democracies are just normal systems – that is, normal historically-first systems. Likewise, all the system's characteristics are well applied to the legal system of an authoritarian state, its autopoietic, operatively closed self-referential core, as well as the environment, which is essential for its survival. Akerlof says that the ill-intentioned second-hand car sellers who have made the market non-democratic will leave and go elsewhere. Since any system is created and maintained by its environment, the authoritarian leadership cannot just stand up and leave it for another market. Another solution to this dilemma Luhmann offers is that the system can self-correct or fix the social memory when citizens are about to erupt (and hence create another market).

Thus, self-correction is the guarantee that the system will avoid pathological conditions. In an authoritarian, asymmetrical information-based system, obedient masses can't bring about progressive ideas and social change because human rights and freedoms are the foundation of democracy (Kelsen, 1955). It is thus up to the system to deal with its adverse selection problem and avoid reaching a pathological condition close to a collapse. As Luhmann remarked, these are communication topics that facilitate the memory of communicative systems (Luhmann, 2000). He continued that by swapping and changing "local" modules of topics, a highly differentiated memory can tolerate rapid topic changes while returning to them later. Taking the trail of events and explanations, let's exaggerate and simplify to see how it happens in Russia:

> *As opposed to capitalism and the United States, we built socialism before transitioning to democracy to create the "Eastern pillar" of Europe. Europe and the U.S. threatened our efforts to establish a sovereign democracy. However, we might discover we don't need Europe and democracy as long as Russia challenges the U.S.*

Each time a significant crisis necessitates a collective regret over an ideology, a new one emerges. Meanwhile, Russia remains self-referential by opposing itself to the United States and the "collective West." Russia positions itself as capable of self-defence in any tough time, so tuning a framework on the fly is just fine (in the absence of freedom of expression), regardless of what and how it does it internally. In Luhmann's definition, "normal interception" and "absorption capacity" are typical cases for any system, whether it is "reciprocal noise, disturbances, and perturbations" (Luhmann, 1992, p. 258). What or, in our case, internal conflicts, such as Prigozhin's *coup*.

Authoritarian leadership, even one that uses asymmetrical information, can survive until it reaches a pathological condition. Luhmann noted that a sense of the pathological occurs only when certain tolerance thresholds are transcended (1992, p. 257). There's pathology when the system's memory "is brought into play" (1992, p. 257) and "experiences of disturbances are stored, combined, represented again, and amplified by reinforcement of deviation and hypercorrection, as well as when increases in these abilities are exhibited" (1992, p. 259). By overusing methods, the system thus runs out of skilful ways to manipulate reality perception, so it risks creating a pathological condition. Liudmila Petranovskaia says it is hard to find too many such methods in Russia because people are so busy making ends meet that they don't think about how they're treated for their rights and freedoms (Poligon.Media, 2022).

As economies get tougher, social memory can also be affected, and Luhmann helps us understand how it happens. One can tune social memory and knowledge over time by delaying psychological memory performances sequentially (1992, p. 235). History is replaced by moulded *memory* that is shaped, for example, by how people share memories about war if they witness it and tell others about it. Social memory can create a false narrative if the first person to share their memory presents it differently from what happened in reality and subsequent witnesses repeat it.

The drawbacks of such asymmetrising information are evident in divination and law (Luhmann, 1992, p. 235). All the earliest written forms of information were in documents that only certain people could access, possess, and read (1992, p. 235). Likewise, accessing confidential documents has been a stumbling block for decades, not just in the Soviet Union, but today, citizens cannot see them. Modernity has everything it needs to make access to information more accessible. Especially after 2012, Russia tried to shape this by censoring books, monitoring the internet, controlling media that spread official propaganda, and imprisoning and exiling opposition leaders. Uncensored writing can achieve something unwelcome in a system based on asymmetrical information, "the basis for forming different opinions" (1992, pp. 258–259).

8.4 Summing Up

We could establish that Akerlof's suggestion regarding asymmetrical information and the adverse selection problem it causes holds to Russia's legal system's limitation of free speech. Communication of asymmetrised data uses binarisation, legal for us but illegal for them, that maintains the self-reference and closure of the boundaries of the system. The situation is that citizens are offered a choice of topics to think about, such as opposing NATO, fighting the elusive Nazis in eastern Ukraine, preserving traditional Russian values, opposing European LGBTQ+ discourse, etc. Despite the binary choices infused by the system and the taxonomies used to formulate laws, there is not much choice in what to conclude after such thinking: either to self-identify as "bad" like the West allied with Ukraine or to be "good" like Russia. No matter what colour plate the broccoli is served on or whether it is on a pink, white, or green plate, the customer is served only broccoli.

Another theoretical dilemma remains: when an asymmetrical information-based system will become a pathology. It is, however, true that some other states rely heavily on information censorship to limit opposition to their policies. Are systems with asymmetrical information or systems opposed to democracy, norms, or pathologies? In terms of Luhmann's systems theory, he could not say whether the principles he devised for them could be applied to general standard or nonpathological social systems. Still, he was not able to deny it either (1992, pp. 258–259).

Akerlof's insights suggest that systems based on asymmetrical information are likely unstable. This relates to the prisoners' dilemma: if both accomplices cooperate, they will receive a minimum sentence or no sentence at all. People who go to great lengths to protect others can take the penalty from their accomplices. Despite this, their punishment will still be less severe since crimes committed in collaboration usually carry more serious penalties. Because of this, all accomplices will receive the maximum sentence if they refuse to work together.

The issue is, thus, who should sacrifice for the benefit of another one? While the system is not going to do it and collects all its inventiveness to self-correct, so does the citizenry who chose not to believe the official narrative; they go to great lengths to protect others. As we witnessed in this book, different societal groups

Figure 8.3. People laying flowers at ad hoc memorials to pay respect to A. Navalny's death

Source: Anonymous

try to resist the system. Those who make these attempts may feel powerless and helpless, but it shows how smart and reflexive they are. True, it is risky to say what you think while in Russia now due to fear of consequences. To stay sane now, it's only safe to have saloon-type discussions, as in the time when the Decembrists revolted and were suppressed. Meanwhile, the authorities are trying their best to control educational activities outside of the curriculum they call enlightening, as if in remembrance of the Decembrists and their Enlightenment.

Yet dissent tactics are also changing and evolving. Flowers brought to ad hoc memorials for oppositionist Aleksei Navalny's death are a testament that many try to resist. After it became clear that the mass protest strategy following the "Bolotnoe Affair" was useless because of the financial and other toll, they had to invent different ways to change. According to Shulman (2022), there is currently "not quite a protest" but "quiet sabotage" from those whose loyalty is essential to the system, educators (teachers and school administrators) and parents. It is possible to protest and end up in prison, but it is also possible to gradually create a climate of something badly wrong. It is a heavy climate for a system that is used to believing in its righteousness and stimulating public support. In the end, there can thus always be some symmetry found against the asymmetrical information.

Note

1 Which, in most general terms, is defined by Kenez as "[n]othing more than the transmission of social and political values in the hope of influencing people's thinking, emotions, and behaviors" (Kenez, 1985, p. 4).

References

Akerlof, G. A. (1970). The market for "lemons": Quality uncertainty and the market mechanism. *The Quarterly Journal of Economics*, *84*(3), 488–500.

Blank, S. (2006). Russia's Project 2008: Reforming the military and preparing a coup. *World Affairs*, *169*(2), 65–79.

Boughton, J. M. (2012). 7 *Russia: From rebirth to crisis to recovery*. International Monetary Fund. www.elibrary.imf.org/display/book/9781616350840/ch007.xml

Eltsov, P. (2019, March 8). The best way to deal with Russia: Wait for it to implode. *Politico*. www.politico.com/magazine/story/2019/08/03/russia-separatism-vladimir-putin-227498

European Parliament Resolution on Russia: Sentencing of Demonstrators Involved in Bolotnaya Square Events. (2014, March 11). B7-0247/2014, 2014/2628(RSP), par. J.

Kelsen, H. (1955). Foundations of democracy, part 2: Foundations of democracy. *Ethics*, *66*(1), 1–10.

Kenez, P. (1985). *The birth of the propaganda state: Soviet methods of mass mobilization 1917–1929*. Cambridge University Press.

Luhmann, N. (1984). *Law as a social system*. Oxford Press.

Luhmann, N. (1992). What is communication? *Communication Theory*, *2*(3), 258–259.

Luhmann, N. (2000). *The reality of the mass media*. Polity Press.

Luhmann, N. (2004). *Law as a social system*. Oxford University Press (in the original German edition, Suhrkamp Verlag Frankfurt am Main, 1993).

Poligon.Media. (2022, March 30). *Real'nost' ne zavisit ot VPN. Liudmila Petranovskaia o tom, kak govorit's temi, kto verit v propagandu* [The reality does not depend on VPN. Liudmila Petranovskaia told us how to talk to those who believe propaganda]. https://poligon.media/lyudmila-petranovskaya/

RF Constitutional Court, Determination No. 1387-O. (2023, May 30). *Ob otkaze v priniatii k rassmotreniiu zhaloby grazhdanki Markus Kristiny na narushenie ee konstitutsionnykh prav chastiiu 1 statii 20.3.3 Kodeksa Rossiiskoi Federatsii of Administrativykh Pravonarusheniiakh* [On inadmissibility of the complaint of citizen Markus Kristina concerning the violation of her constitutional rights by part 1 of article 20.3.3 of the Russian Federation's code on administrative offenses]. https://legalacts.ru/sud/opredelenie-konstitutsionnogo-suda-rf-ot-30052023-n-1387-o/?ysclid=lpsf30dclc88103881257

Rodgers, J., & Lanoszka, A. (2023). Russia's rising military and communication power: From Chechnya to Crimea. *Media, War & Conflict*, *16*(2), 135–152.

Shulman, E. (2022). The mobilisation of the demobilised. Neither society nor the political system are ready for ideological indoctrination, ideologies. *Expertise*. https://re-russia.net/en/expertise/022/

Appendix

An example of applying the LCT-grounded analysis with the framework theory of asymmetrical information to the issue of foreign agent legislation in Russia

Before an extended analysis of multiple data sources is made, an initial analysis of connections between the formal concepts of the law can be made with the help of the LCT-derived clausing tool. This tool, proposed by Maton and Doran (2017), allows analysing a text vis-à-vis relating theories and concrete legal issues with a view to finding out which clausing strategy (taxonomising, coordinating, characterising, or establishing) is used in the formulations of the document, which is the result of condensing the meaning of the document. The scale of techniques used to formulate the laws by condensing the complex meanings and assumptions to technical legal provisions, thus, moves from taxonomising to establishing. Each strategy's relative strength of condensing the message (i.e. how much or little they "pack in" meanings) is represented by using plus (+) and minus (–) symbols, with (++) and (–) indicating the strongest and weakest condensation, respectively. Stringer condensation (EC+) implies that more meaning is related to other meanings, while weaker condensation (EC–) implies that less meaning is connected to the previous meaning (Wilmot, 2020, p. 21). In other words, more substantial condensation shows that more complex meaning is built into the message in one go, while weaker condensation indicates less knowledge-building. As applied to our goals, the benefit of this tool is its capacity to show how the narrative in the laws, official interpretations, and case law is constructed and which key themes or triggers it relies on.

LCT-grounded analysis, as applied to the meaning and further political and societal implications of extending the application of laws on foreign agent status from organisations to natural persons, related to the laws amending the "foreign agent" legislation (data), would mean an analysis consisting of several stages:

> An initial analysis of the definition of a foreign agent in the 2022 Federal Law, "On control over the activities of persons under the influence of a foreign entity," with a clausing tool shows that the law relies on a straightforward

technique of taxonomising between foreign agents, on the one hand, and ordinary law-abiding persons, on the other hand:

> A foreign agent means a person who has received support and (or) is under the foreign influence in other forms and carries out activities, the types of which are established by Article 4 of this Federal Law.
>
> (RF Federal Law No. 255-FZ, 2022)

Taxonomising is performed by establishing a binary distinction between individuals who received foreign support while carrying out activities mentioned in Article 4 (i.e. political activities) and individuals who are outside of the scope of this law, and by further classifying meanings within a schema of foreign support and foreign influence that is prohibited by law, indicating that one act of receiving a foreign grant or donation makes up a part of the other more serious condition, remaining under the influence of foreign states and therefore outside the law-abiding realm, endangering Russia's security.

References

Maton, K., & Doran, Y. J. (2017, March). Semantic density: A translation device for revealing complexity of knowledge practices in discourse, part 1 – wording. *Onomázein*, 46–76.

RF Federal Law No. 255-FZ. (2022, July 14). *O kontrole za deital'nost'u lits nahodiashchihksia pod inostrannym vliianiem* [On control of the activities of persons influenced by foreign agents]. Sobranie zakonodatel'stva rossiiskoi Federatsii, 2022, No. 29 (part II) item 5222.

Wilmot, K. (2020). Building knowledge with theory: Unpacking complexity in doctoral writing. *Critical Studies in Teaching and Learning*, *8*(2), 18–38.

Index

Kolibri 360 GmbH
Ferdinand-Jühlke-Straße 7
99095 Erfurt, Deutschland
produktsicherheit@kolibri360.de